Welcome to Volume One of Mary Matters Rhymes

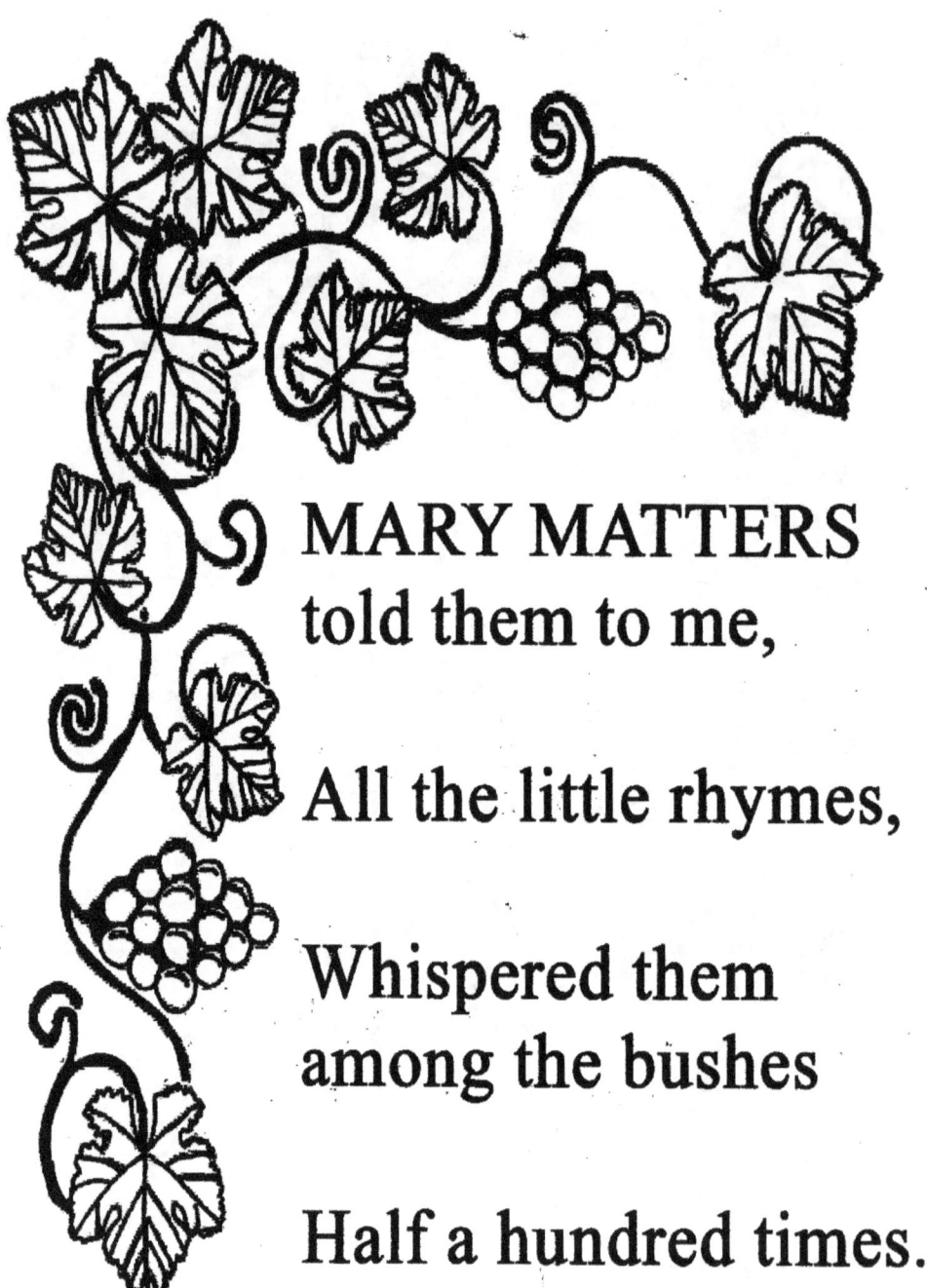

MARY MATTERS
told them to me,

All the little rhymes,

Whispered them
among the bushes

Half a hundred times.

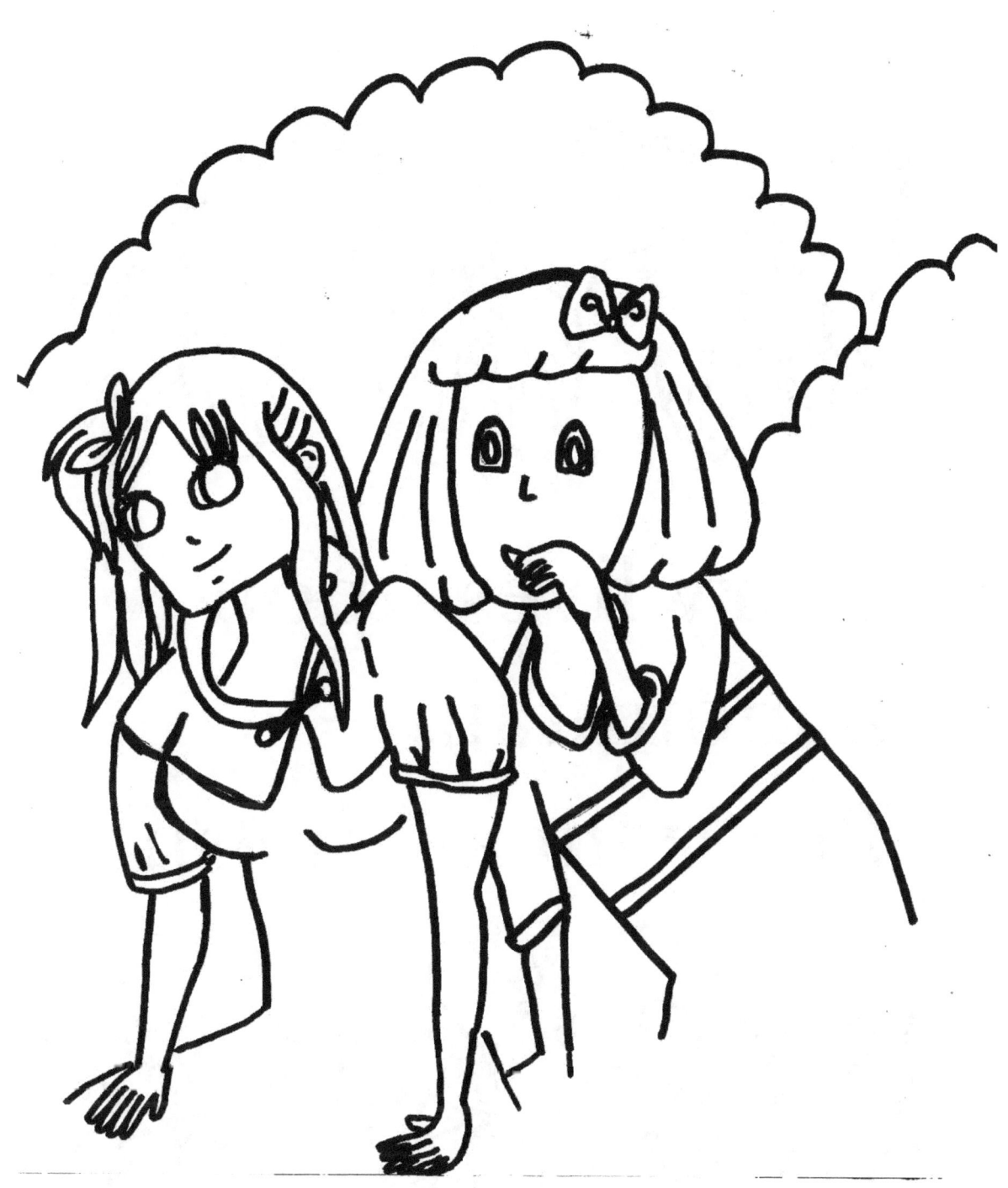

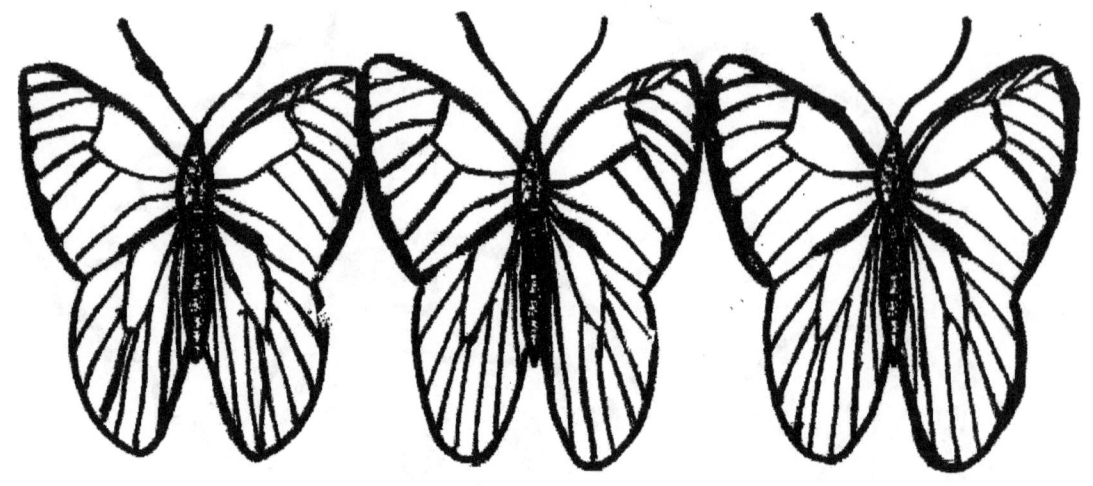

Mary lives upon
a mountain
Pretty near the sun,

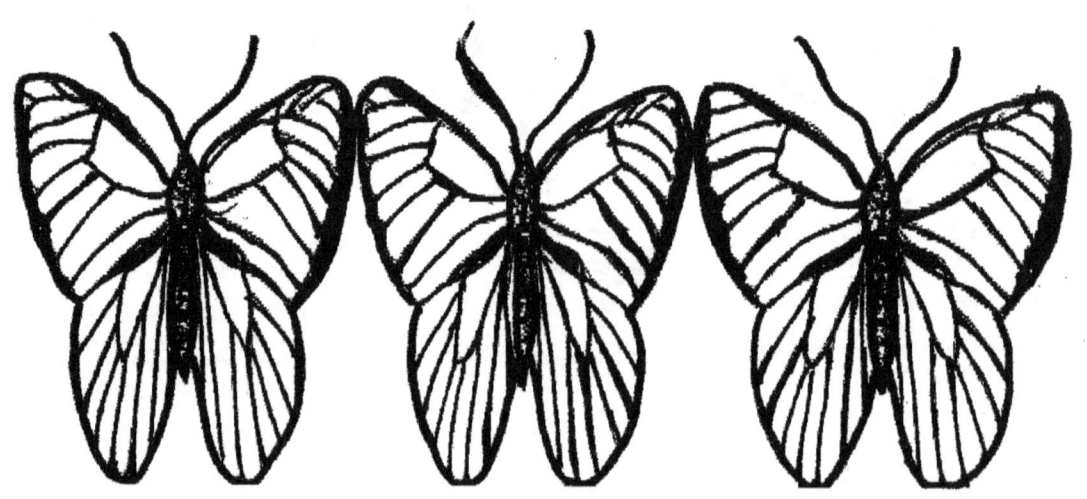

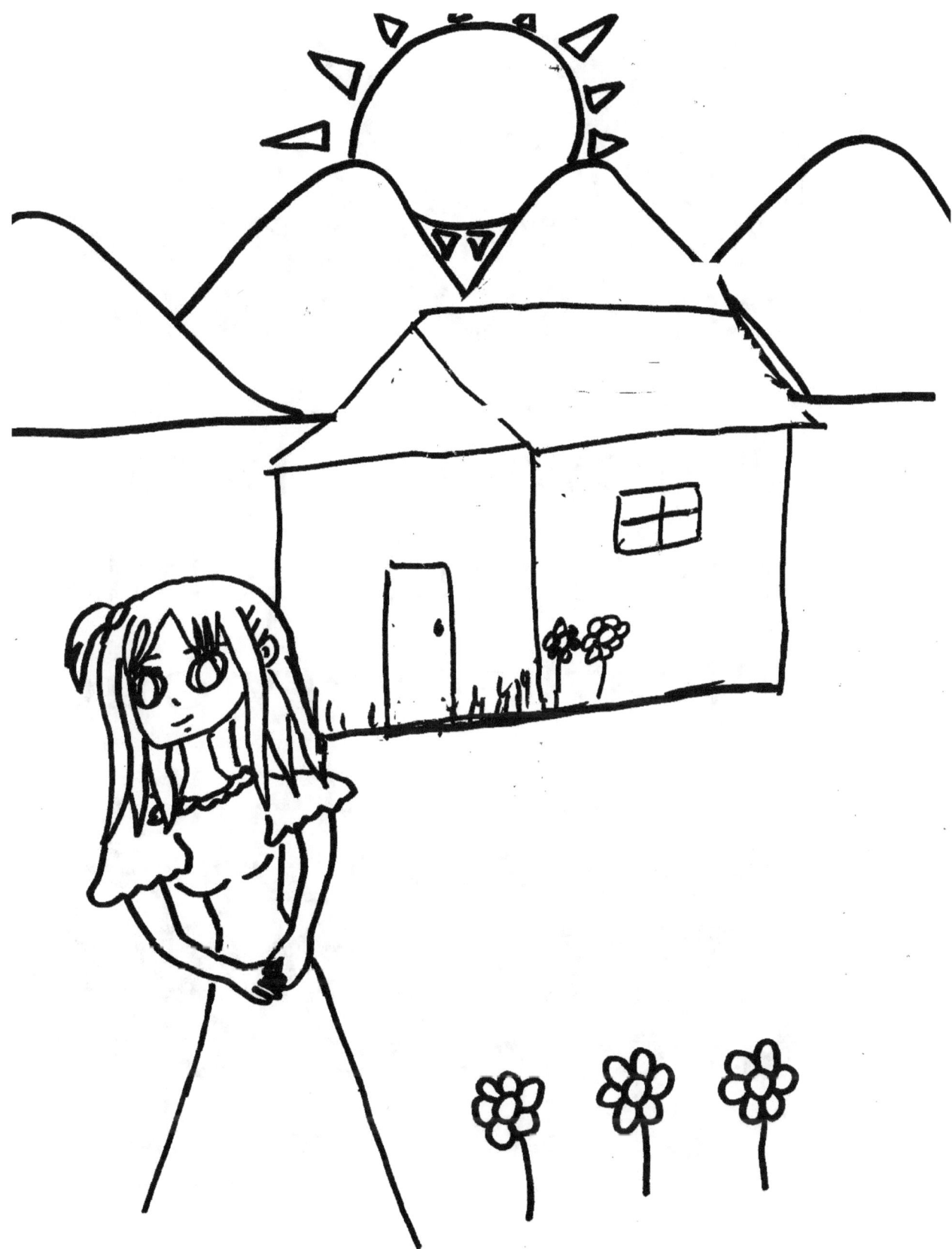

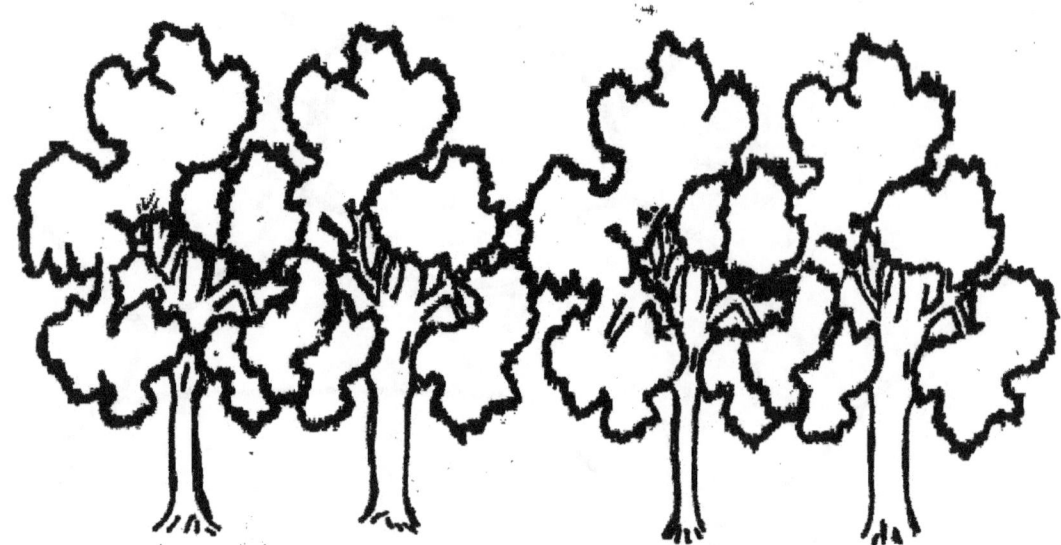

Knows the bears,
birds and rabbits
Nearly every one;

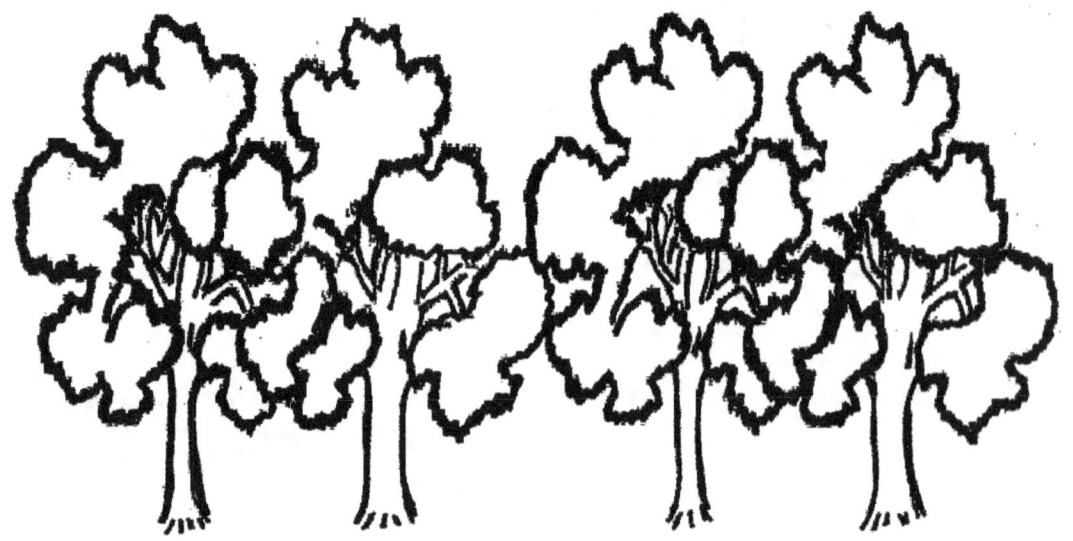

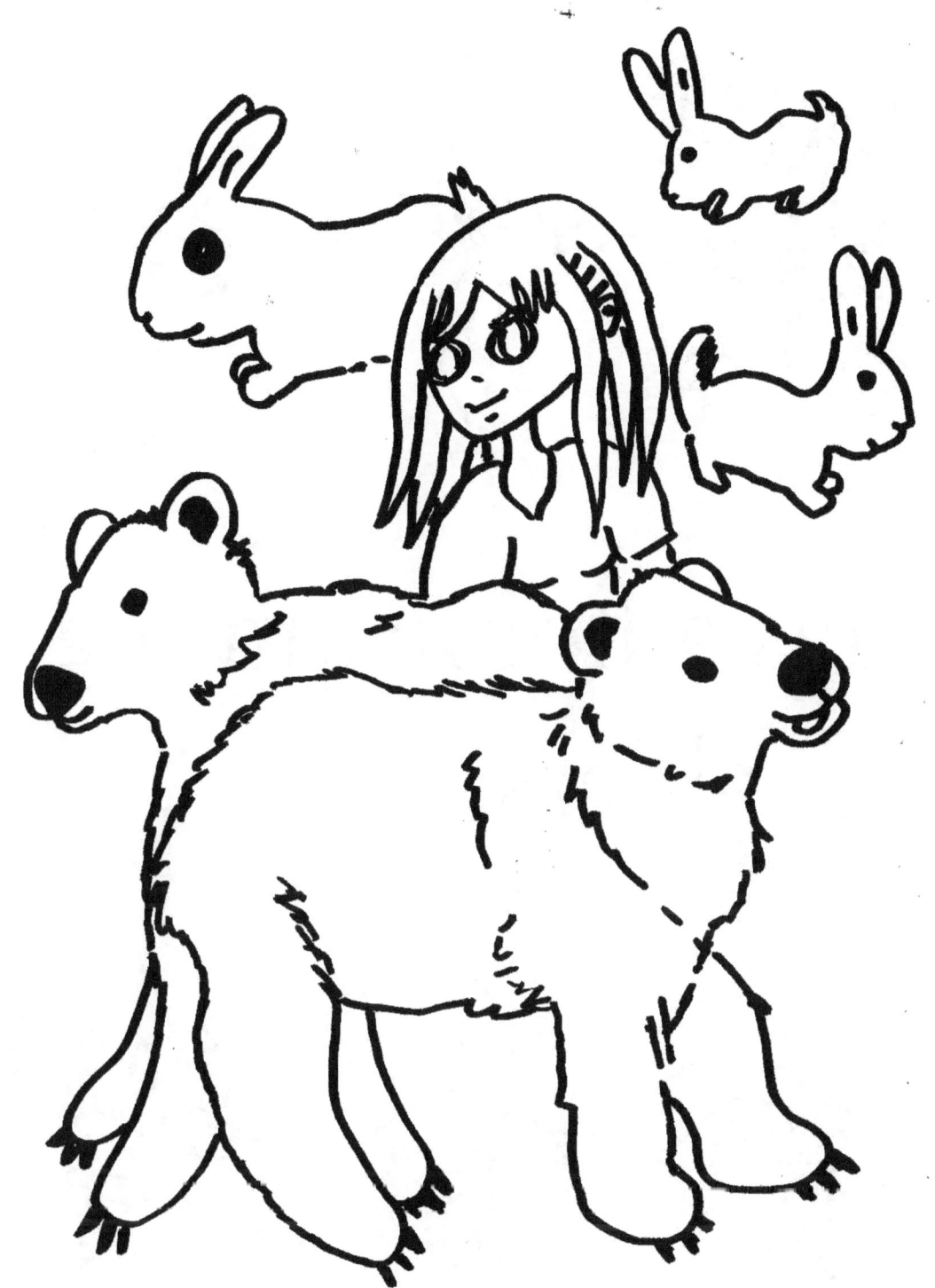

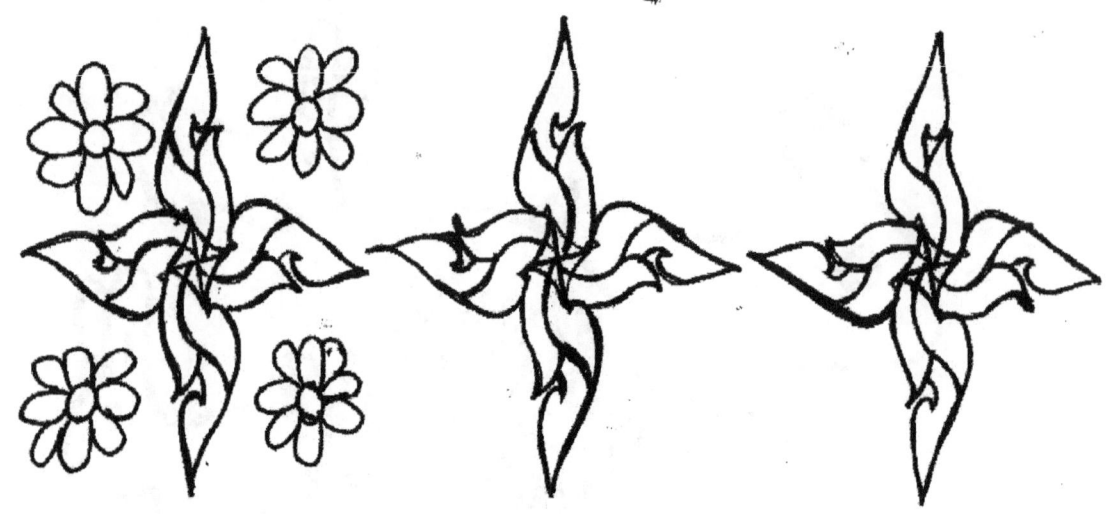

Has a home among
the alders,

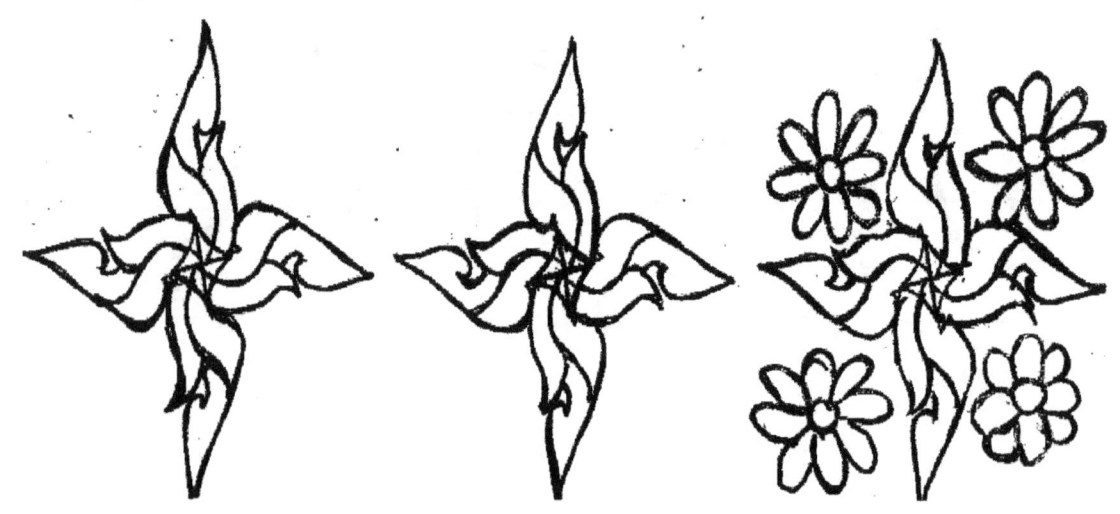

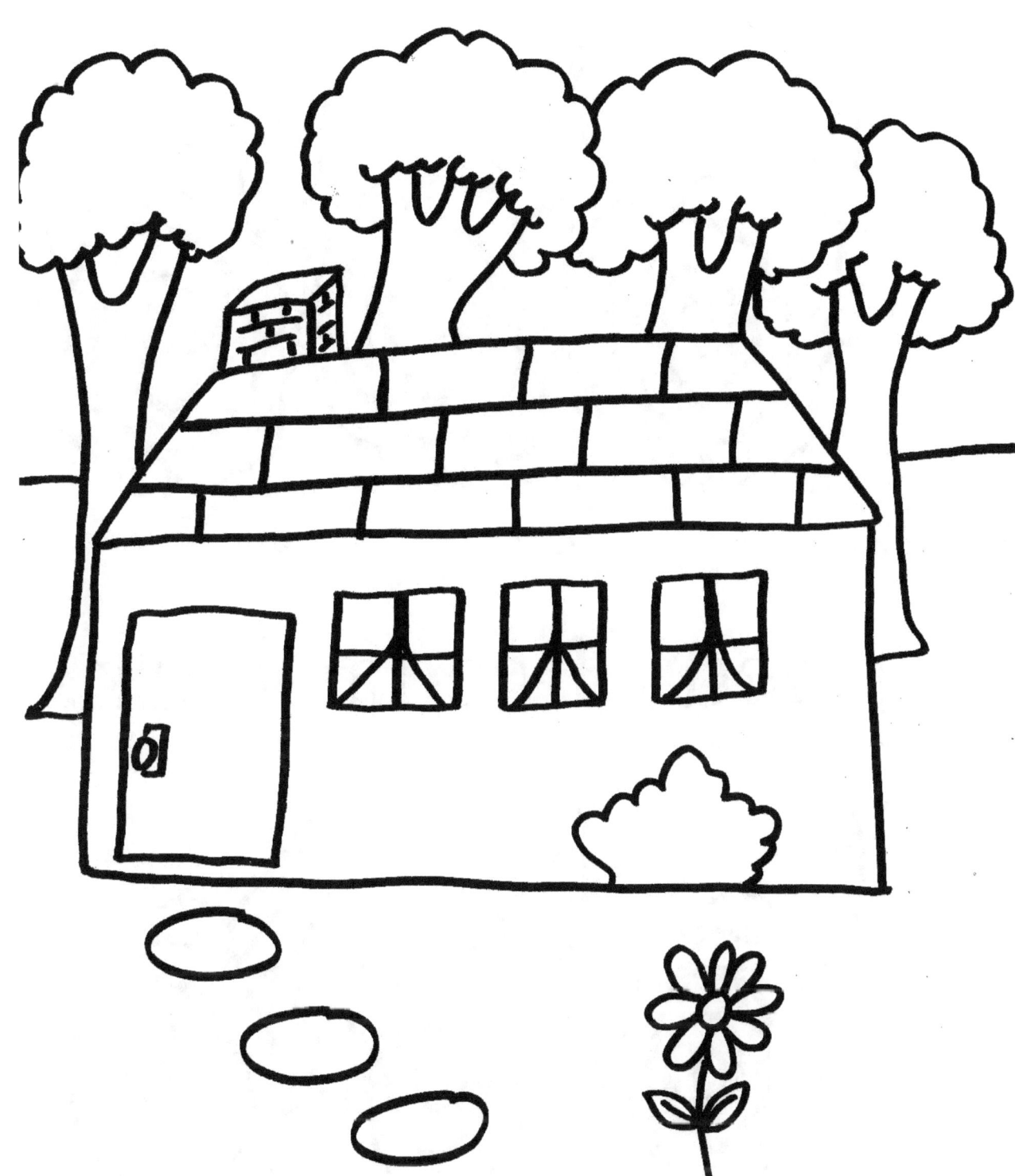

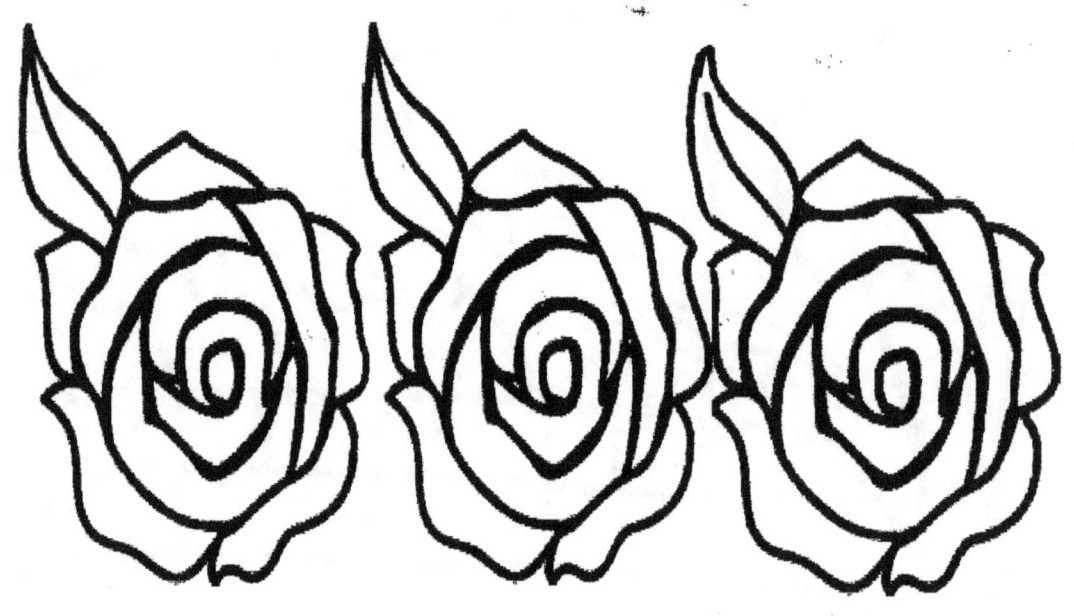

Bed of cedar bark,

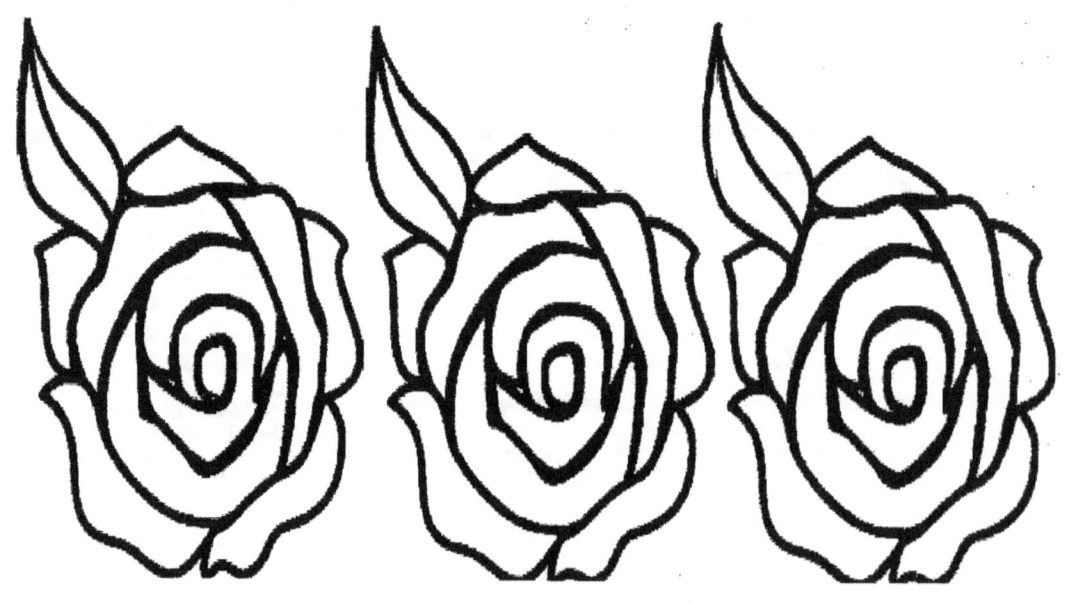

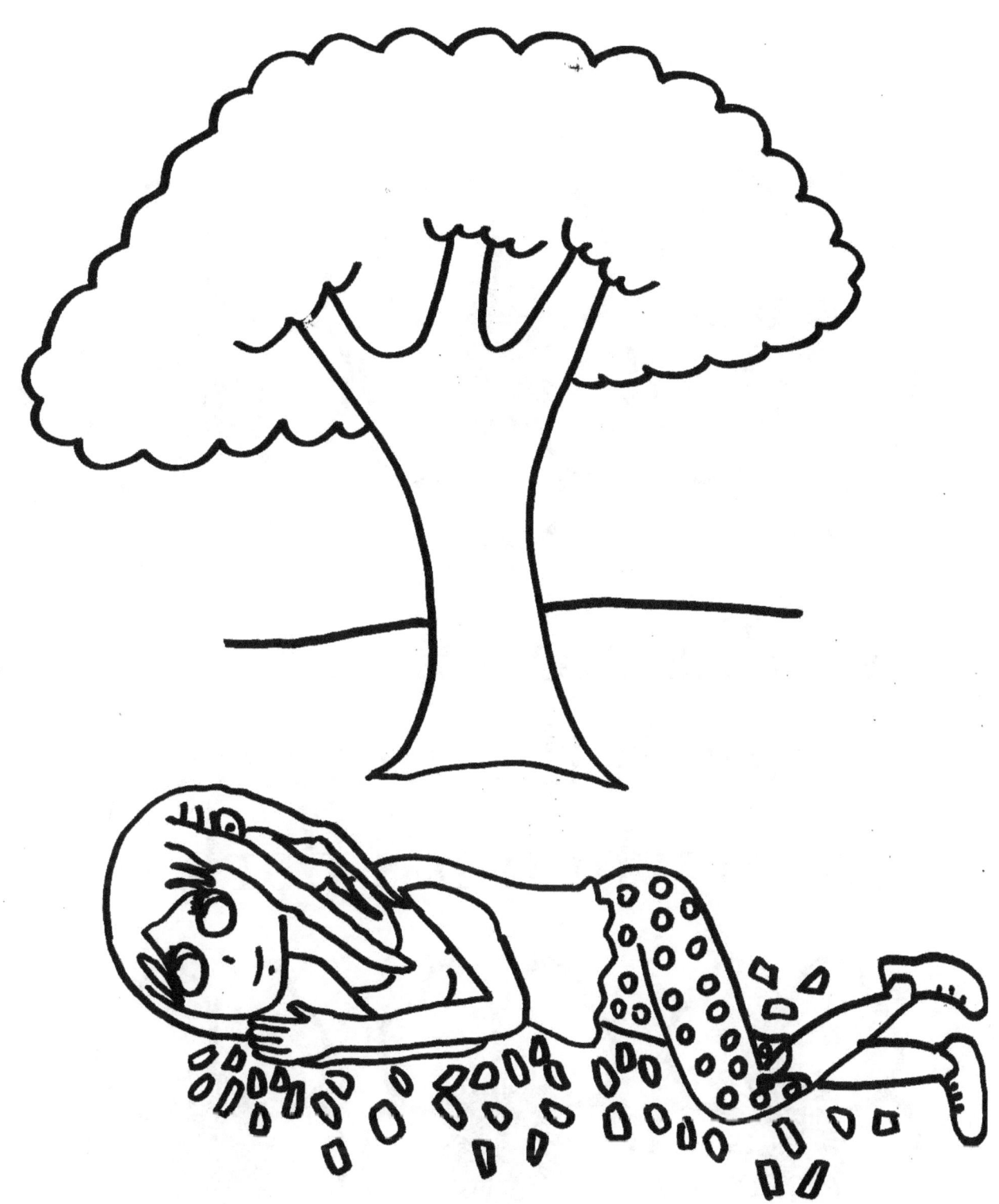

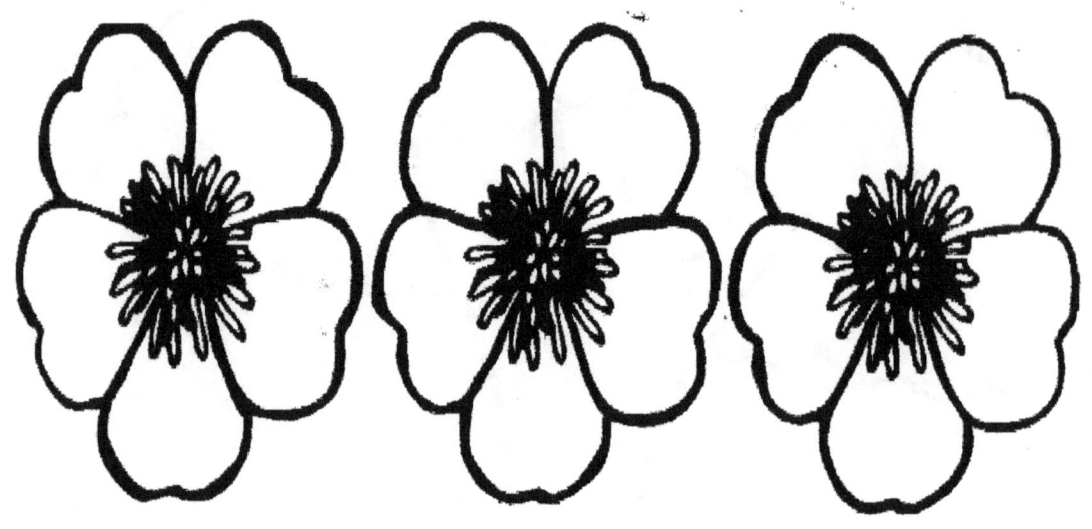

Walks alone
beneath the pine trees
Even when it's dark.

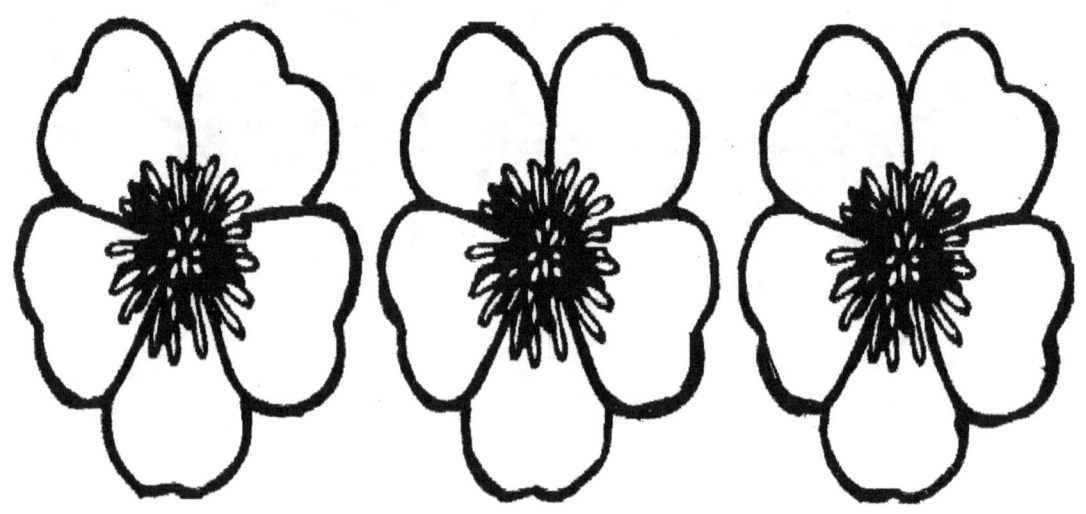

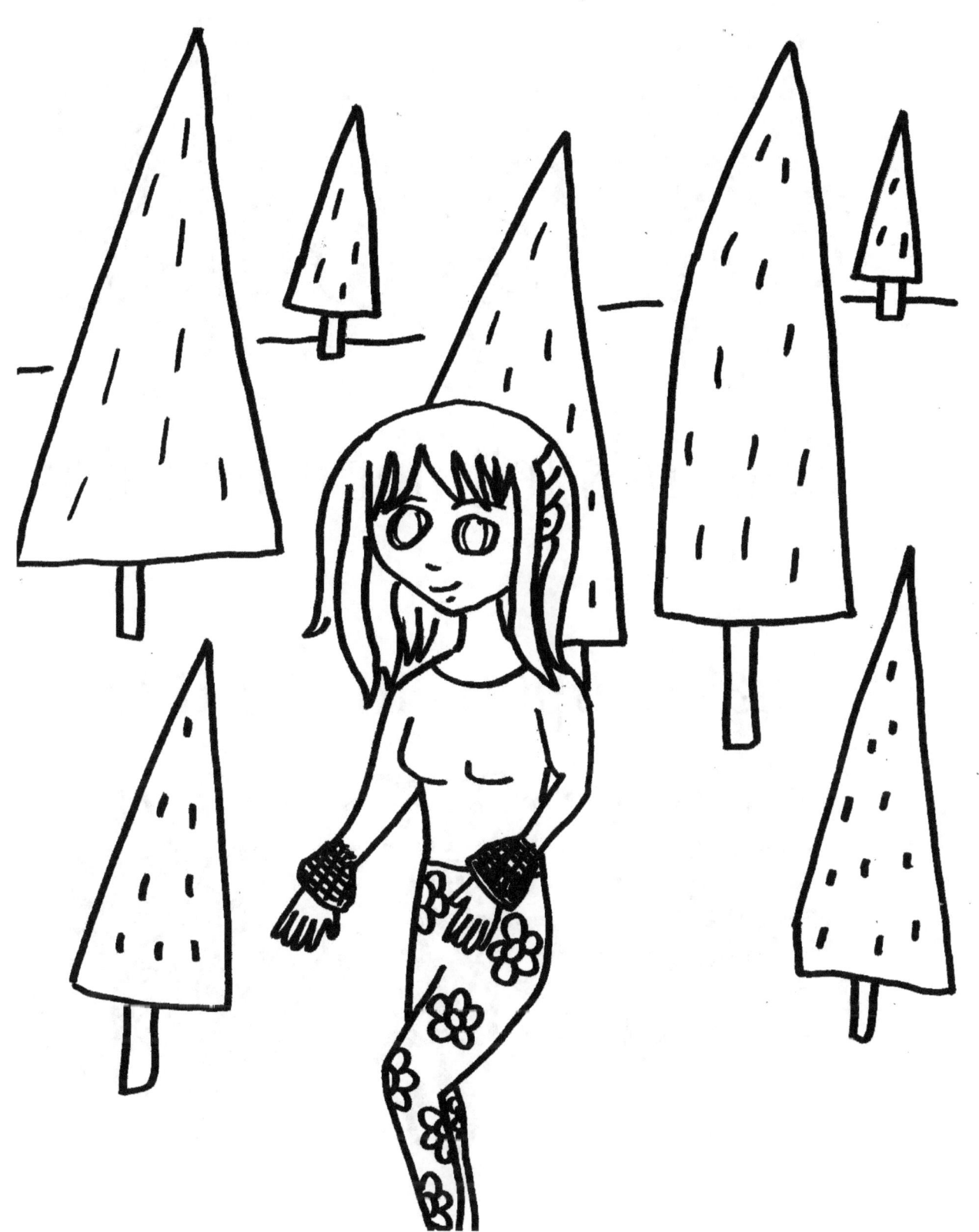

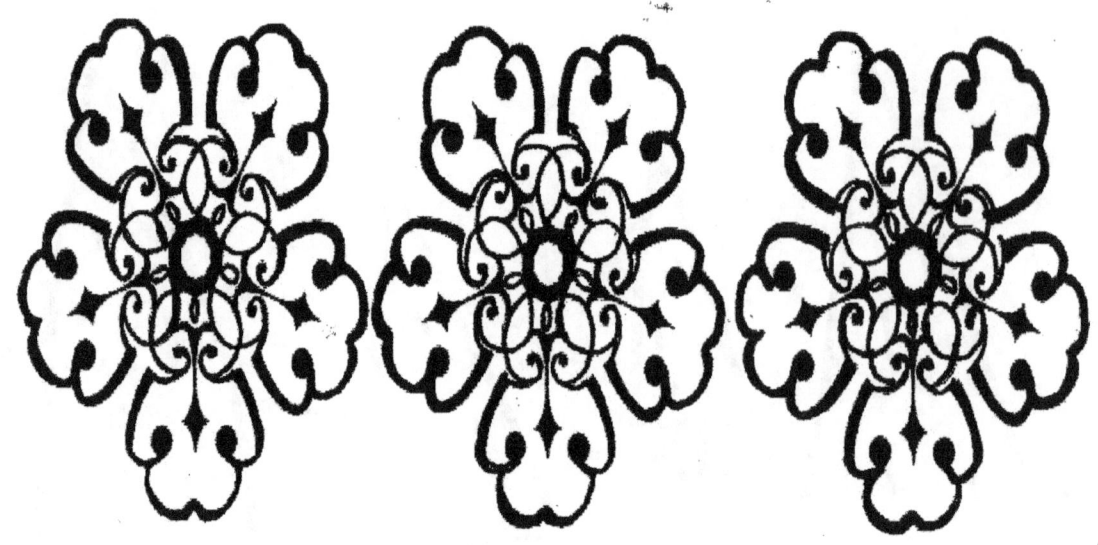

Squirrels tell her everything

That happens in the trees,

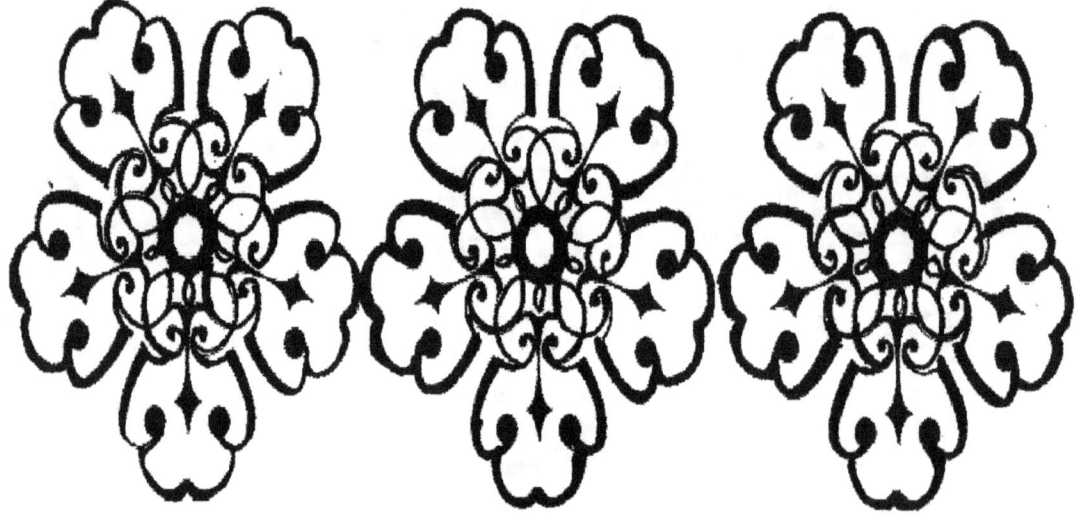

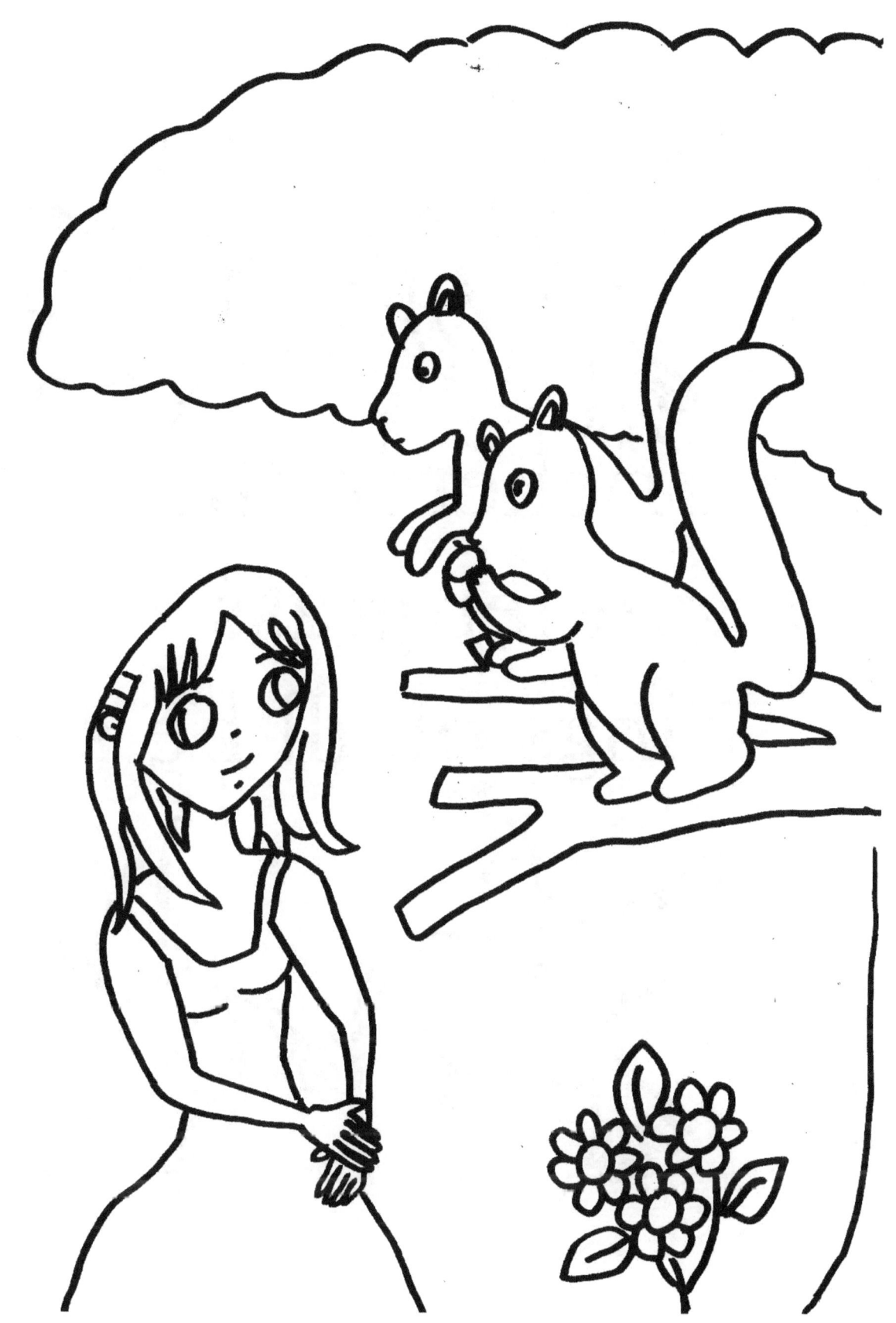

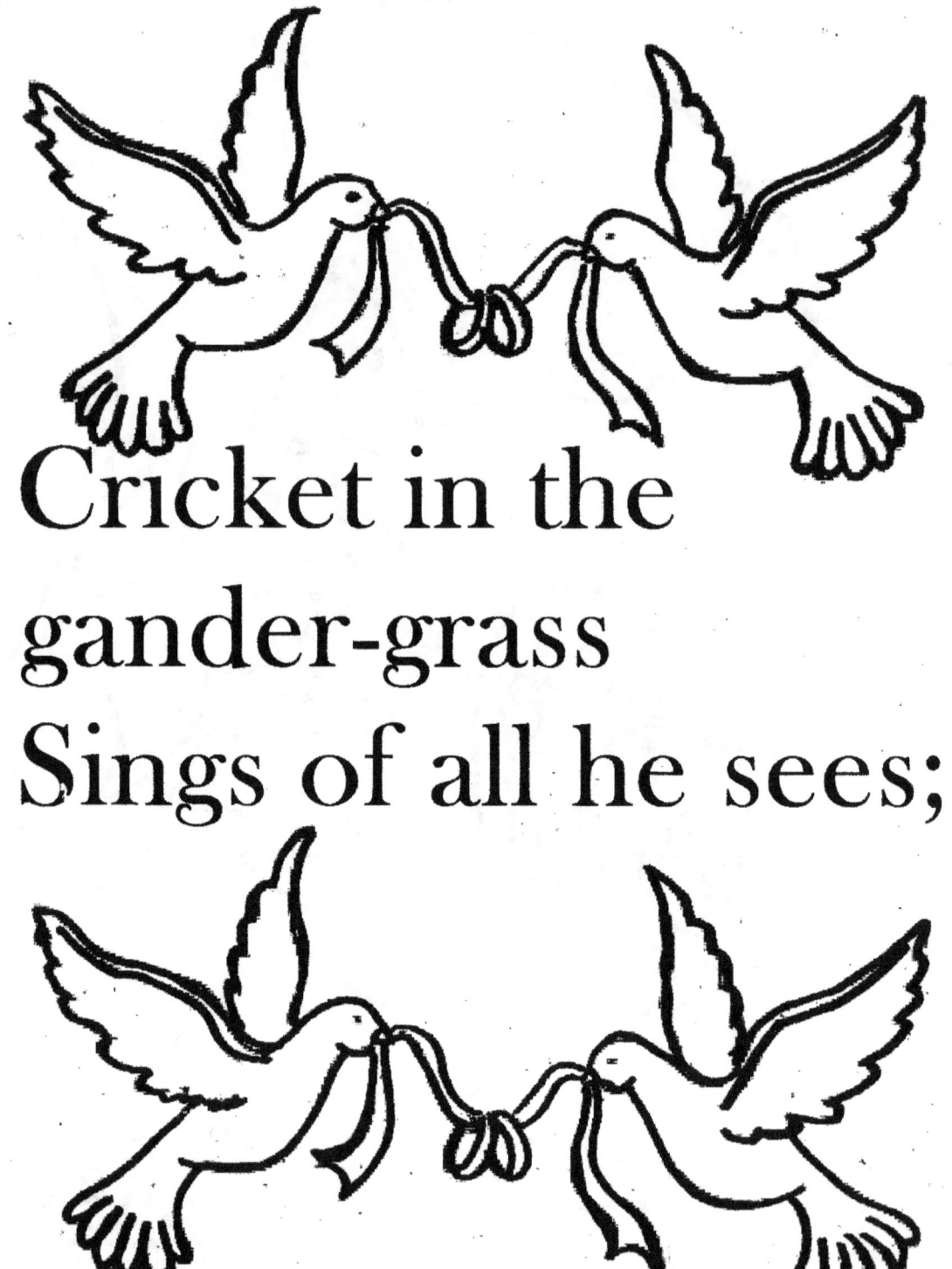

Cricket in the
gander-grass
Sings of all he sees;

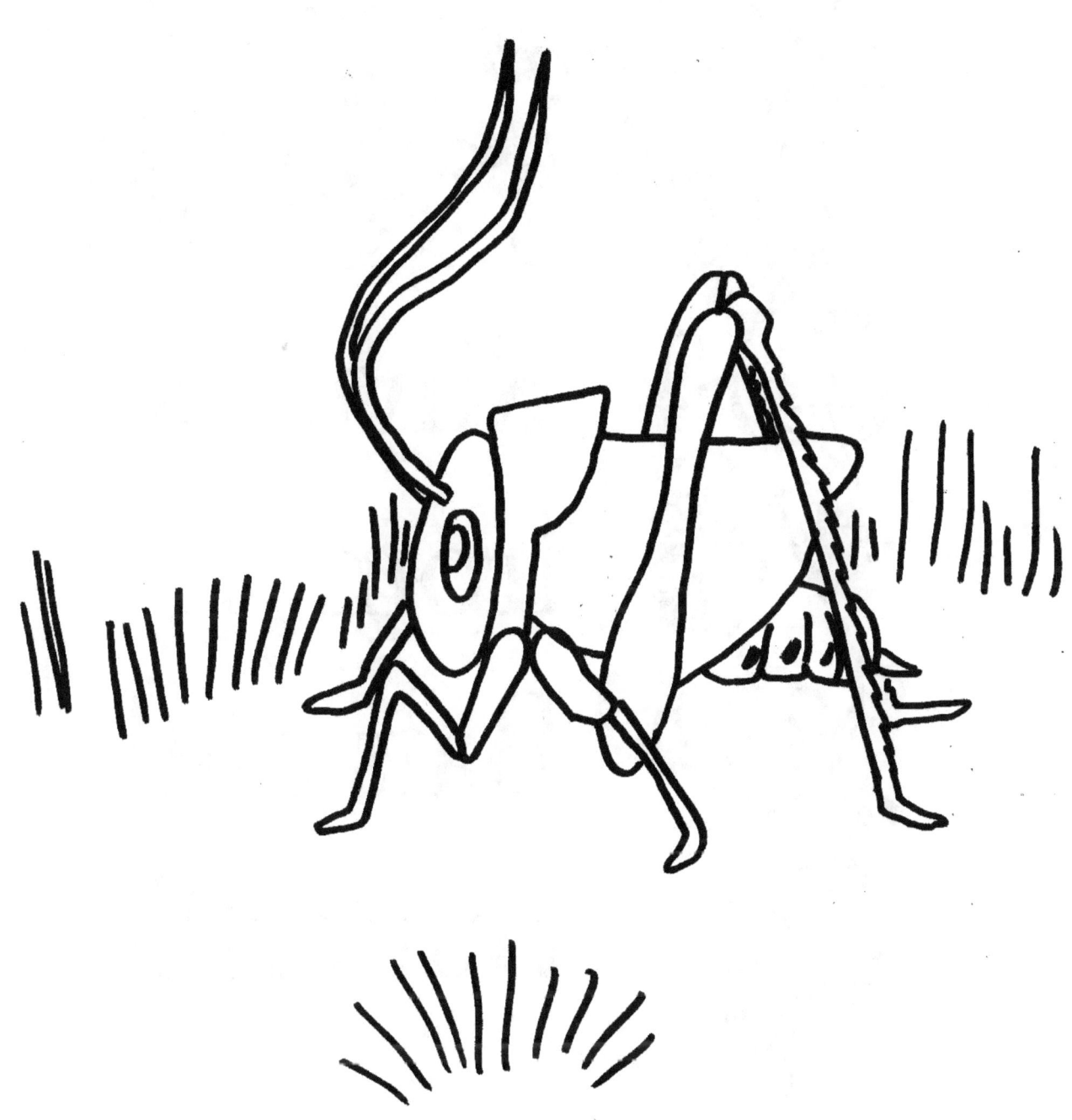

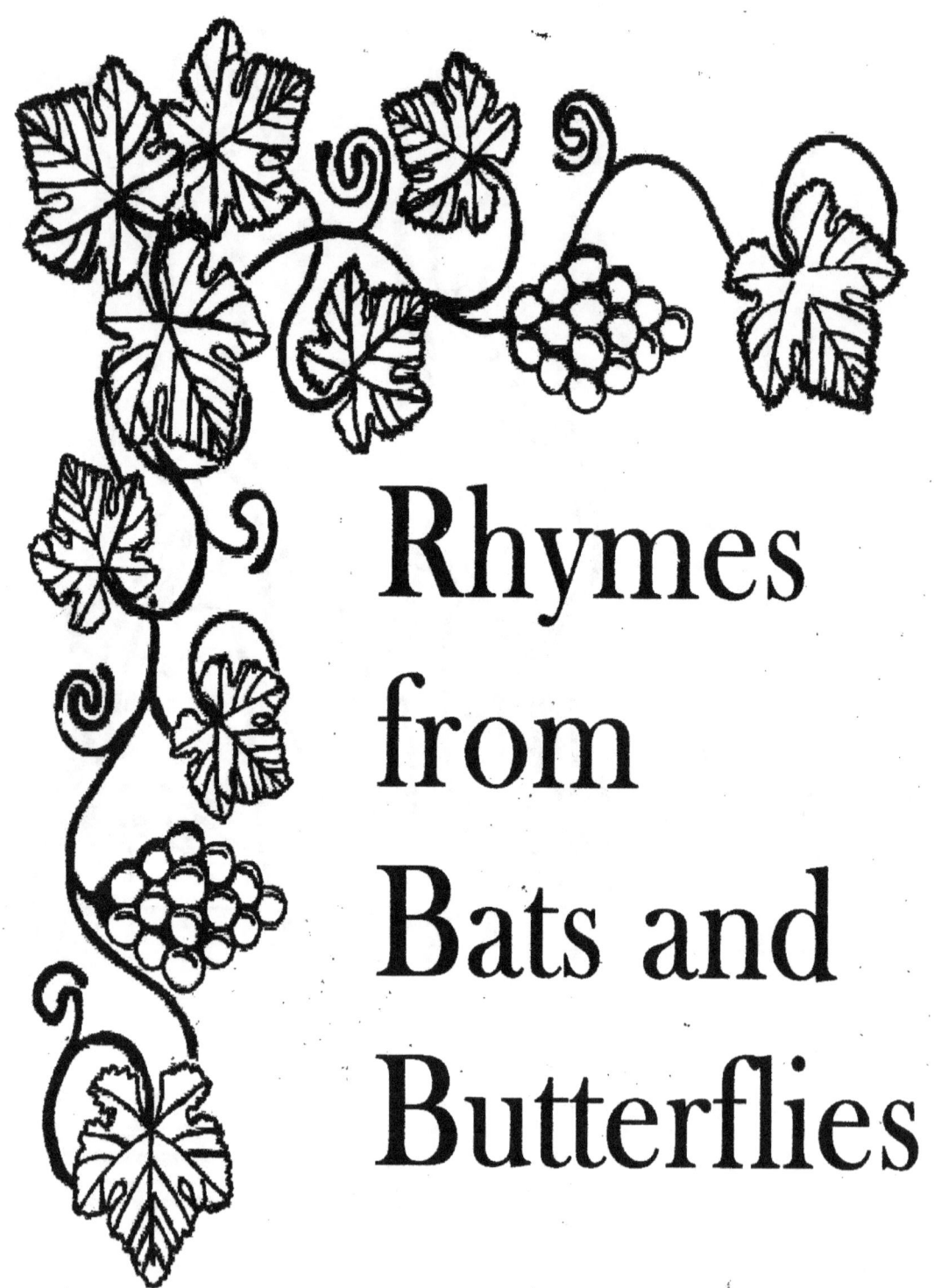

Rhymes from Bats and Butterflies

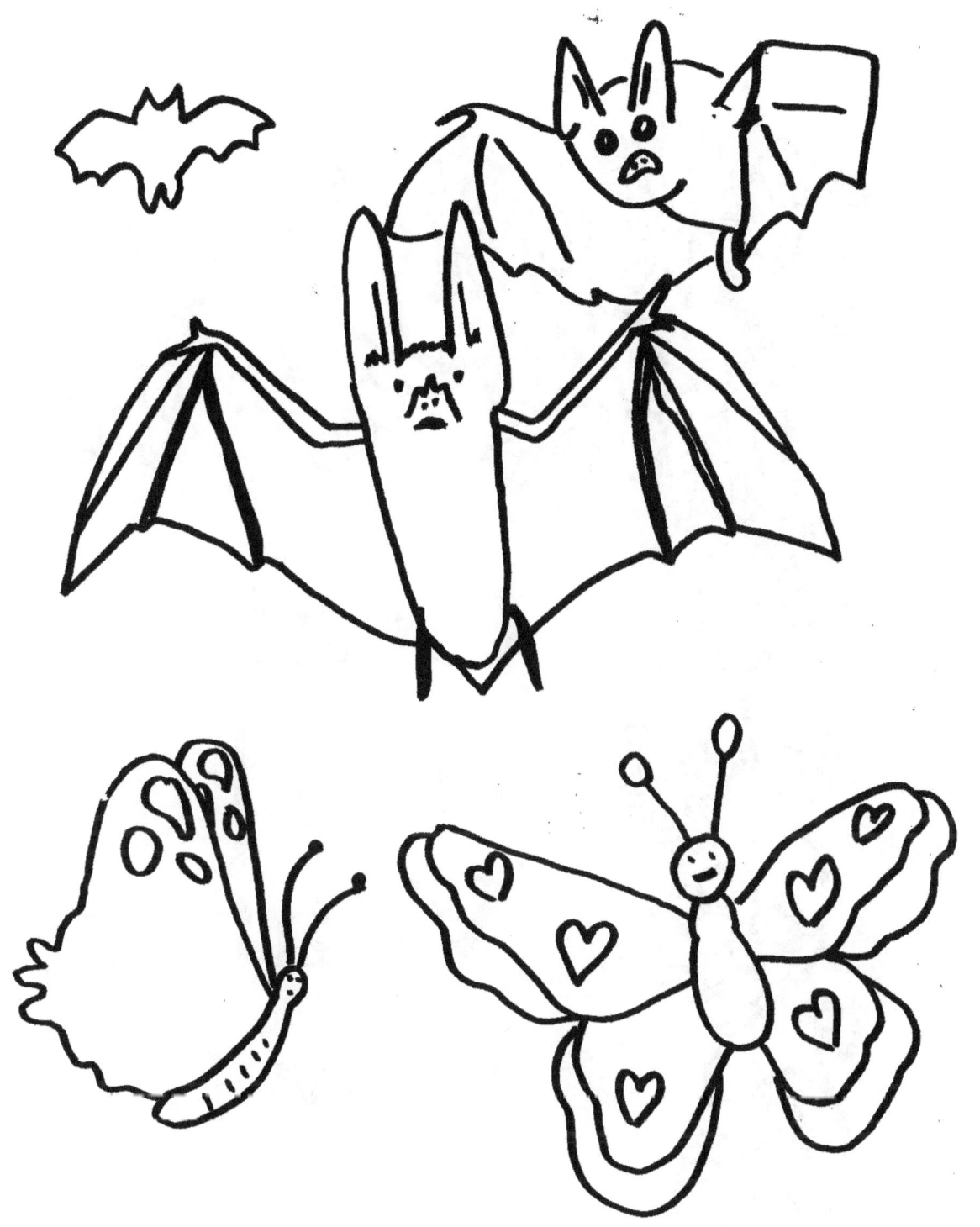

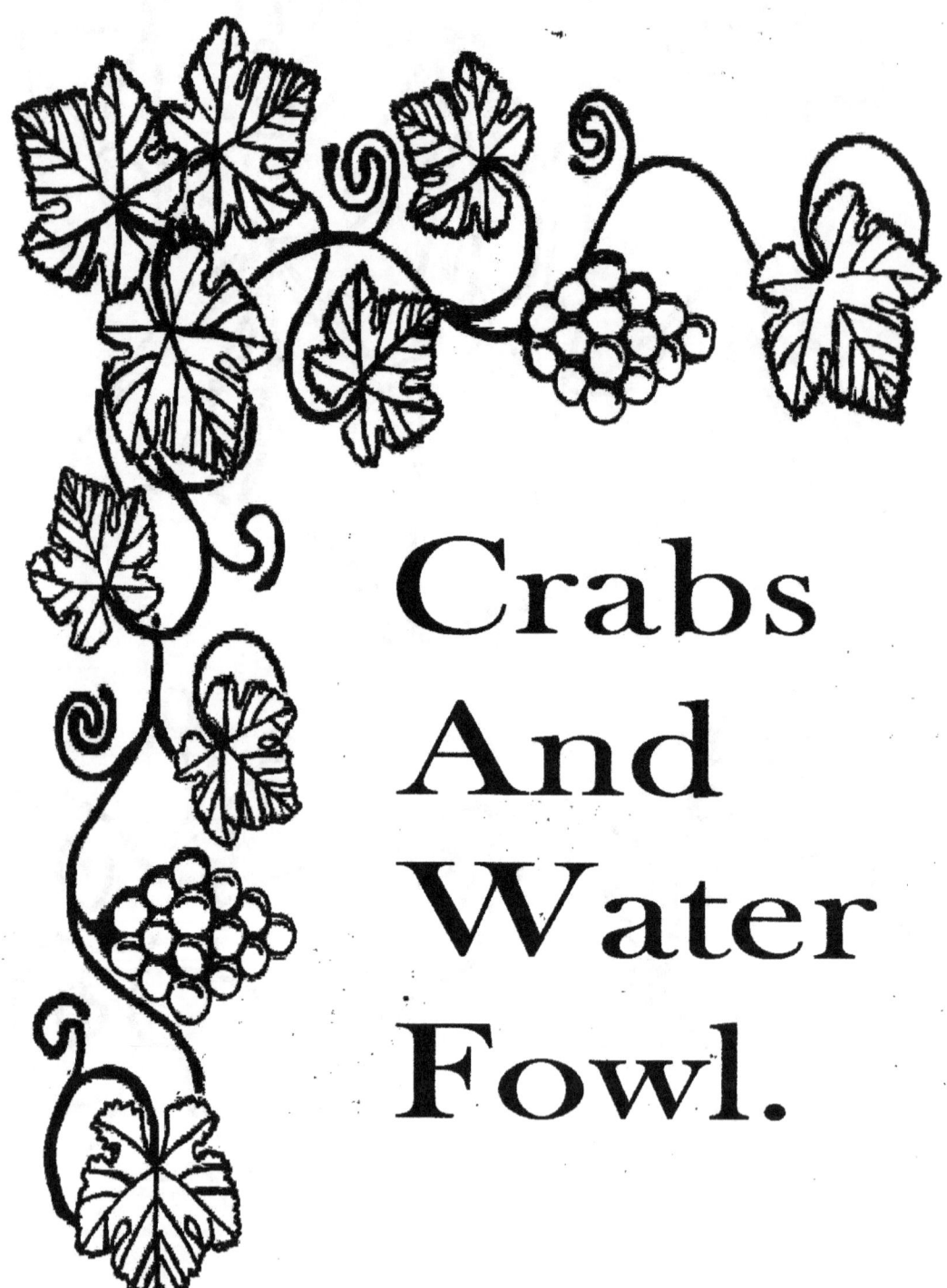

Crabs And Water Fowl.

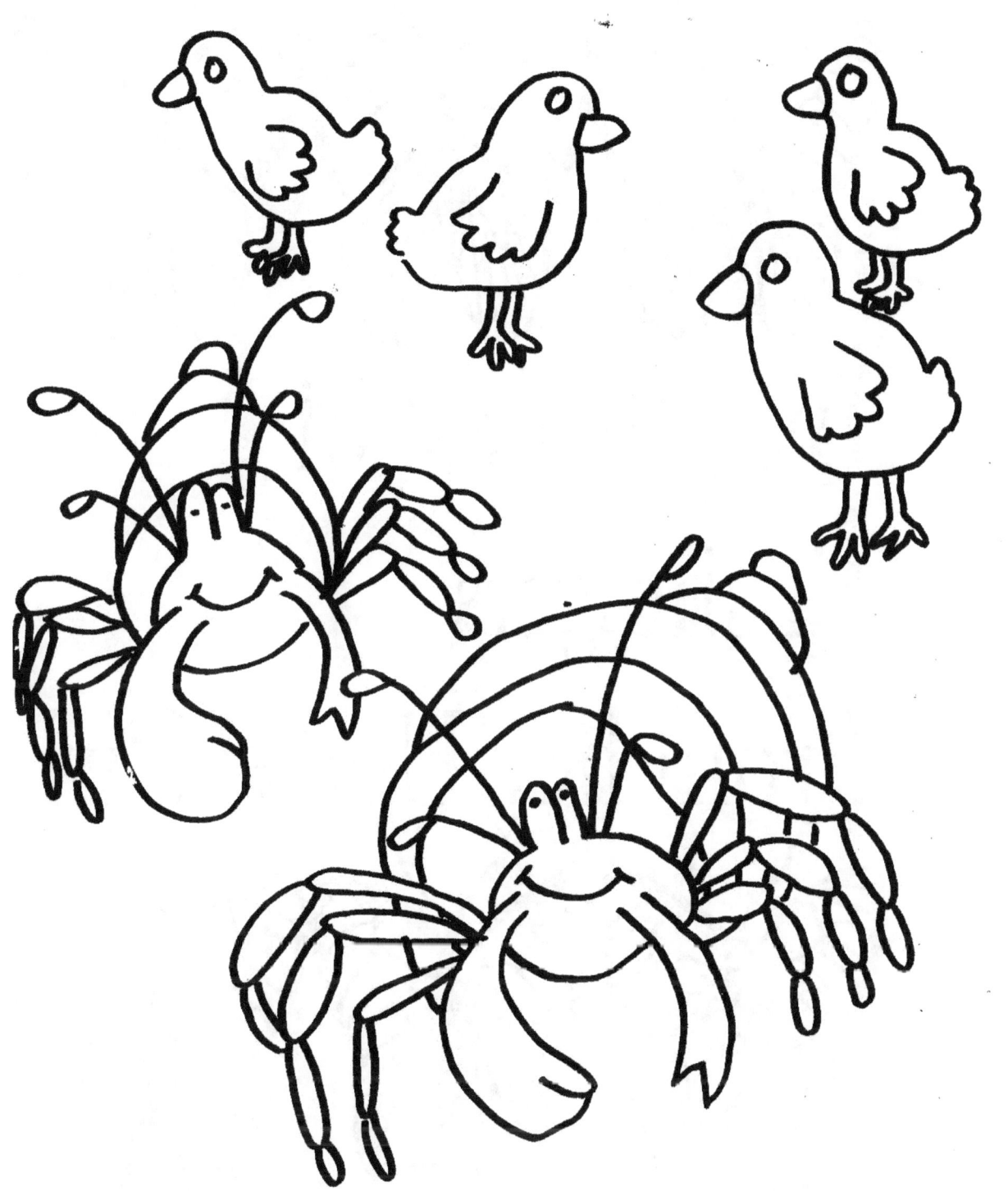

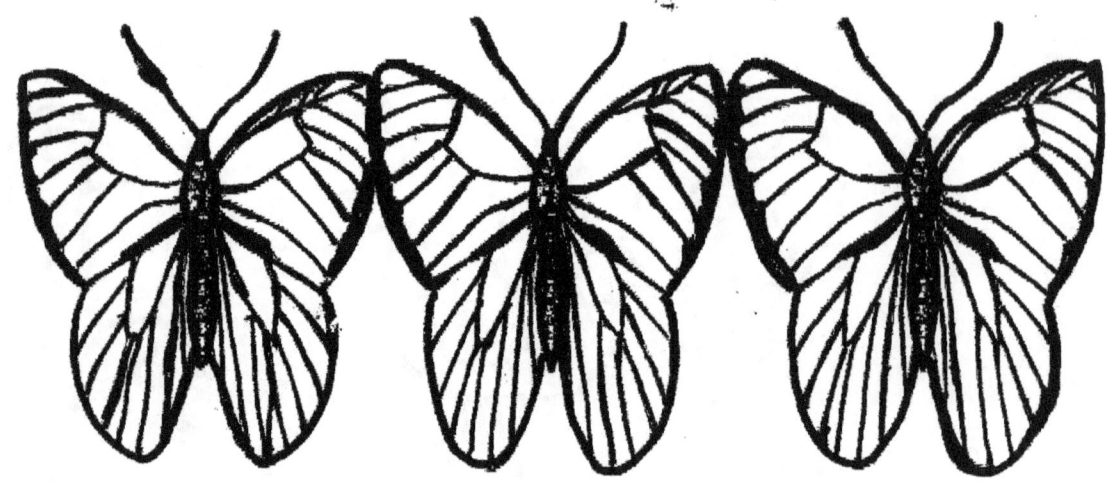

But the best of
all she gets
From her Uncle Owl.

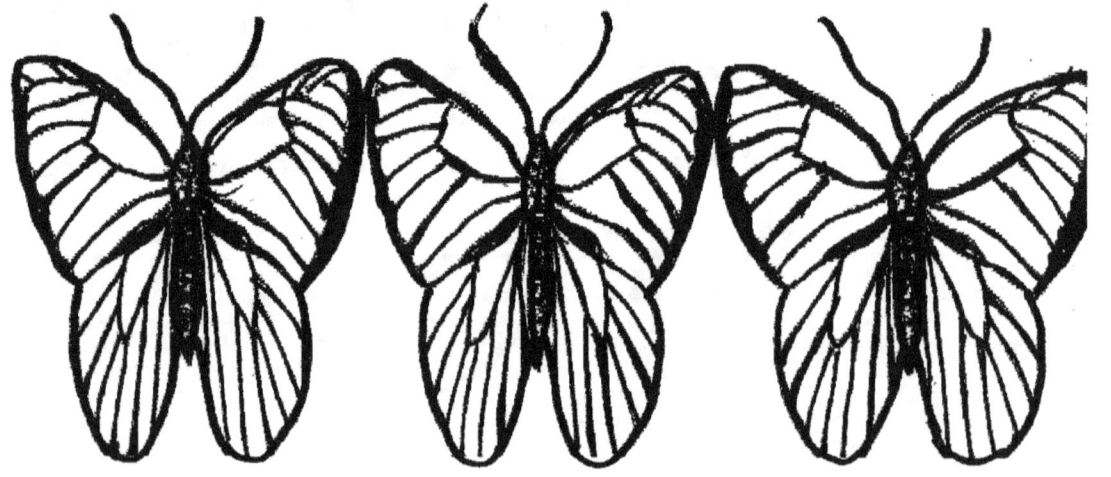

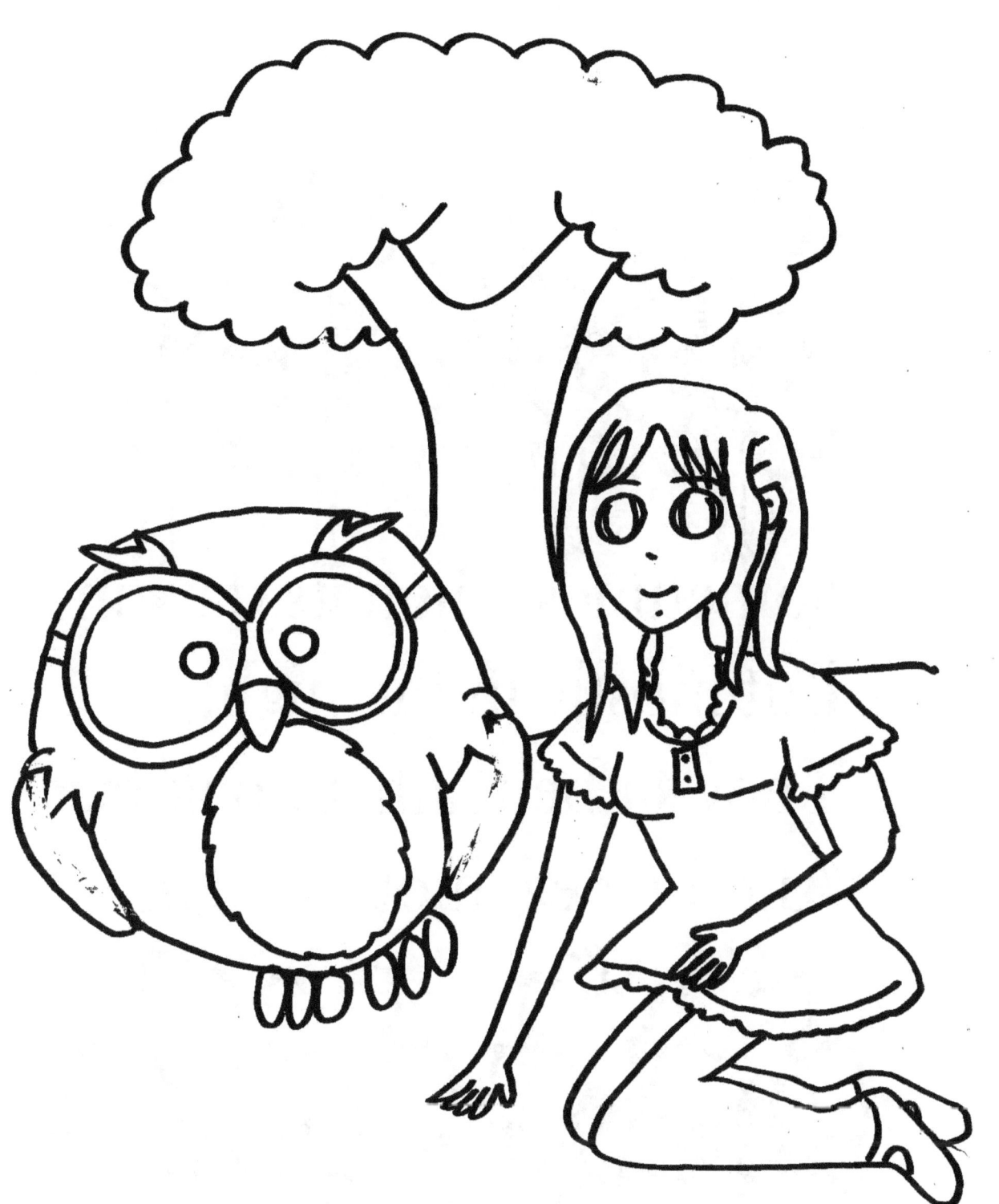

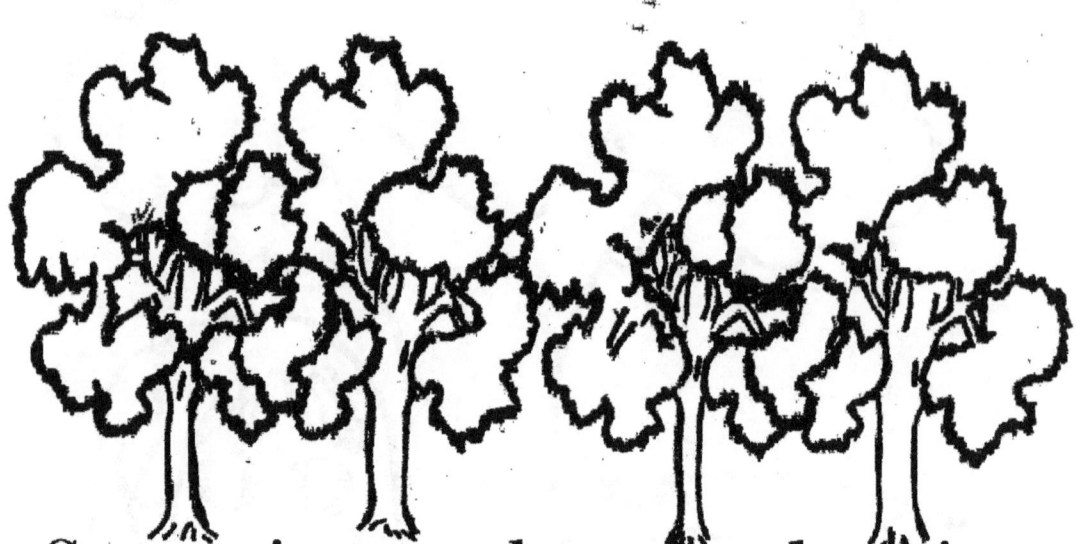

Sometimes when its day-time,
But mostly in the night,
They sit beneath an oak tree
And hug each other tight,

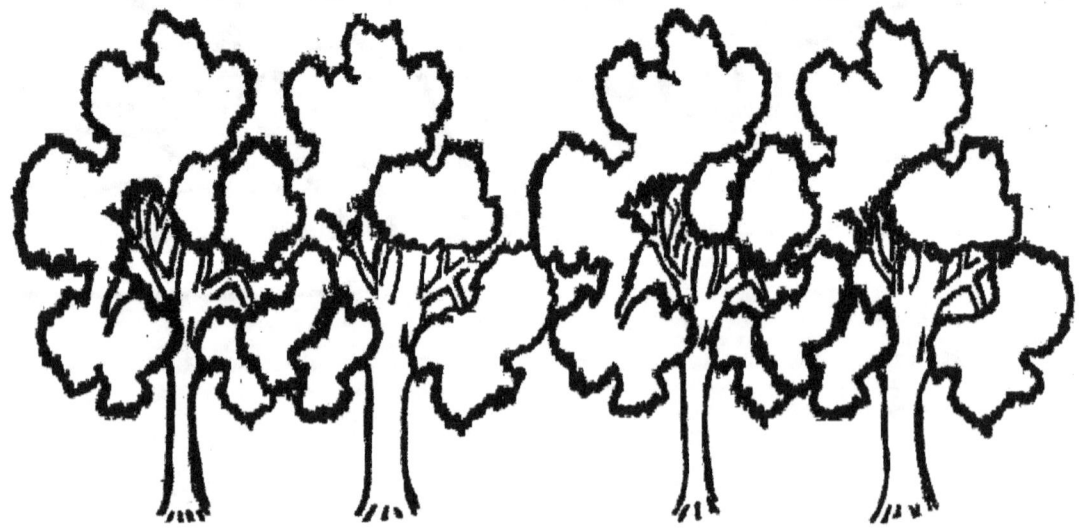

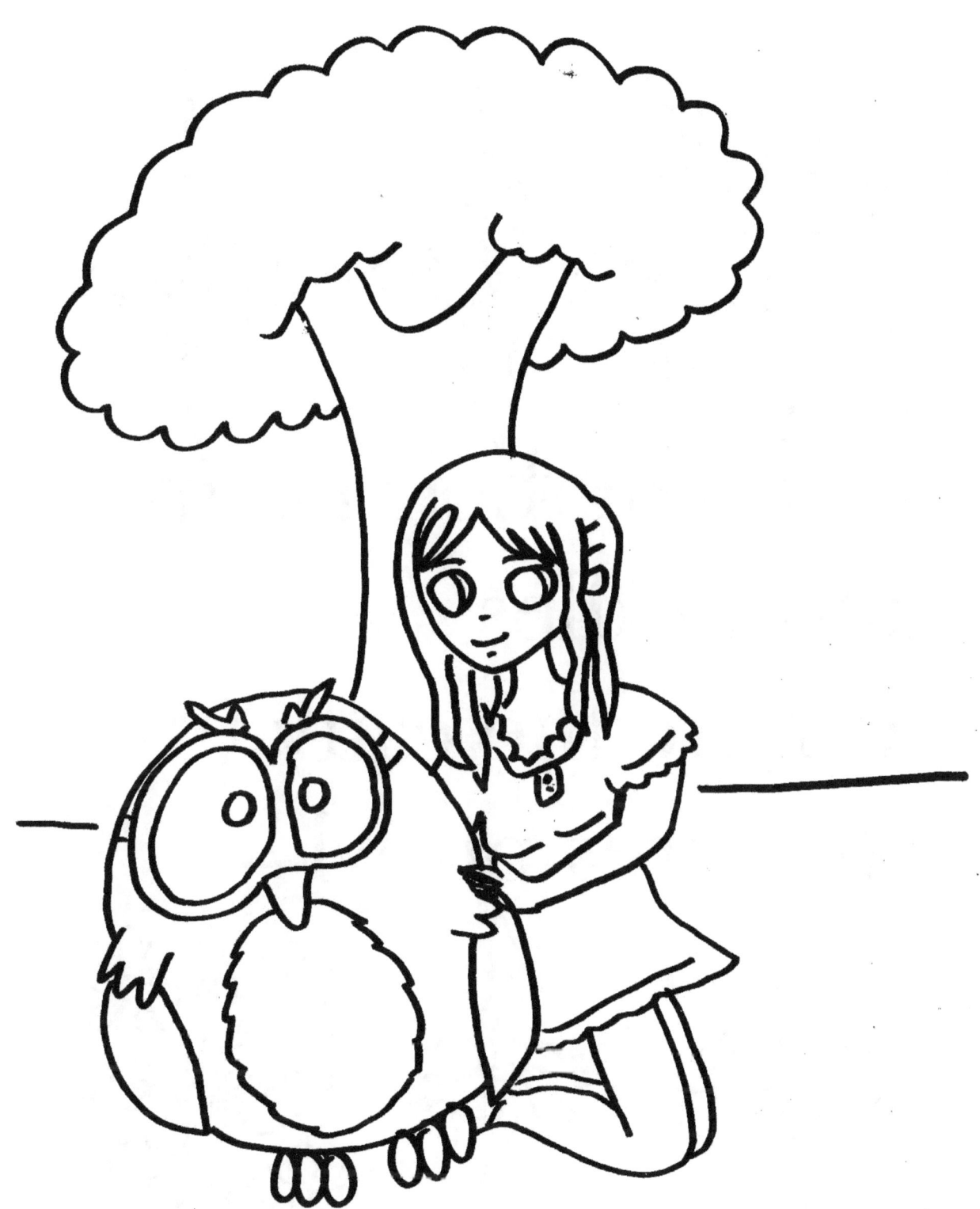

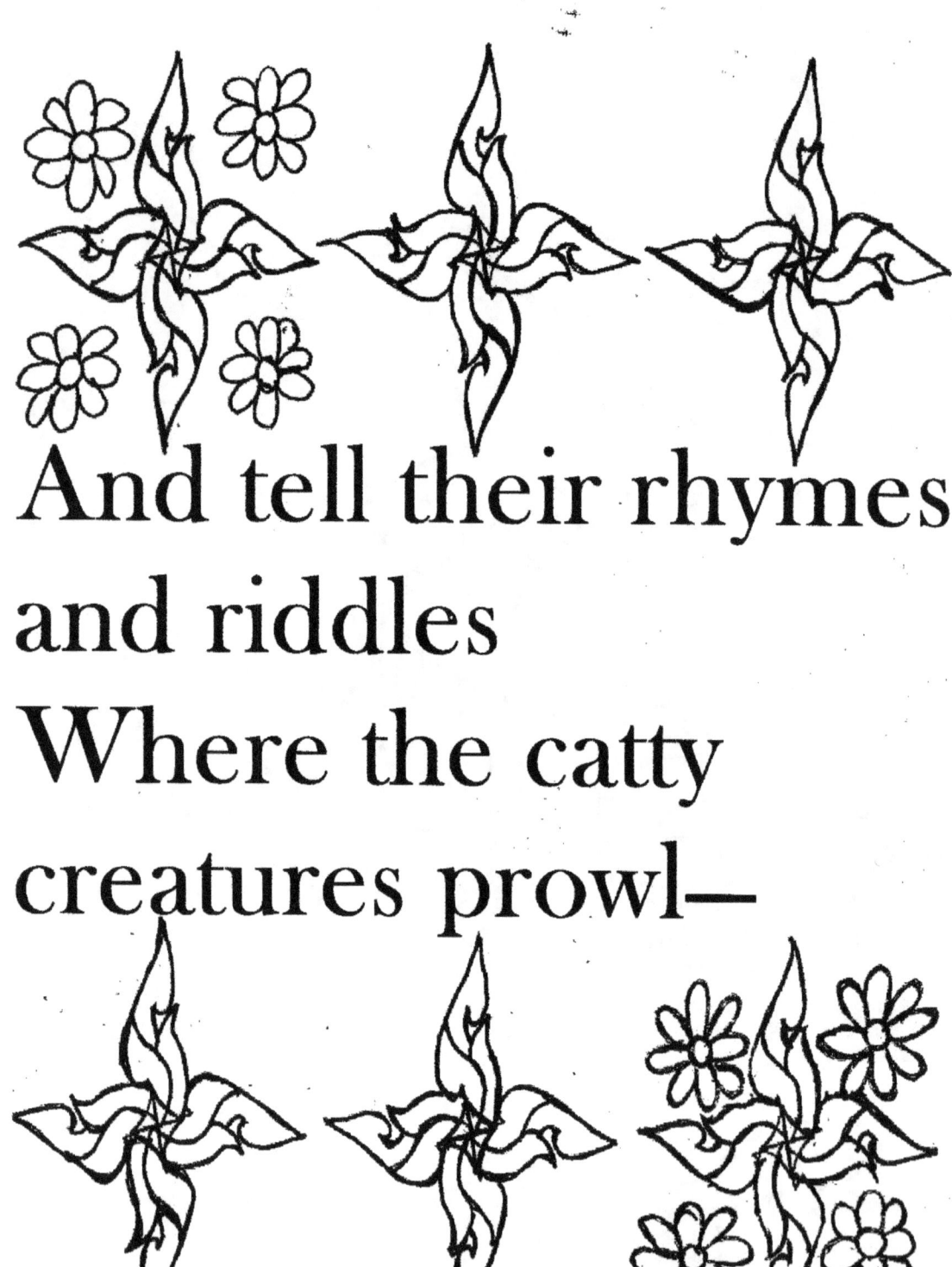

And tell their rhymes
and riddles
Where the catty
creatures prowl—

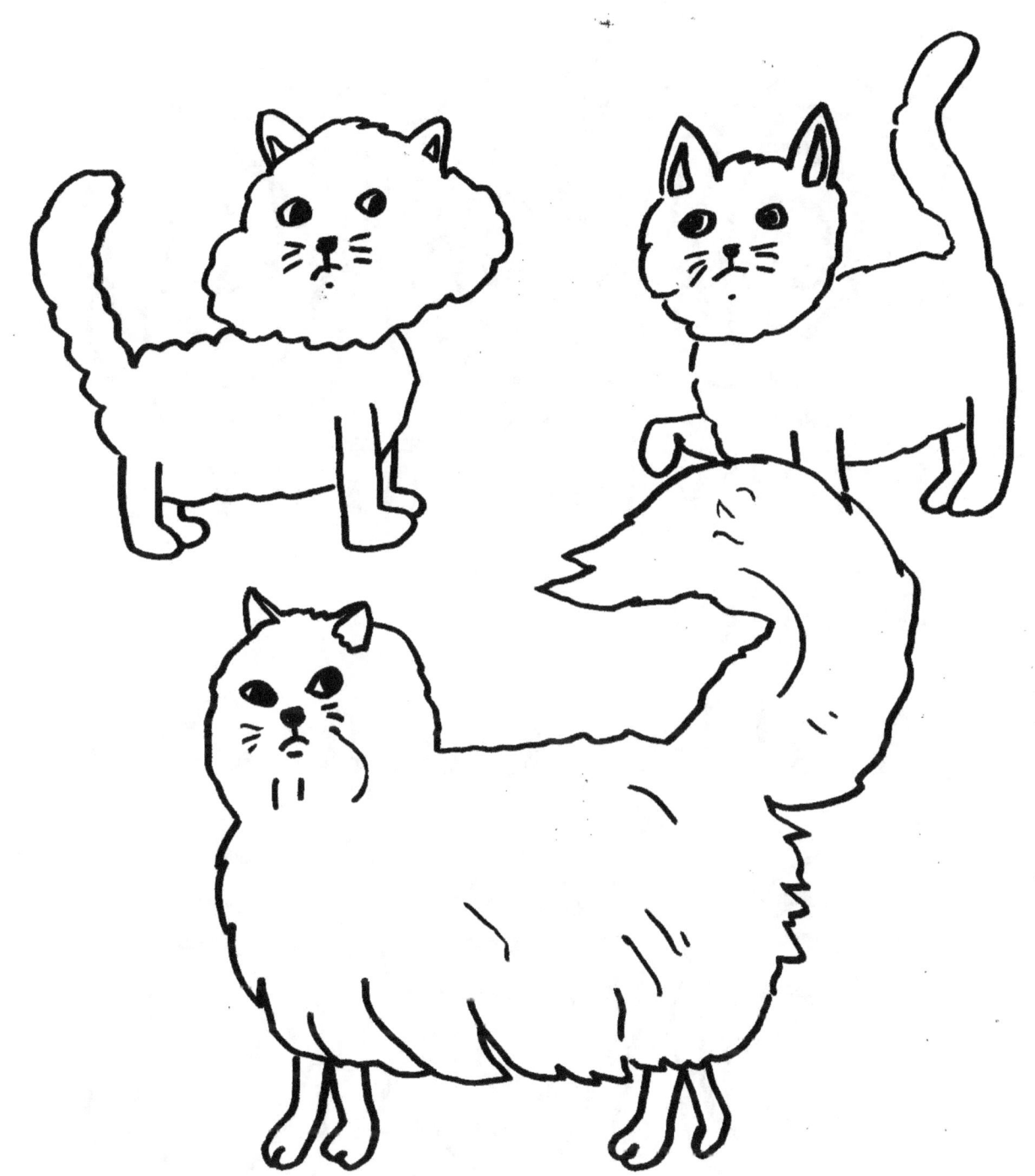

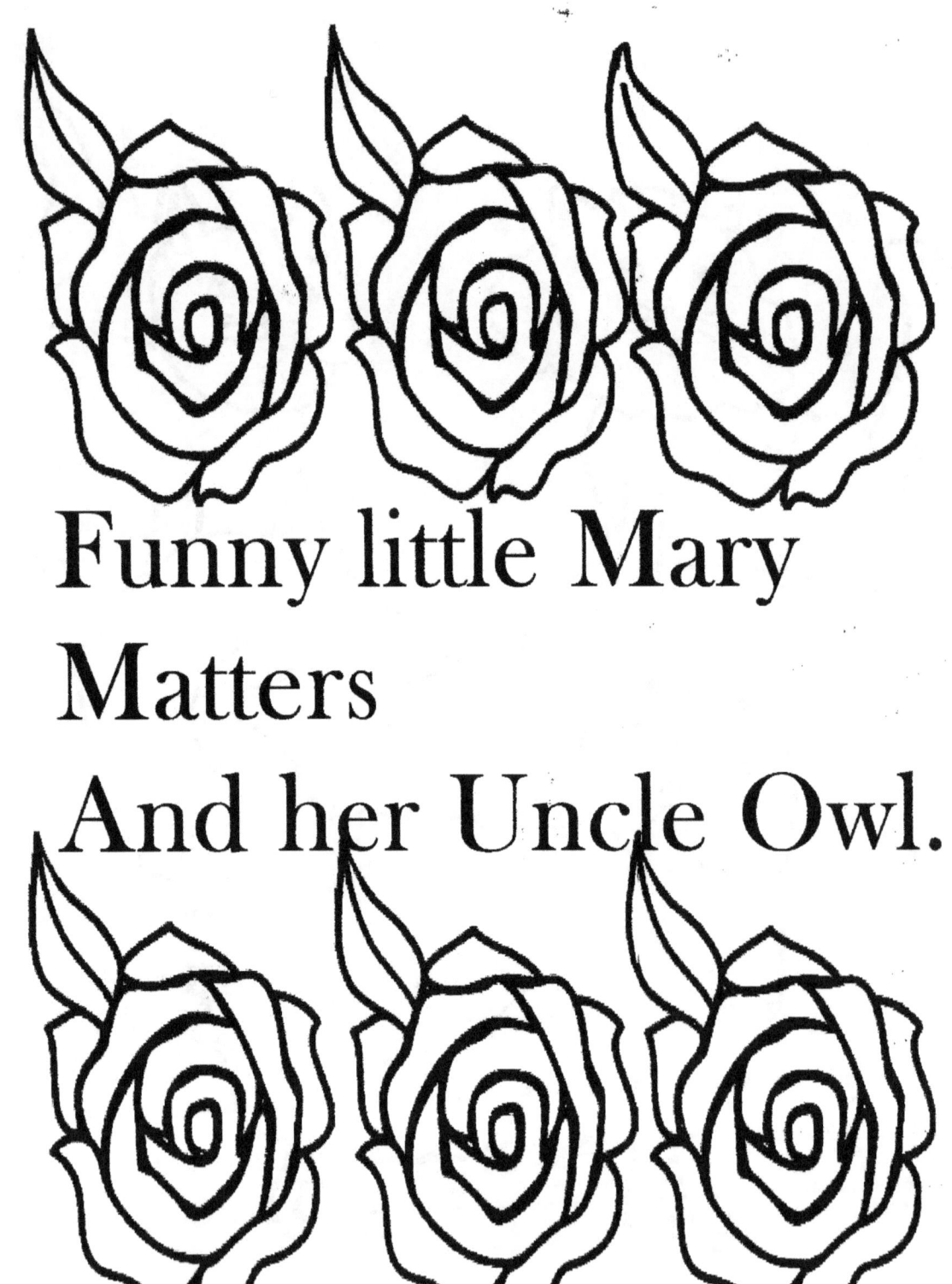

Funny little Mary
Matters
And her Uncle Owl.

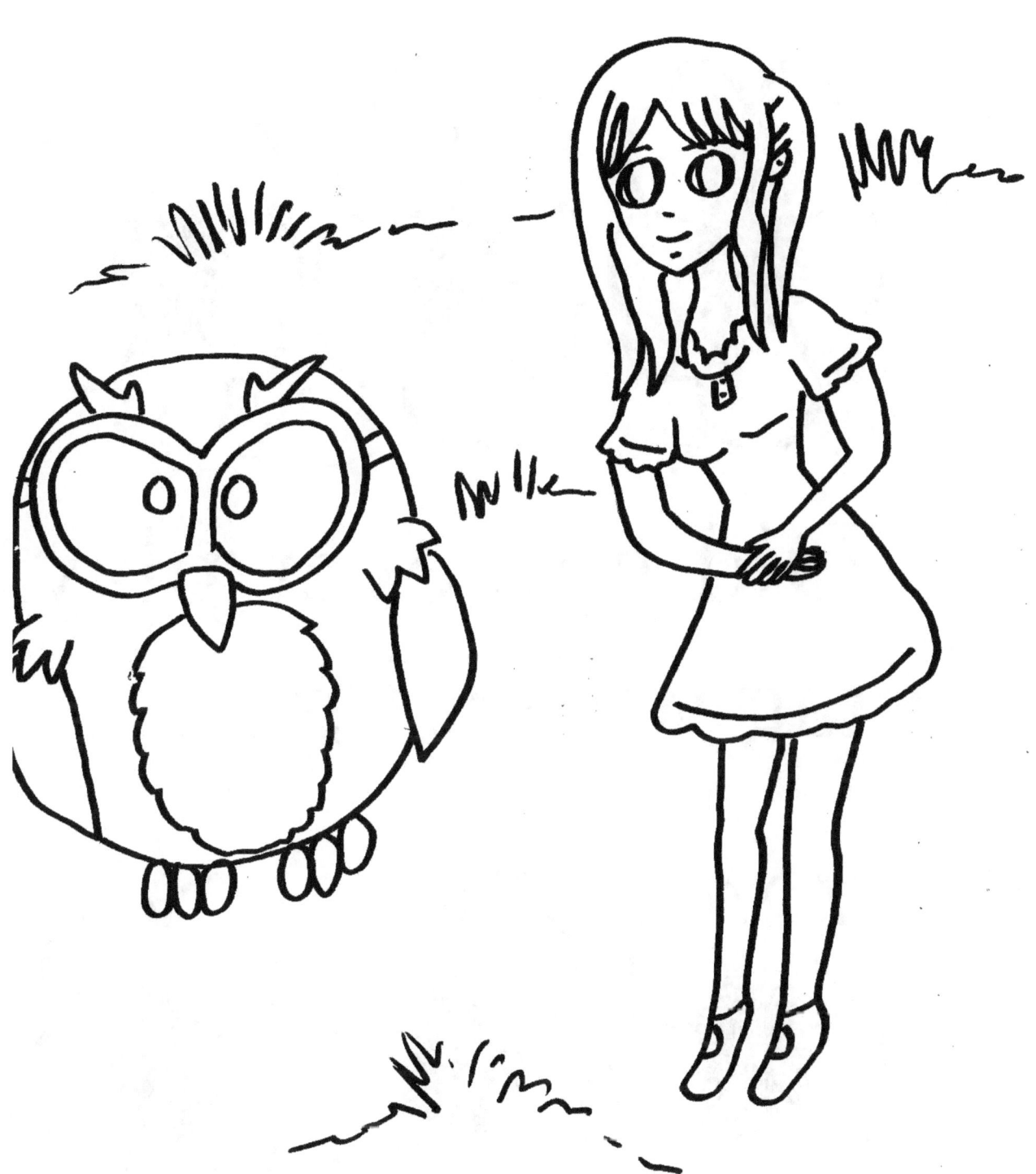

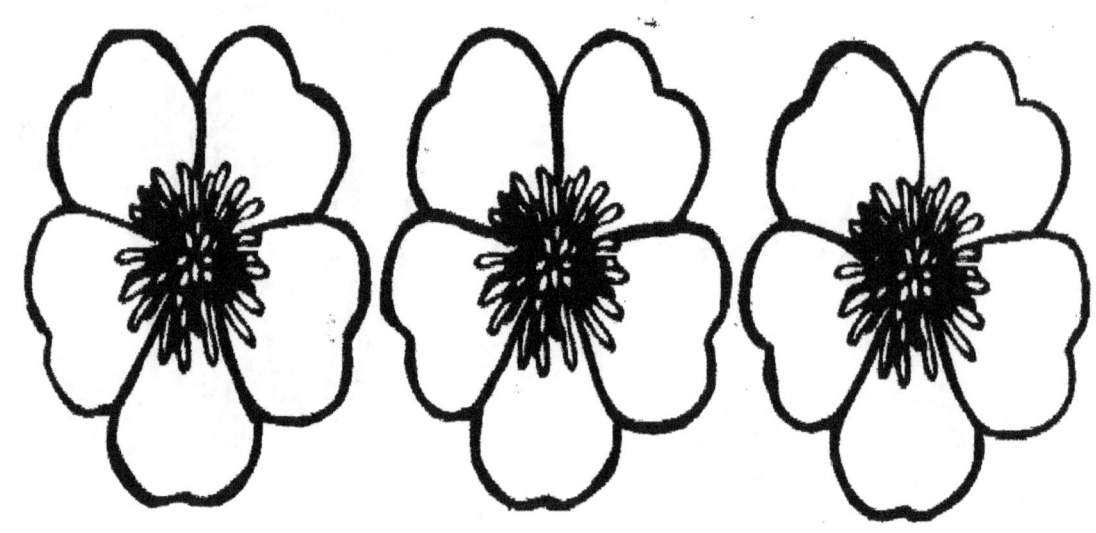

Did you ever play
tag with a tiger,

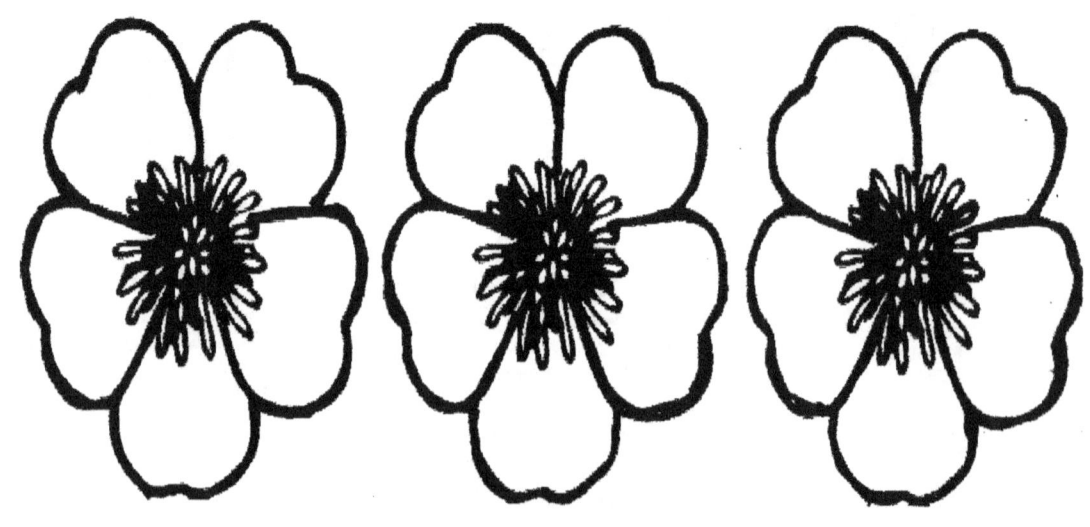

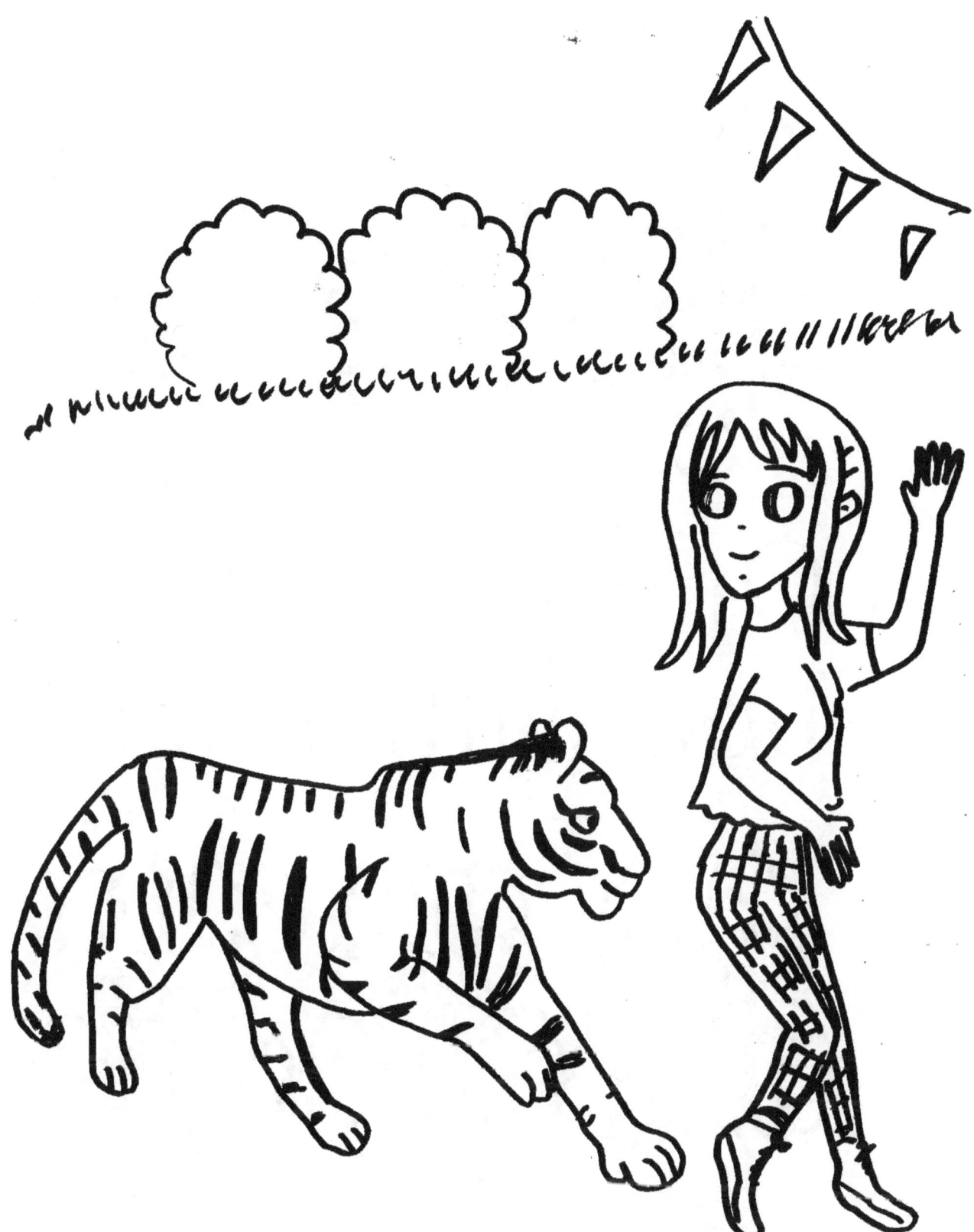

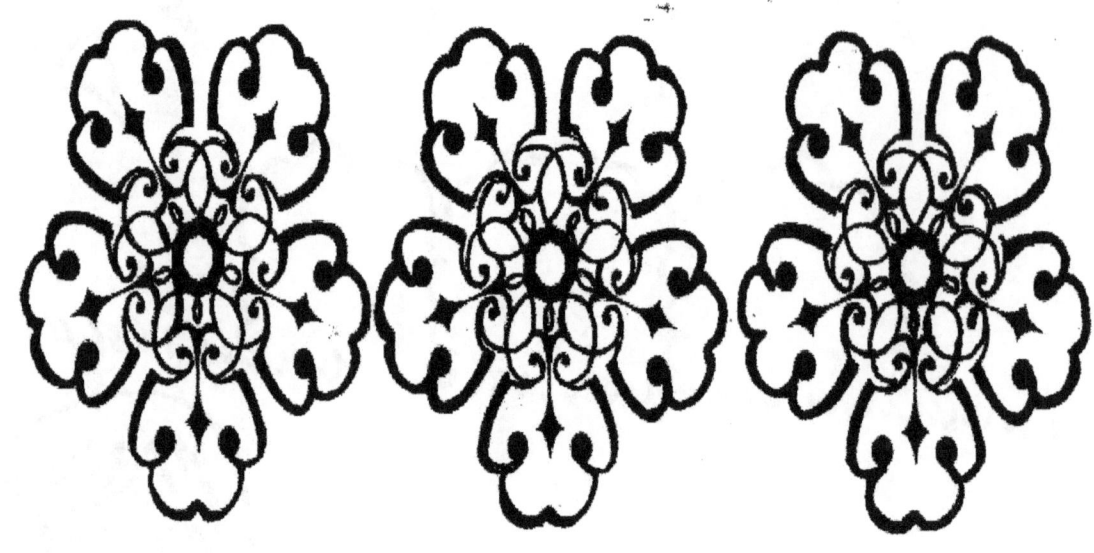

Or ever play
boo with a bear;

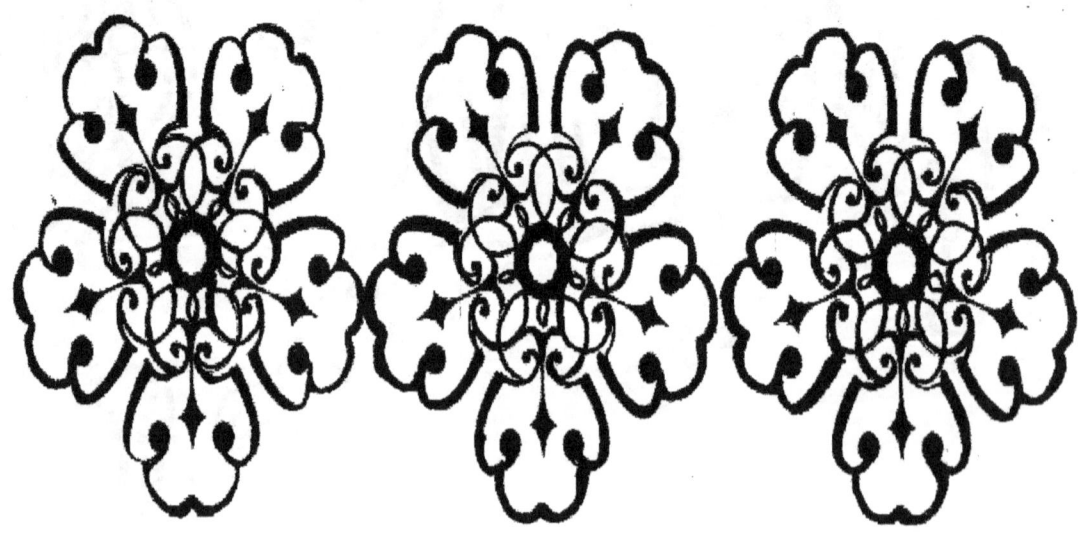

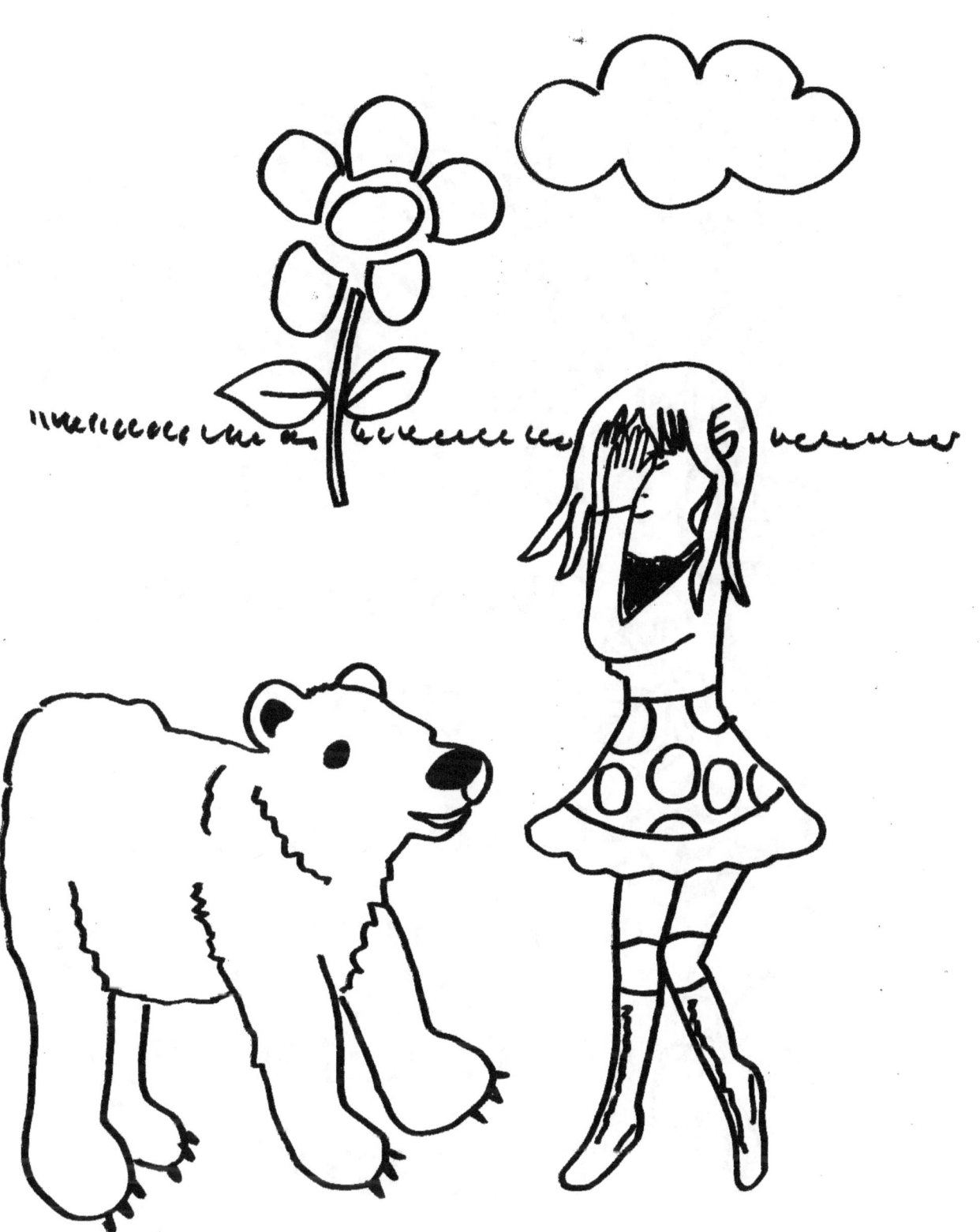

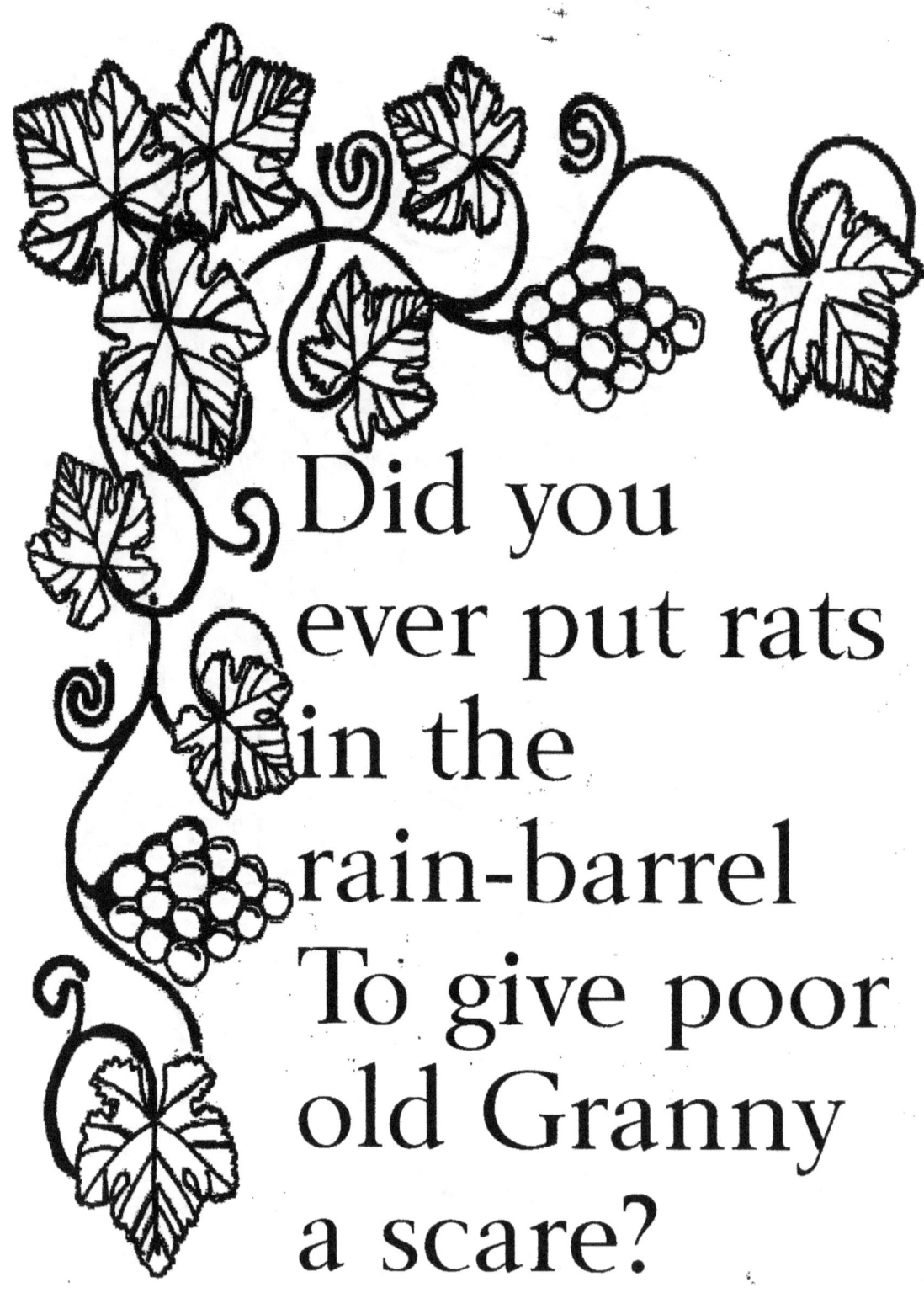

Did you
ever put rats
in the
rain-barrel
To give poor
old Granny
a scare?

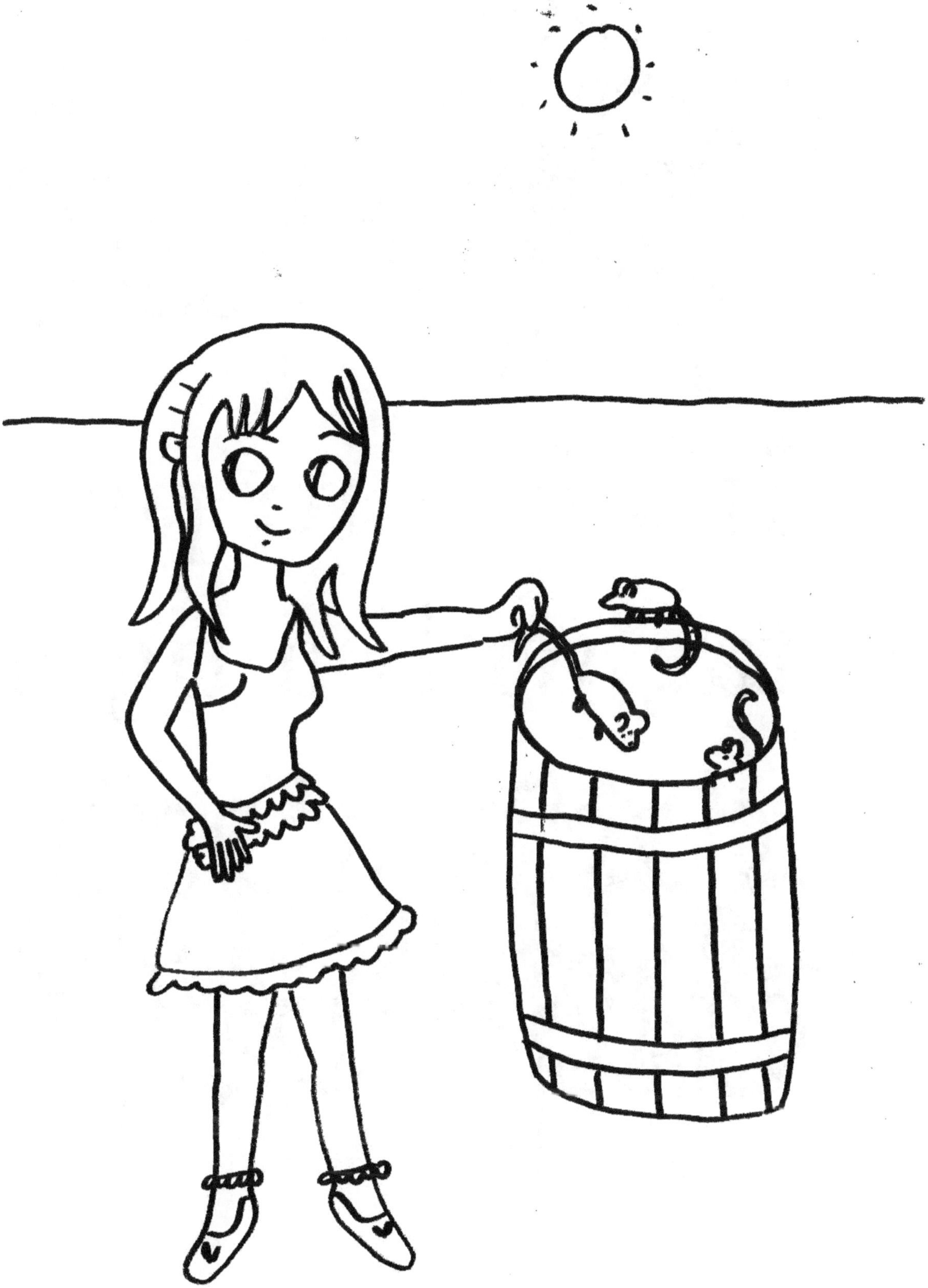

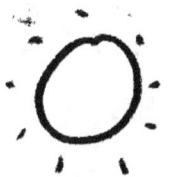

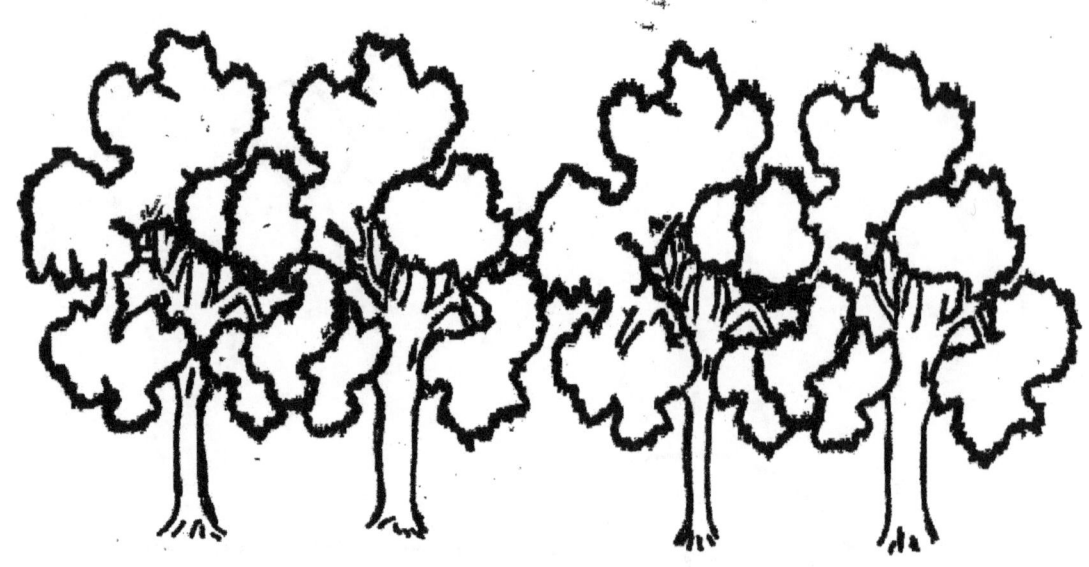

It's fun to play
tag with a tiger,

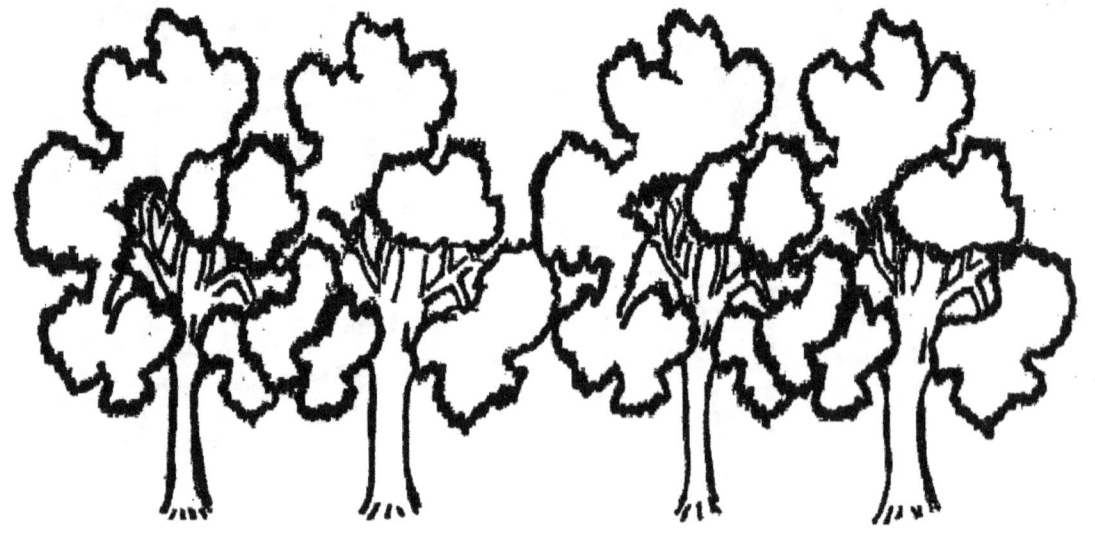

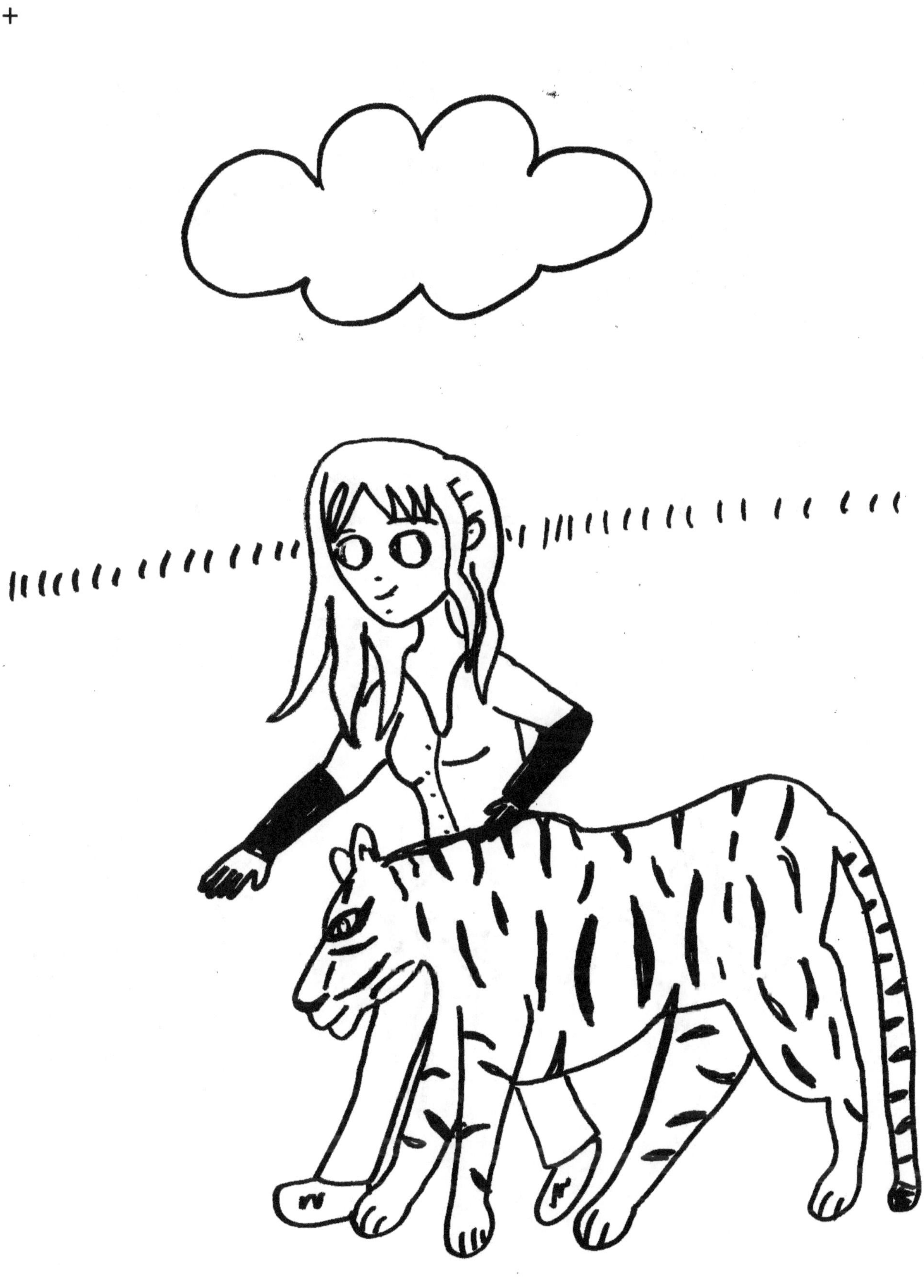

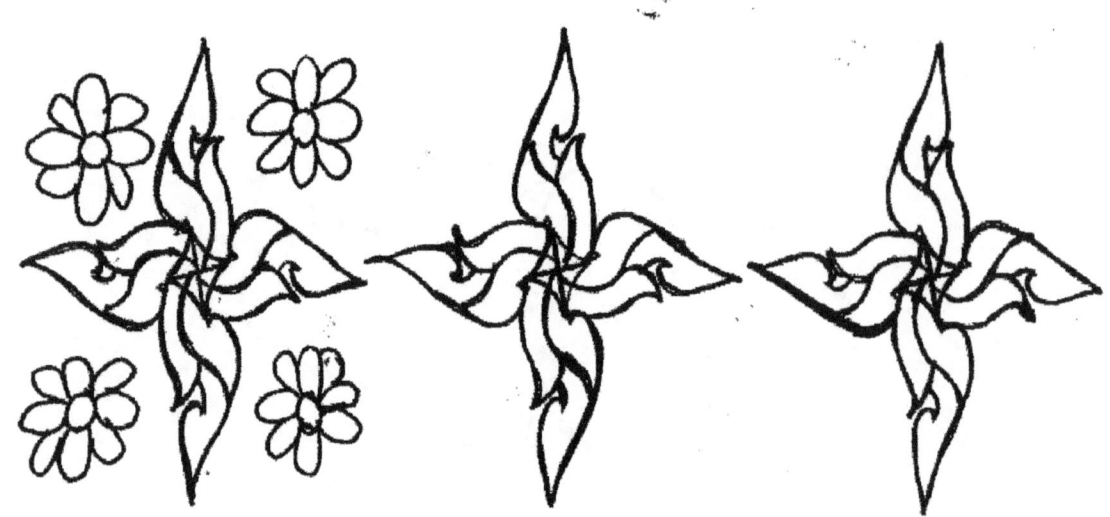

It's fun for the
bear to say "boo,"

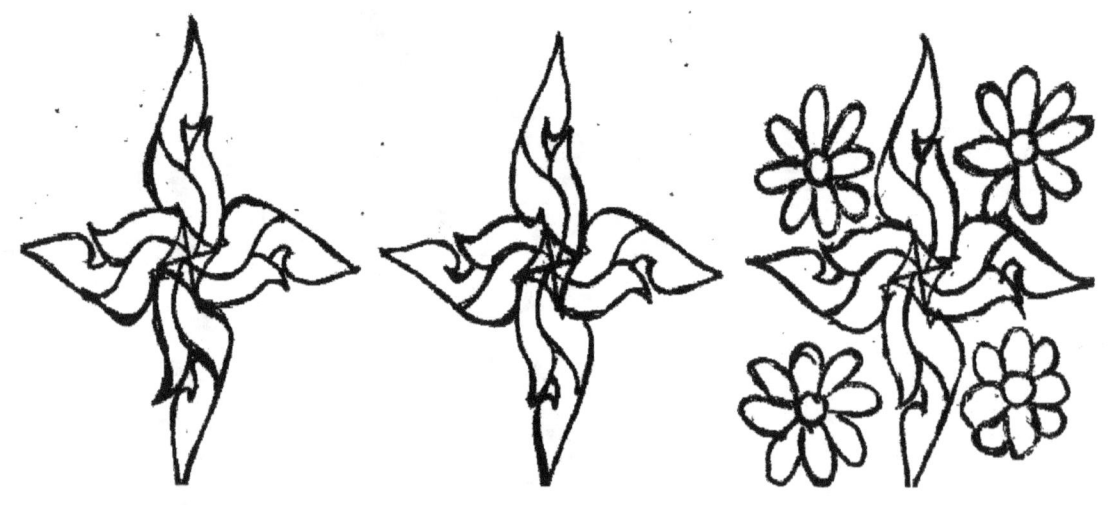

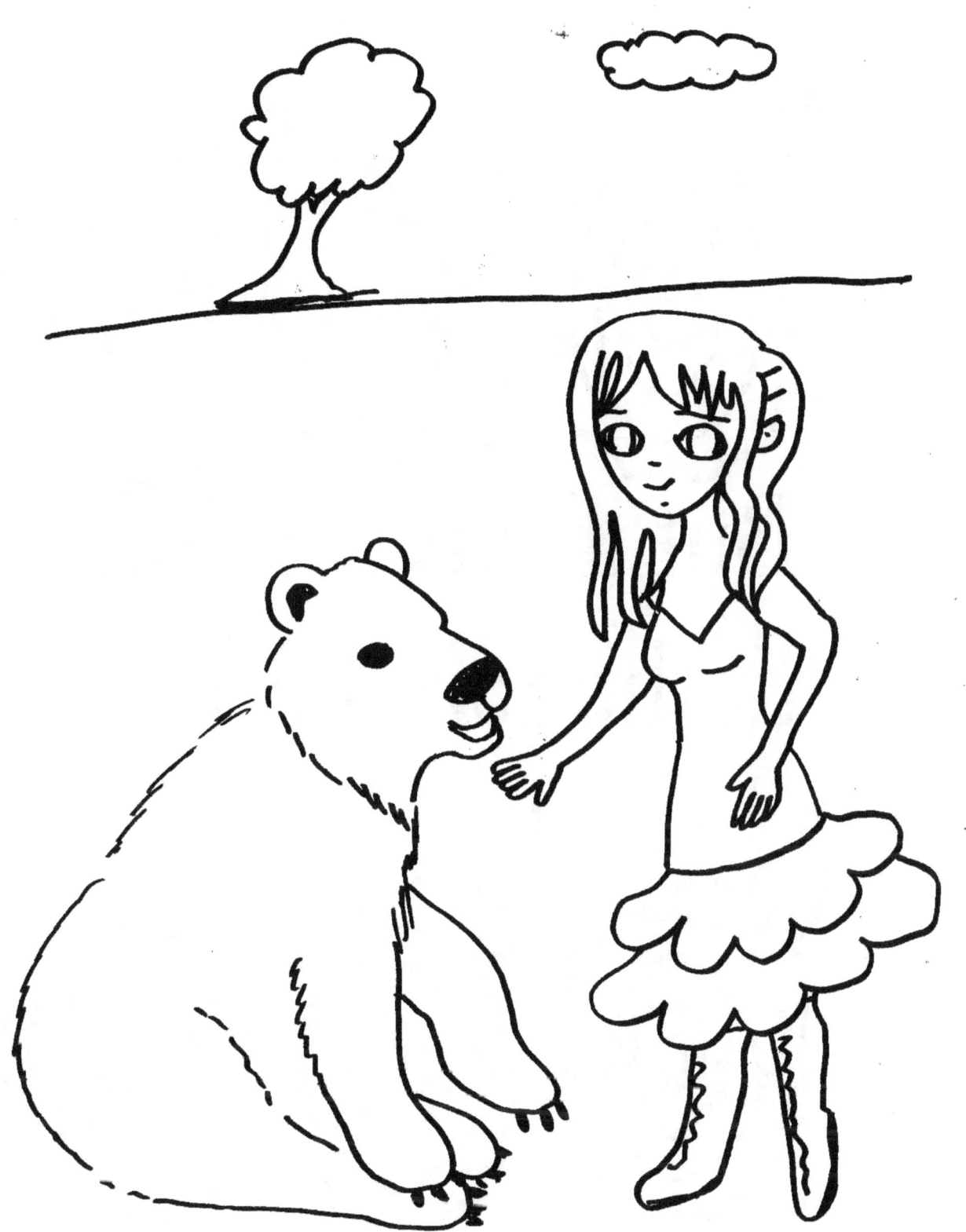

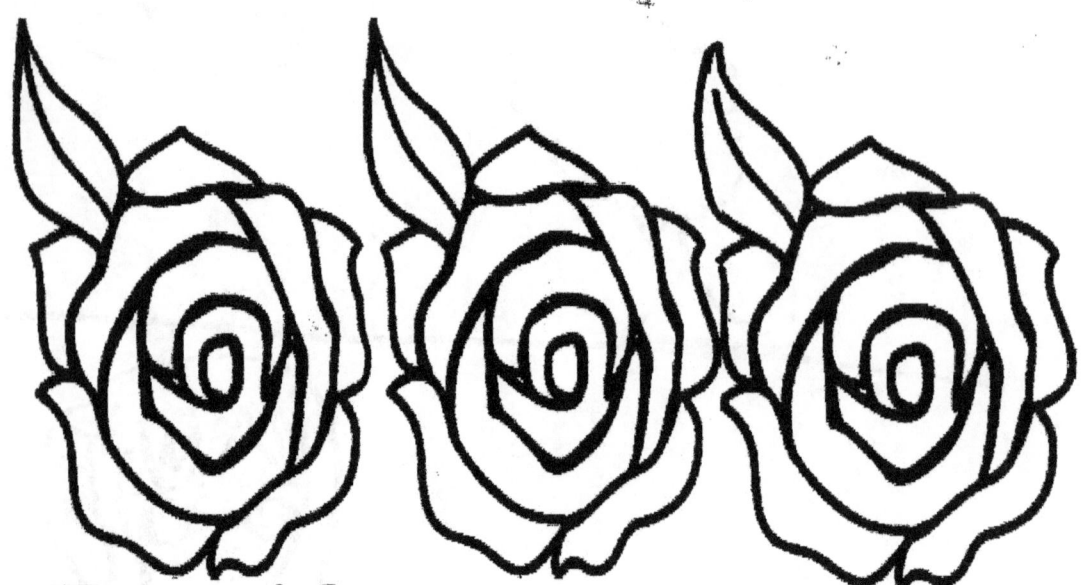

But if rats are found
in the rain-barrel

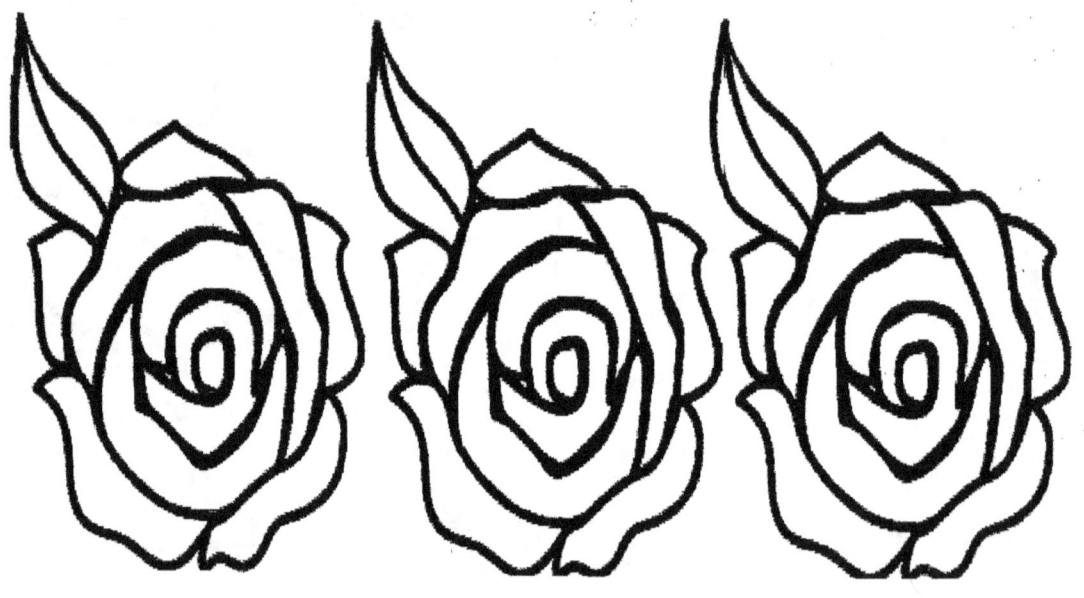

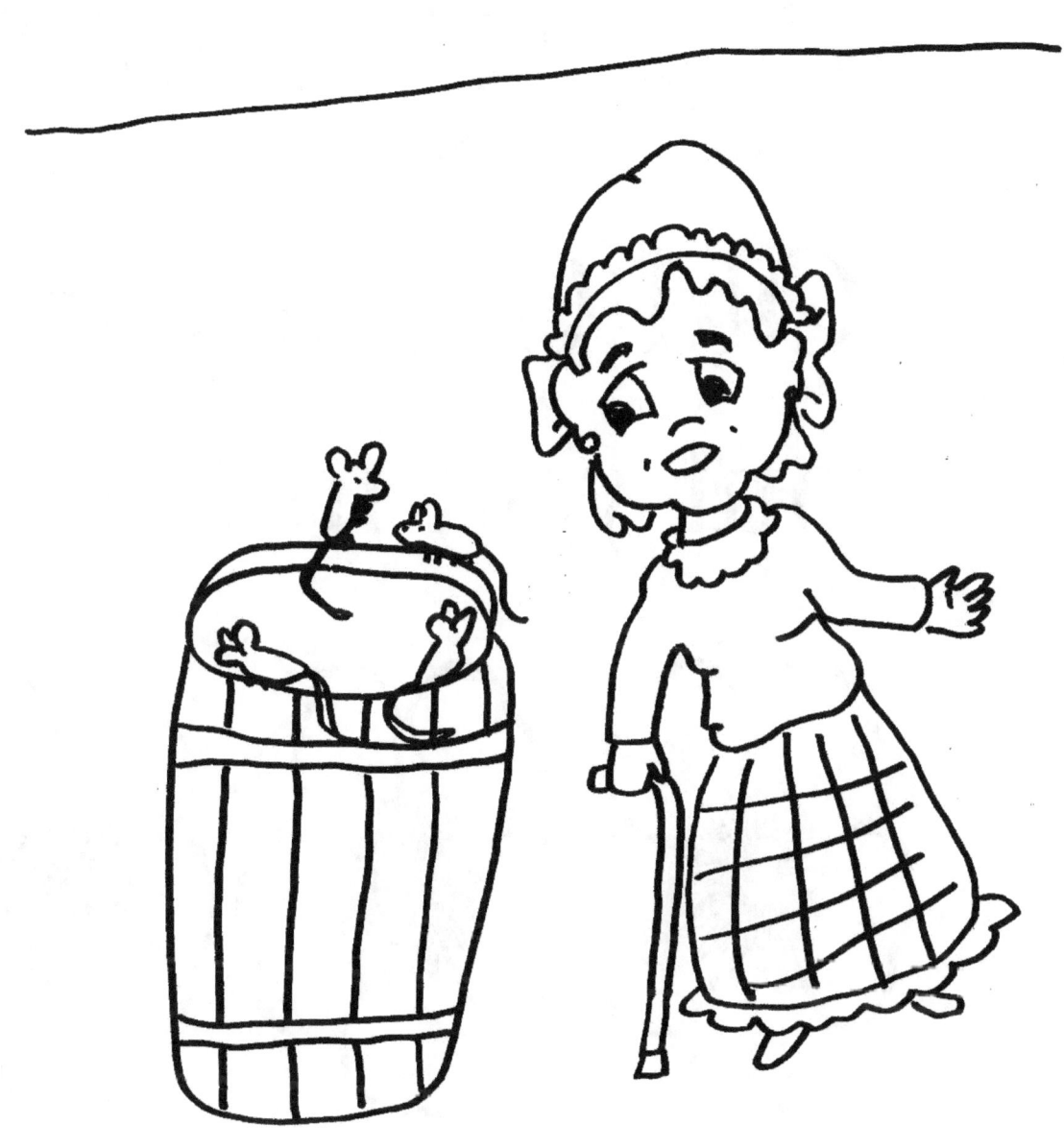

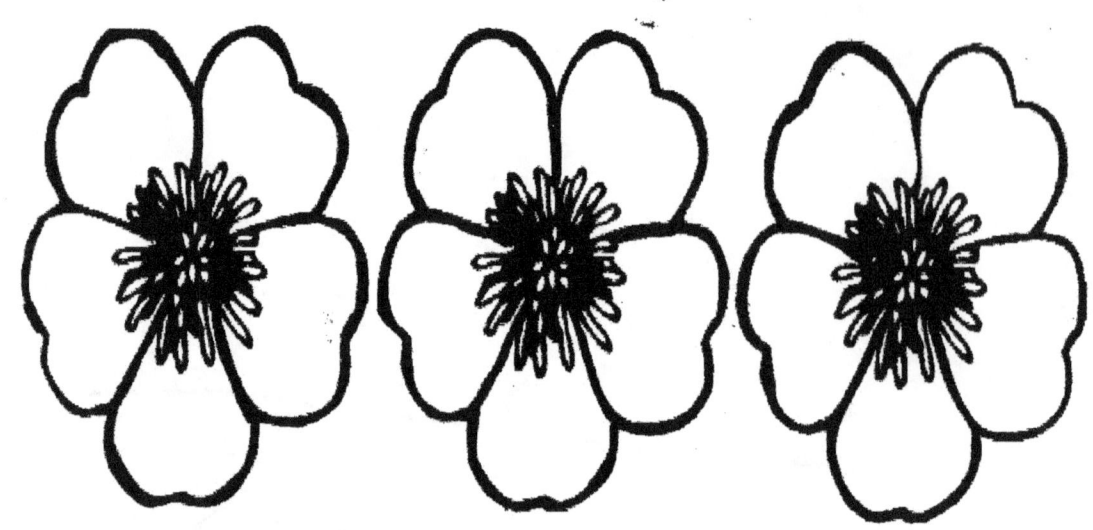

Old Granny will
put you in too.

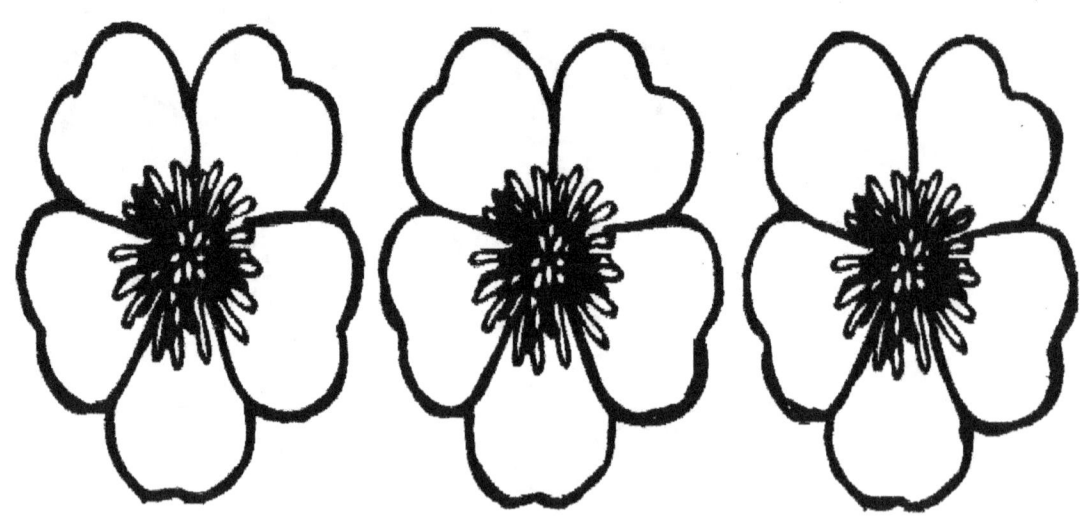

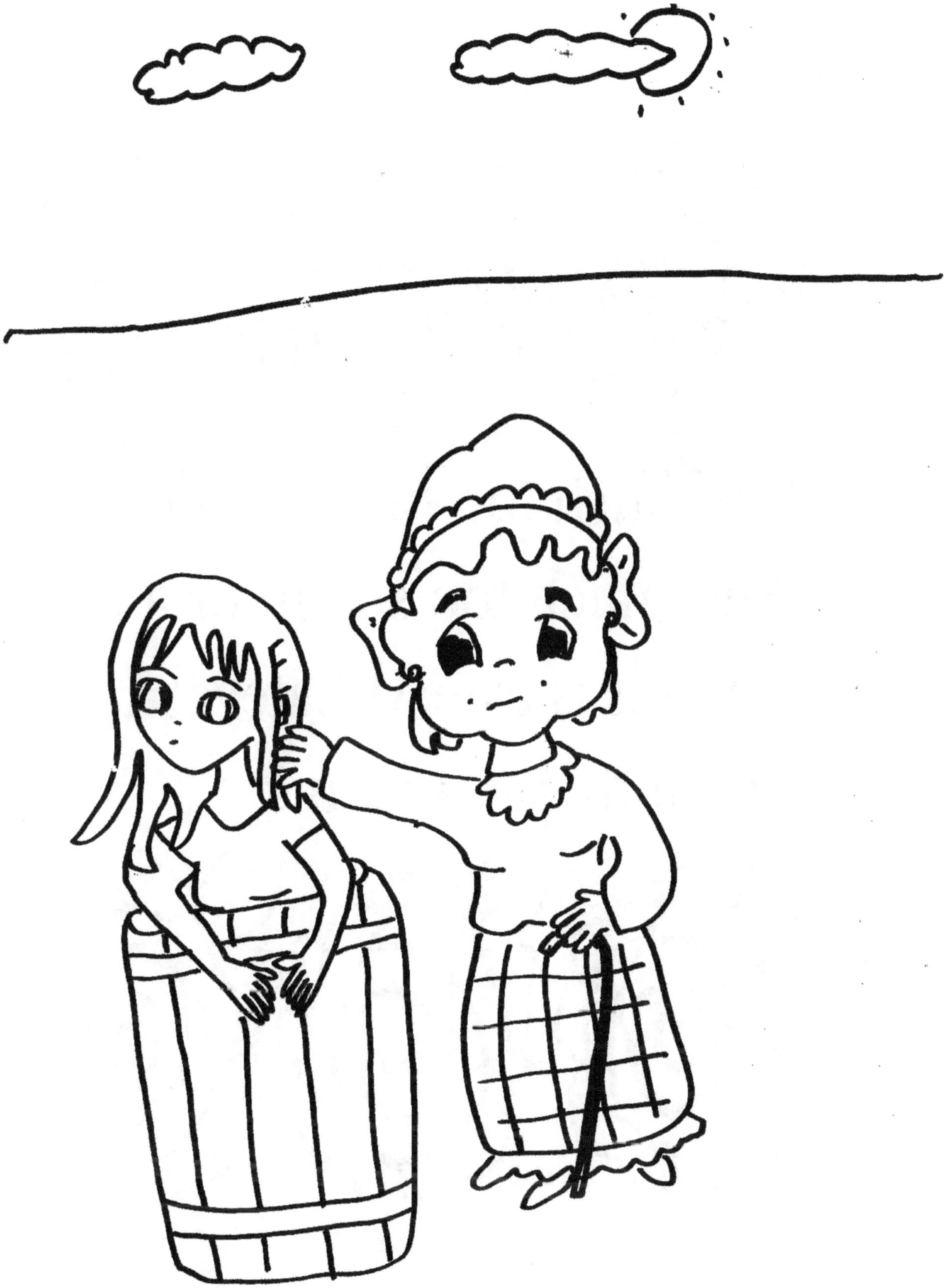

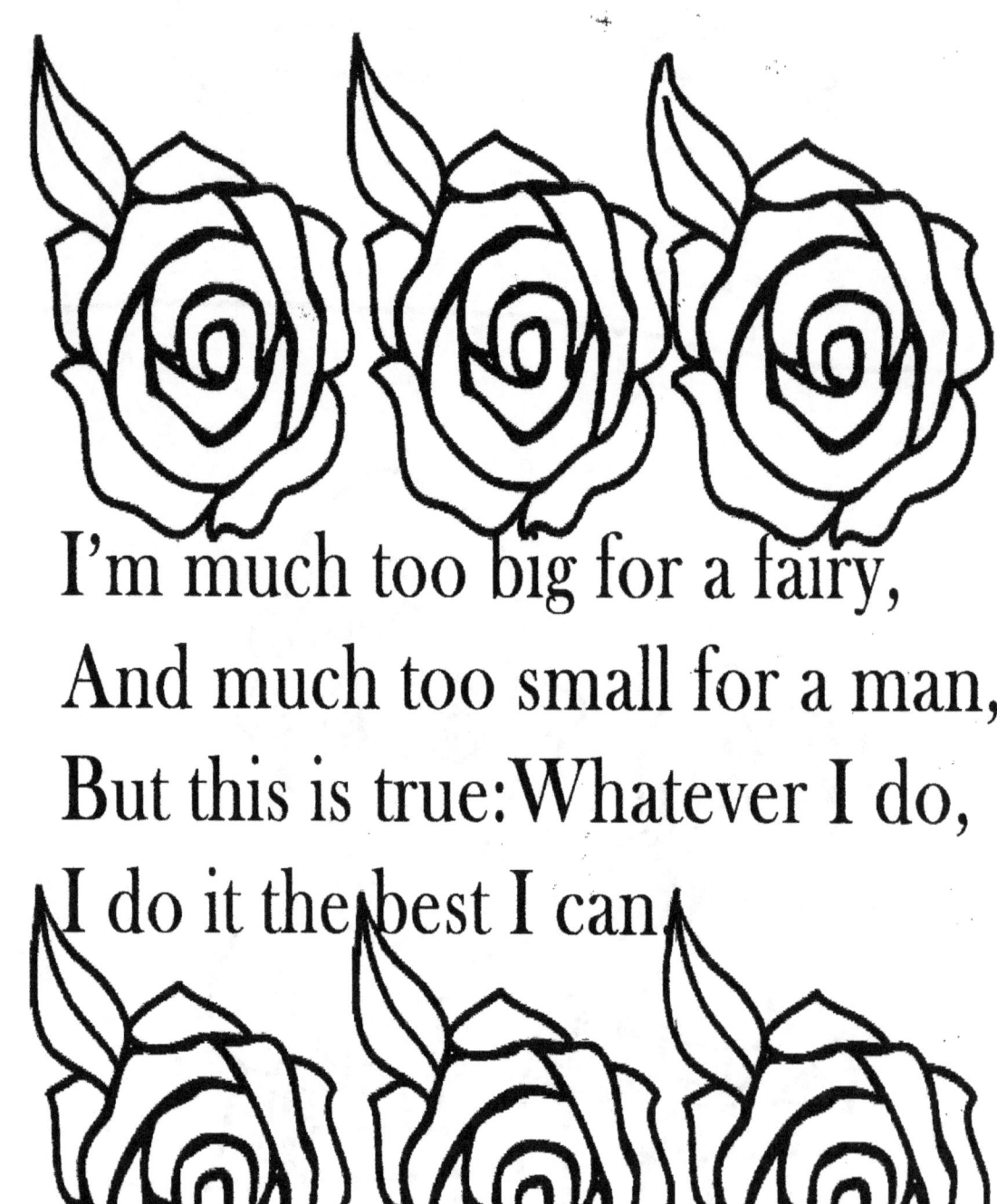

I'm much too big for a fairy,
And much too small for a man,
But this is true:Whatever I do,
I do it the best I can.

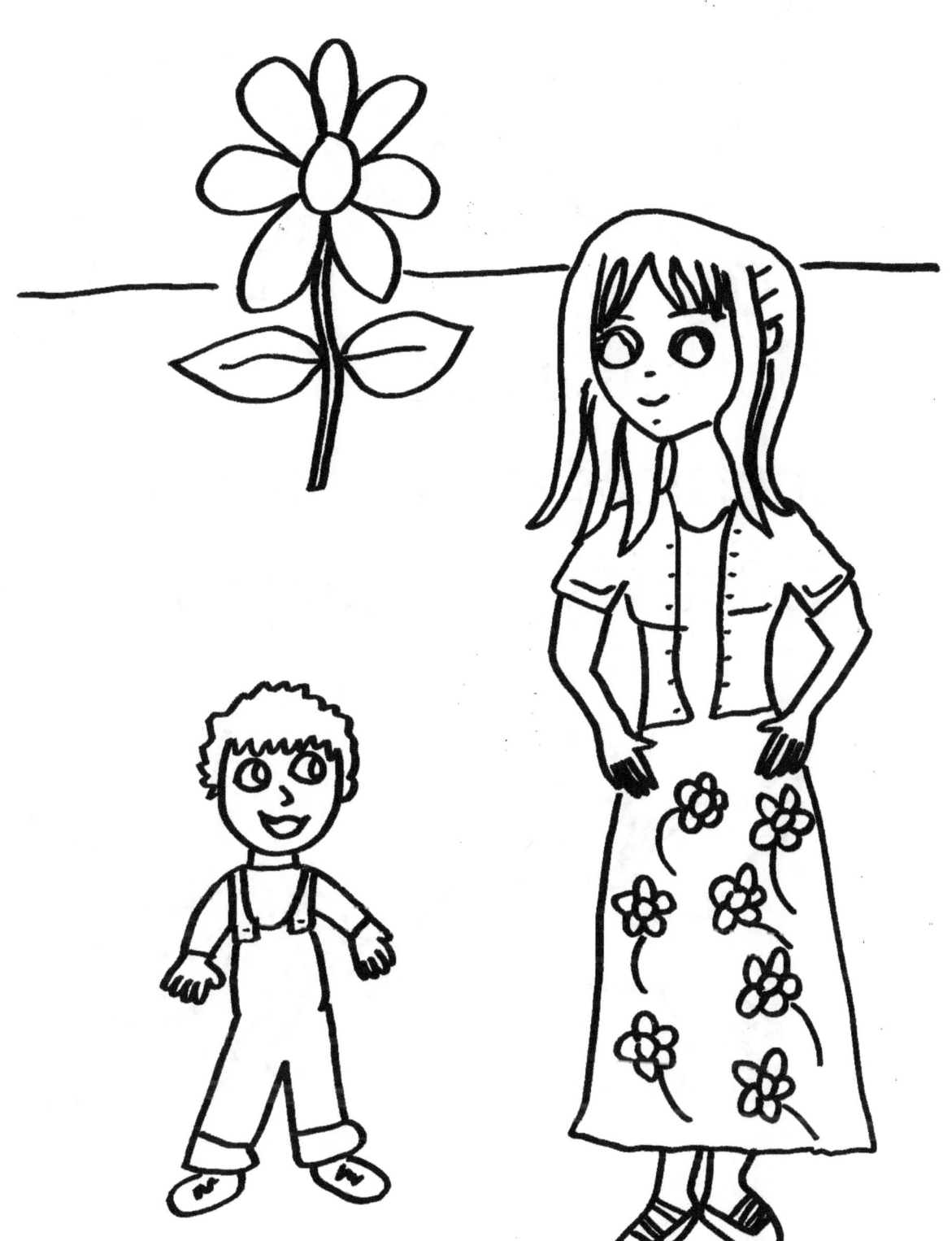

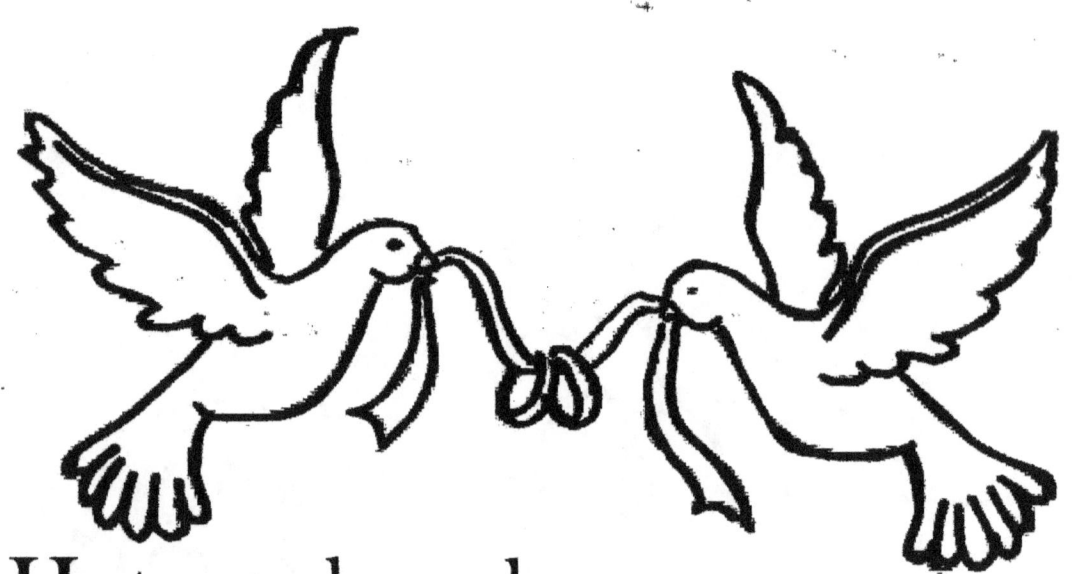

Hot mush and
molasses all in a blue bowl—
Eat it, it's good for you, Mary.

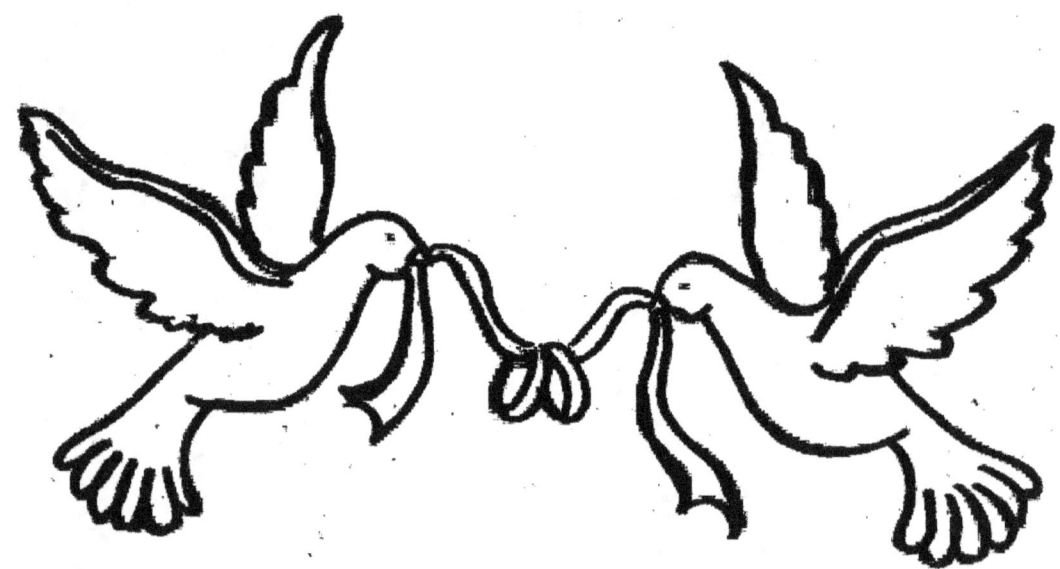

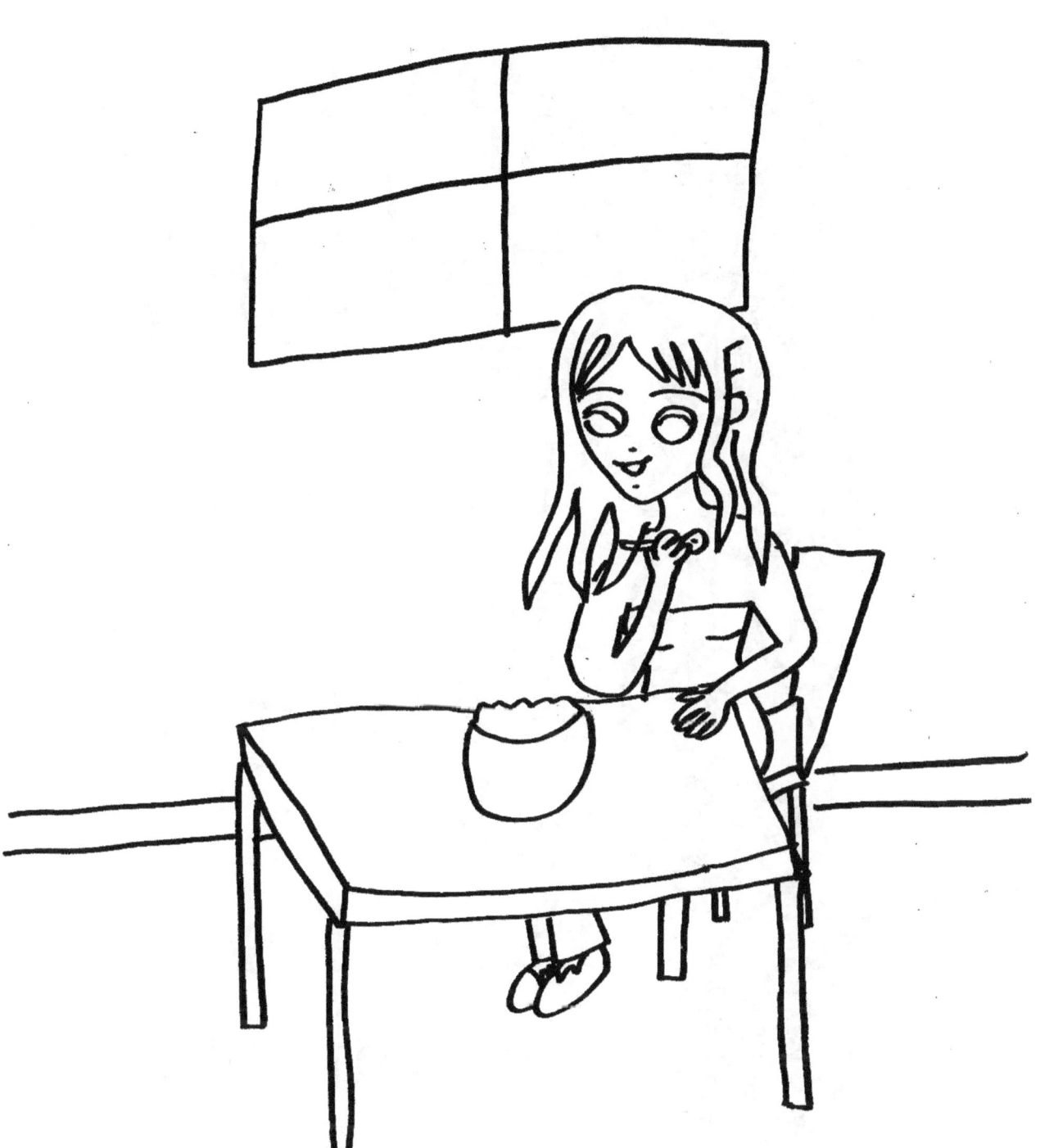

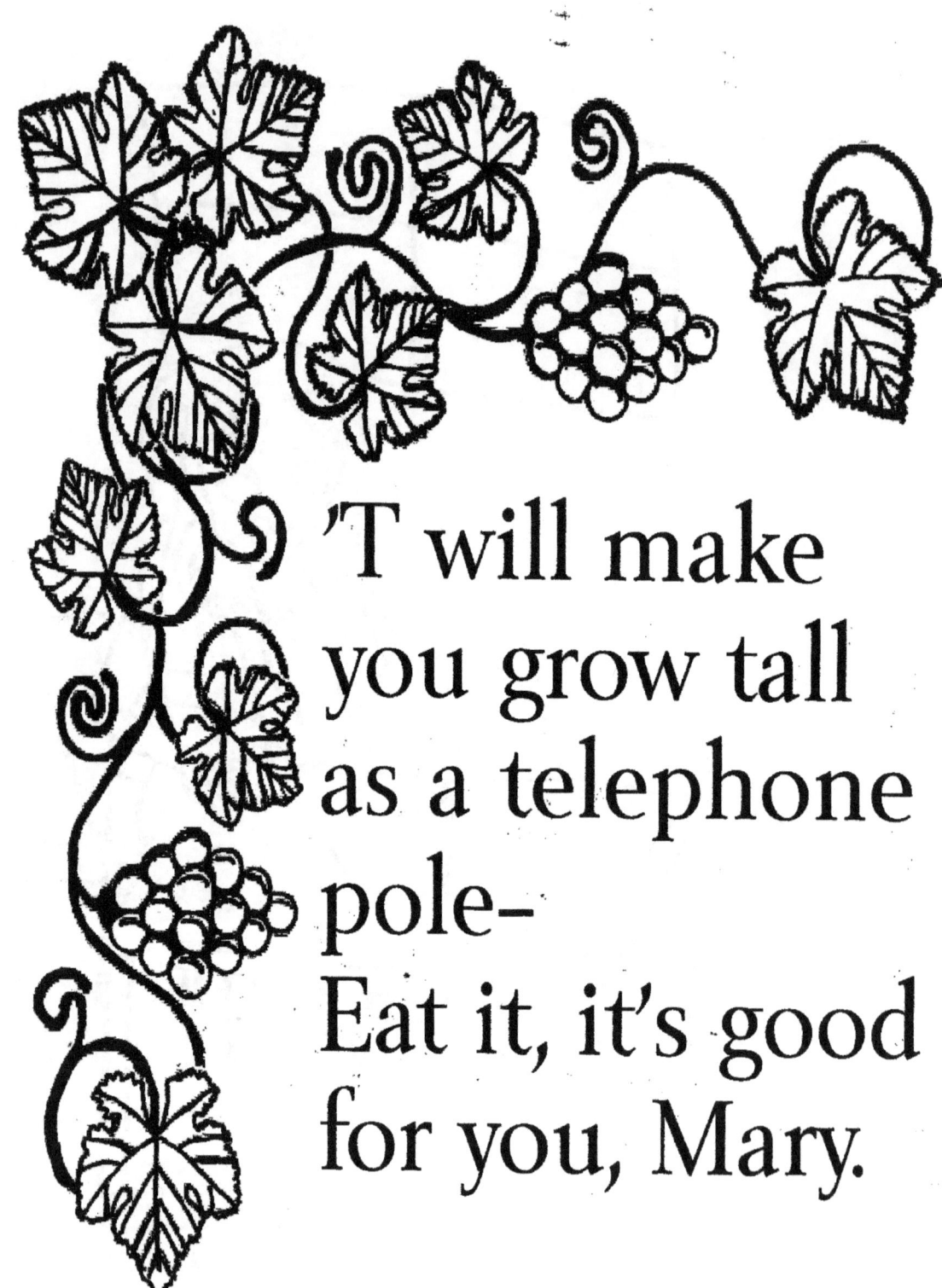

'T will make
you grow tall
as a telephone
pole–
Eat it, it's good
for you, Mary.

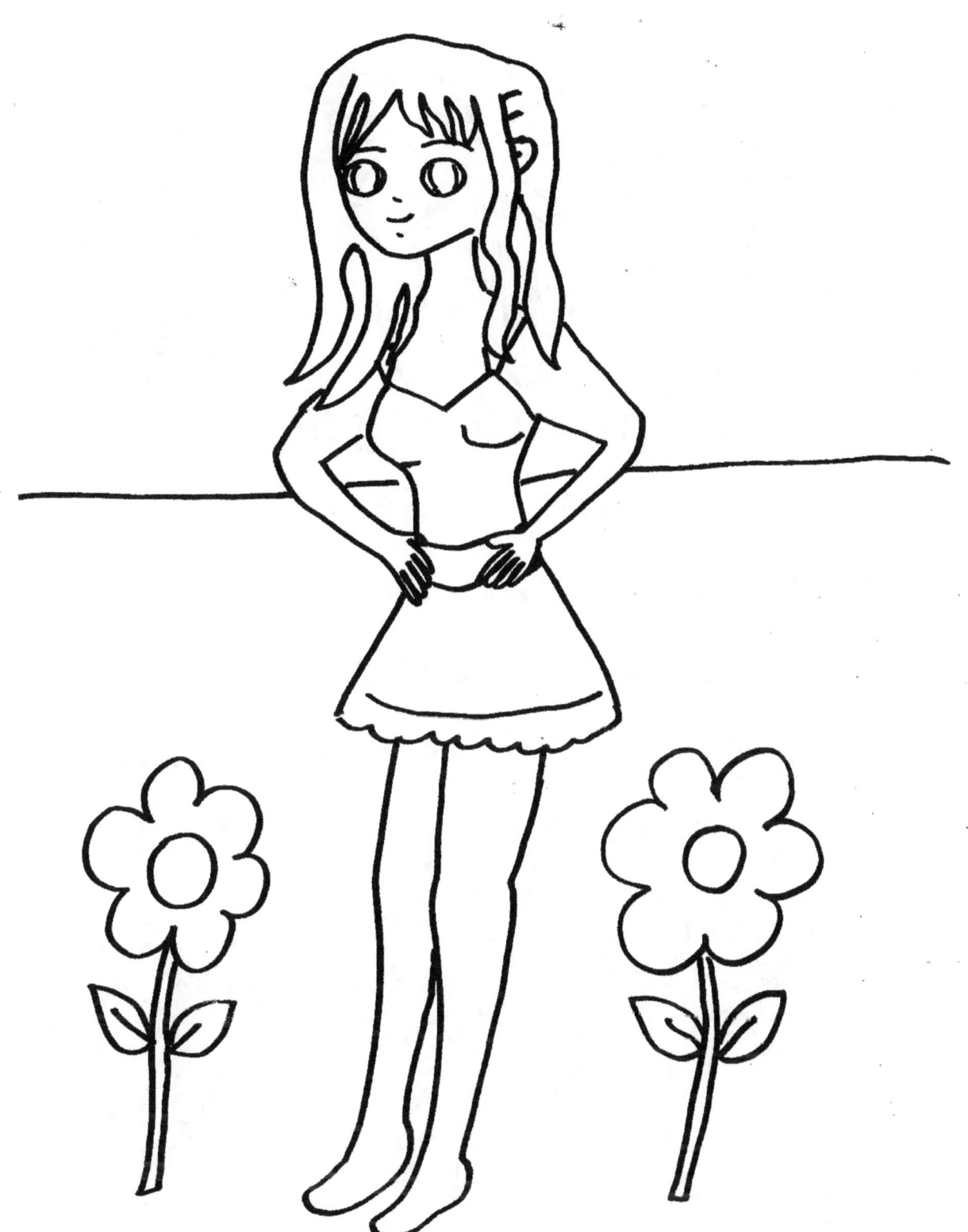

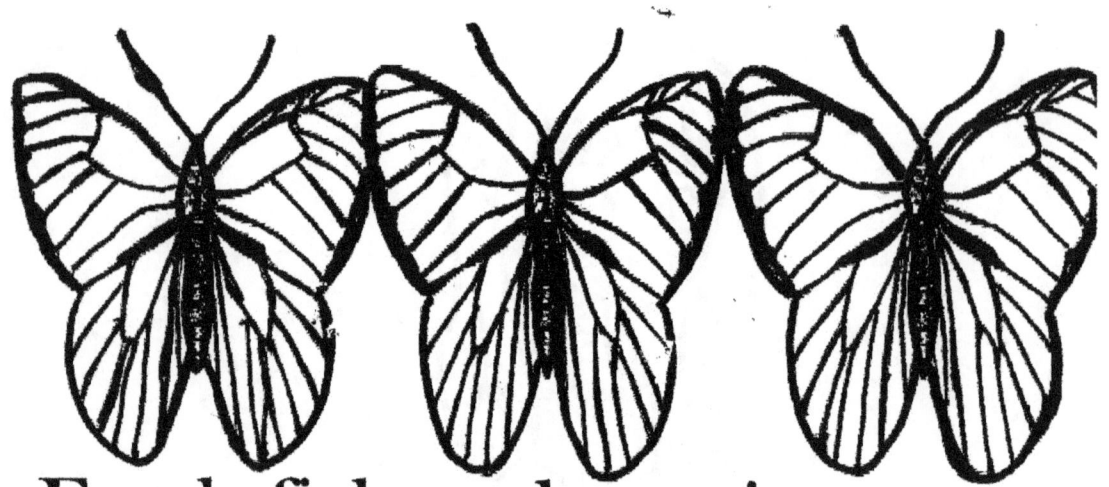

Fresh fish and veggies
all on a blue plate—
Eat it up smart now, Mary.
T 'will make you as
stong and tall as Aunt Kate—
Eat it up quick now, Mary.

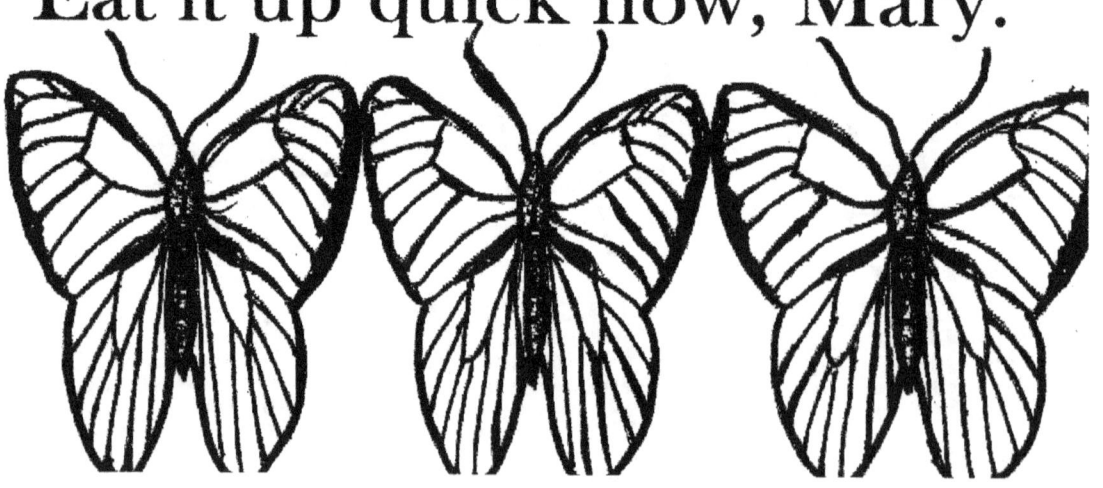

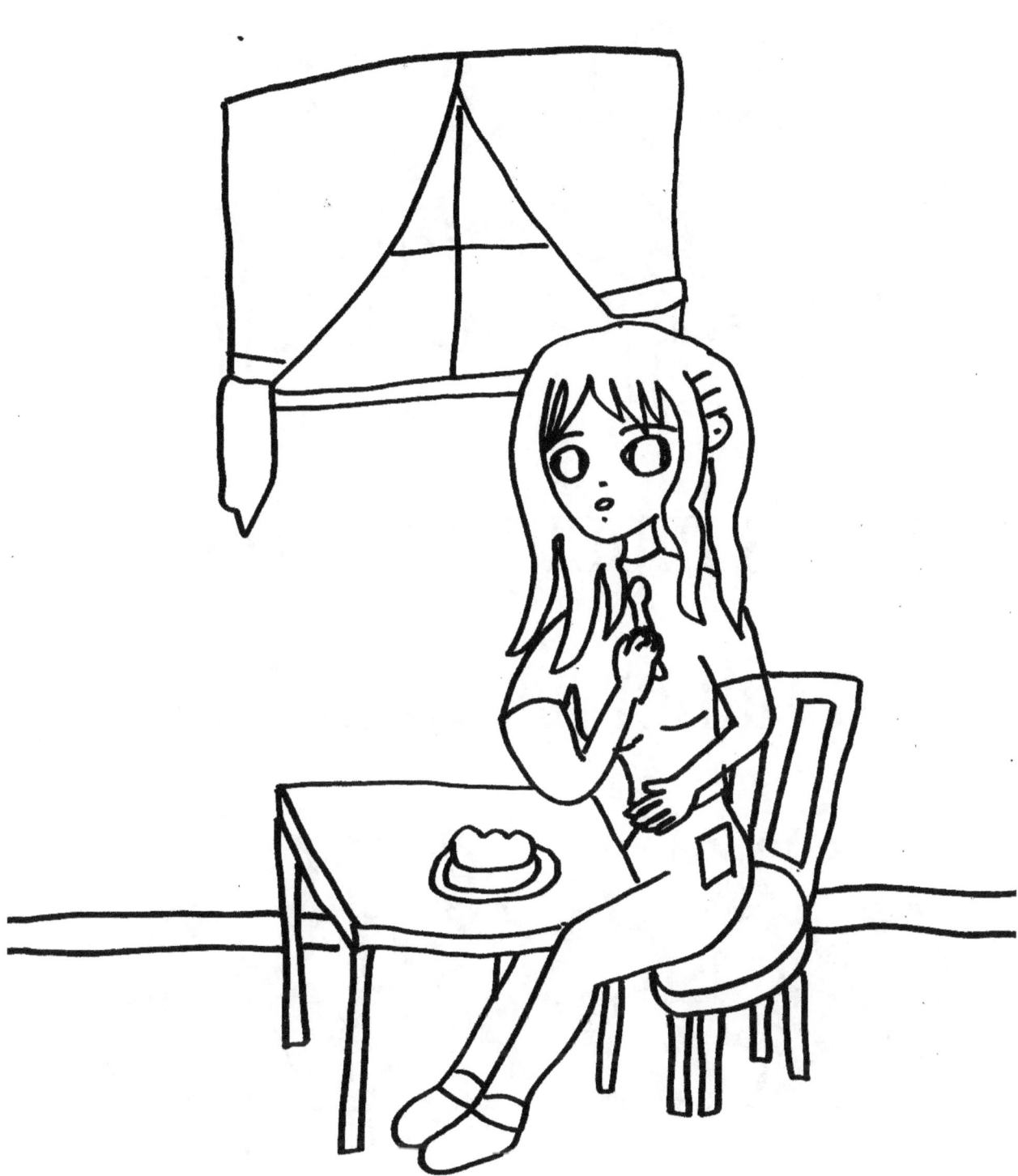

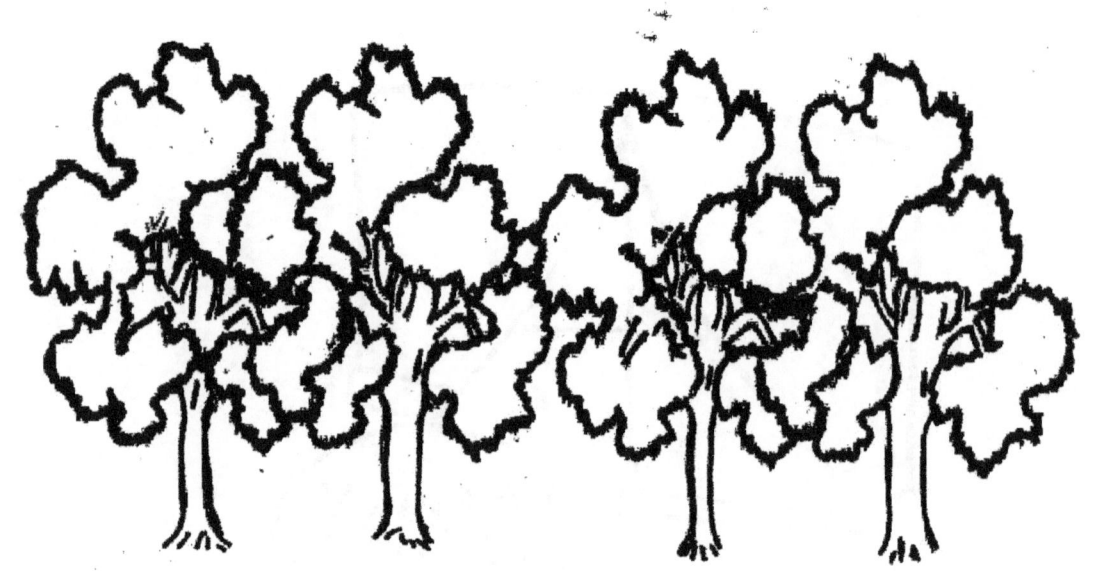

O it's hippity hop to bed!

I'd rather sit up instead.

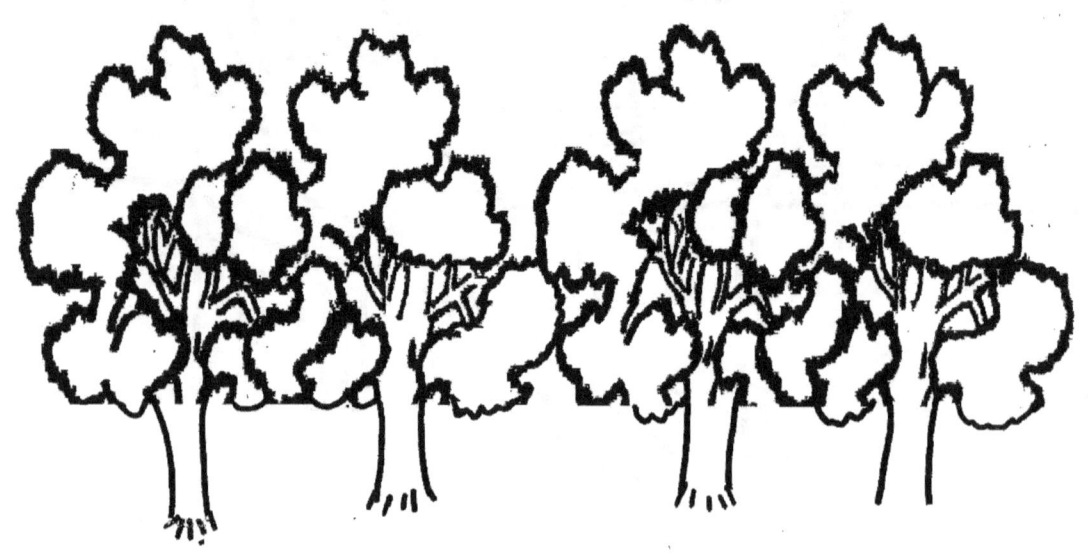

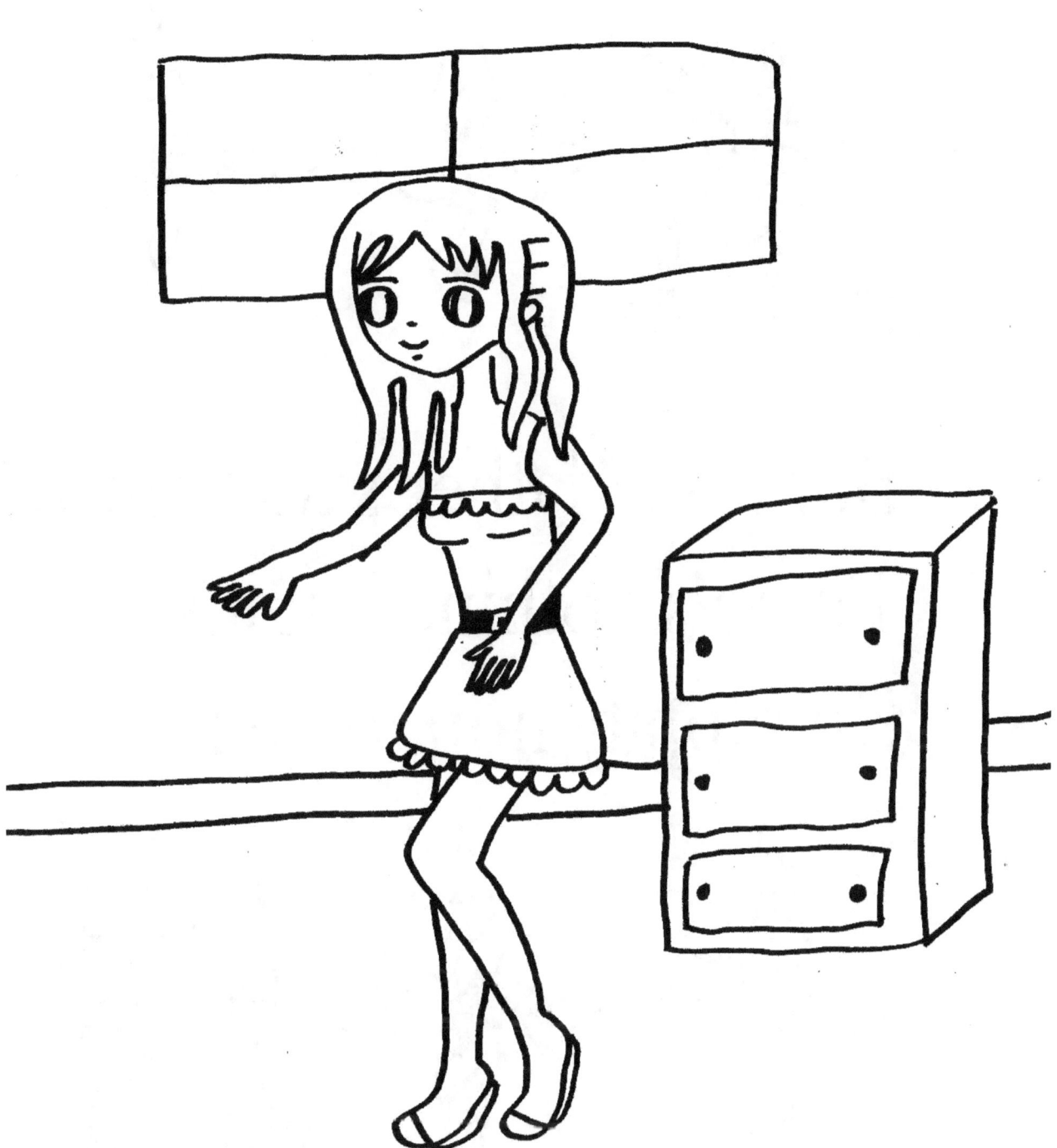

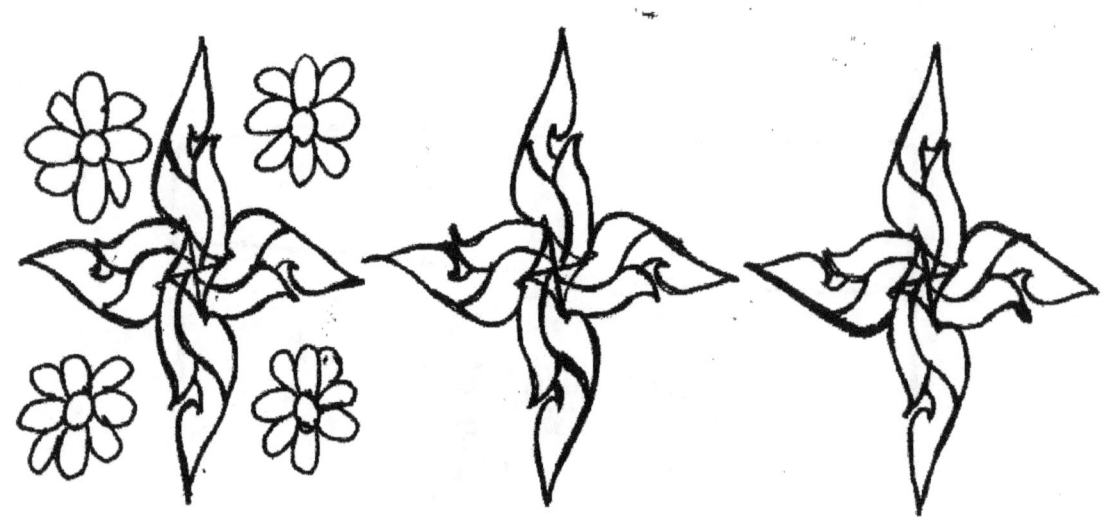

But when father says "must,"
There's nothing but just
Go hippity hop to bed.

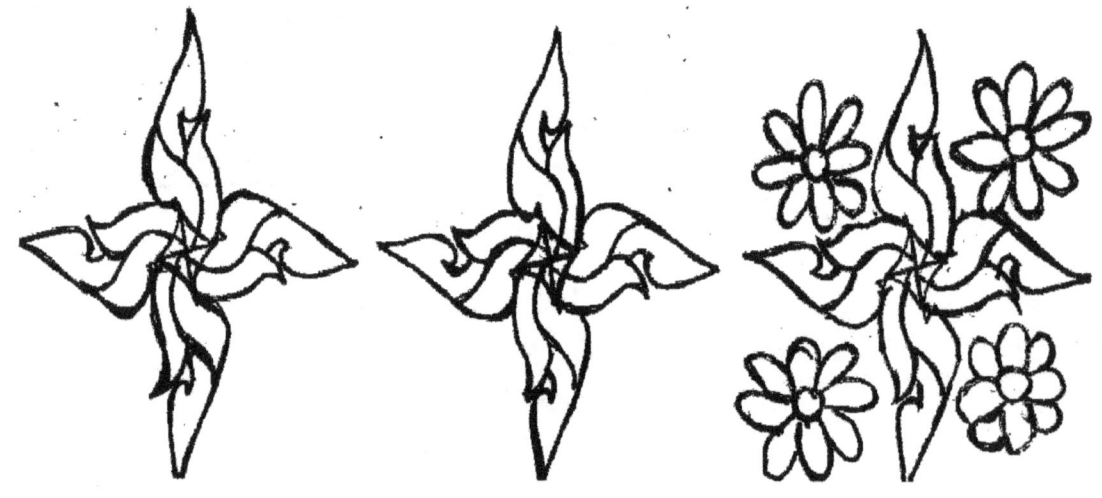

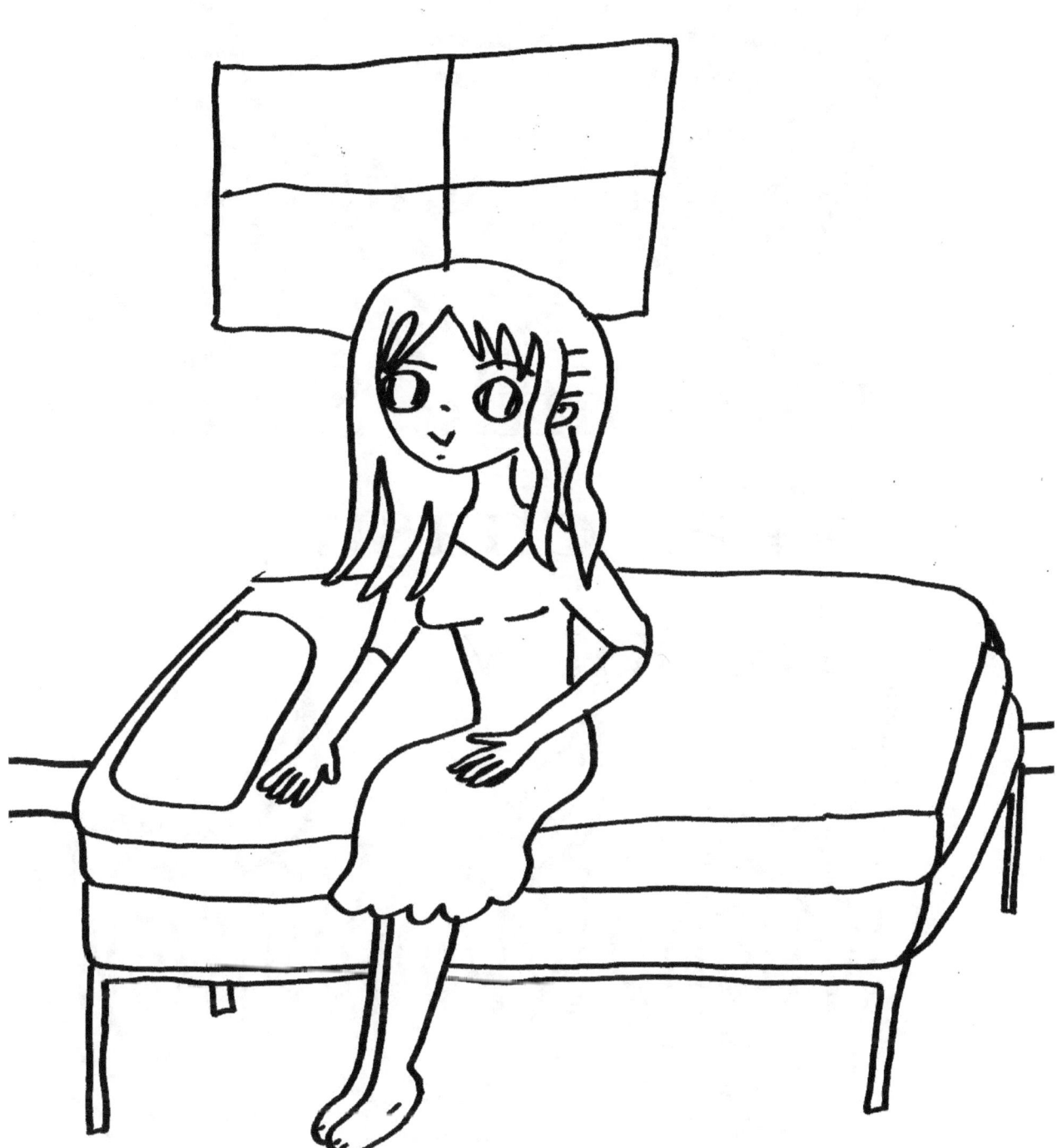

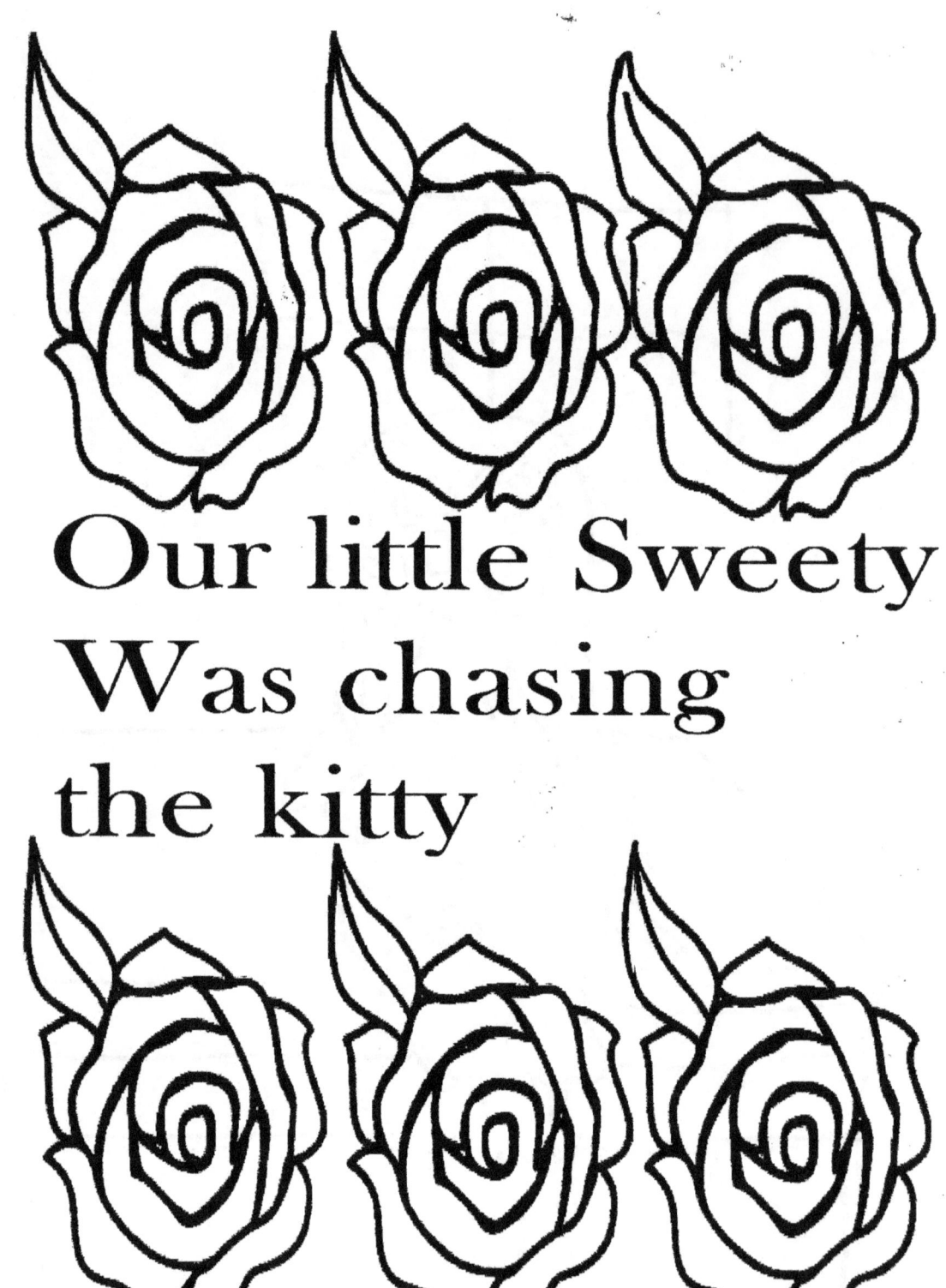

Our little Sweety Was chasing the kitty

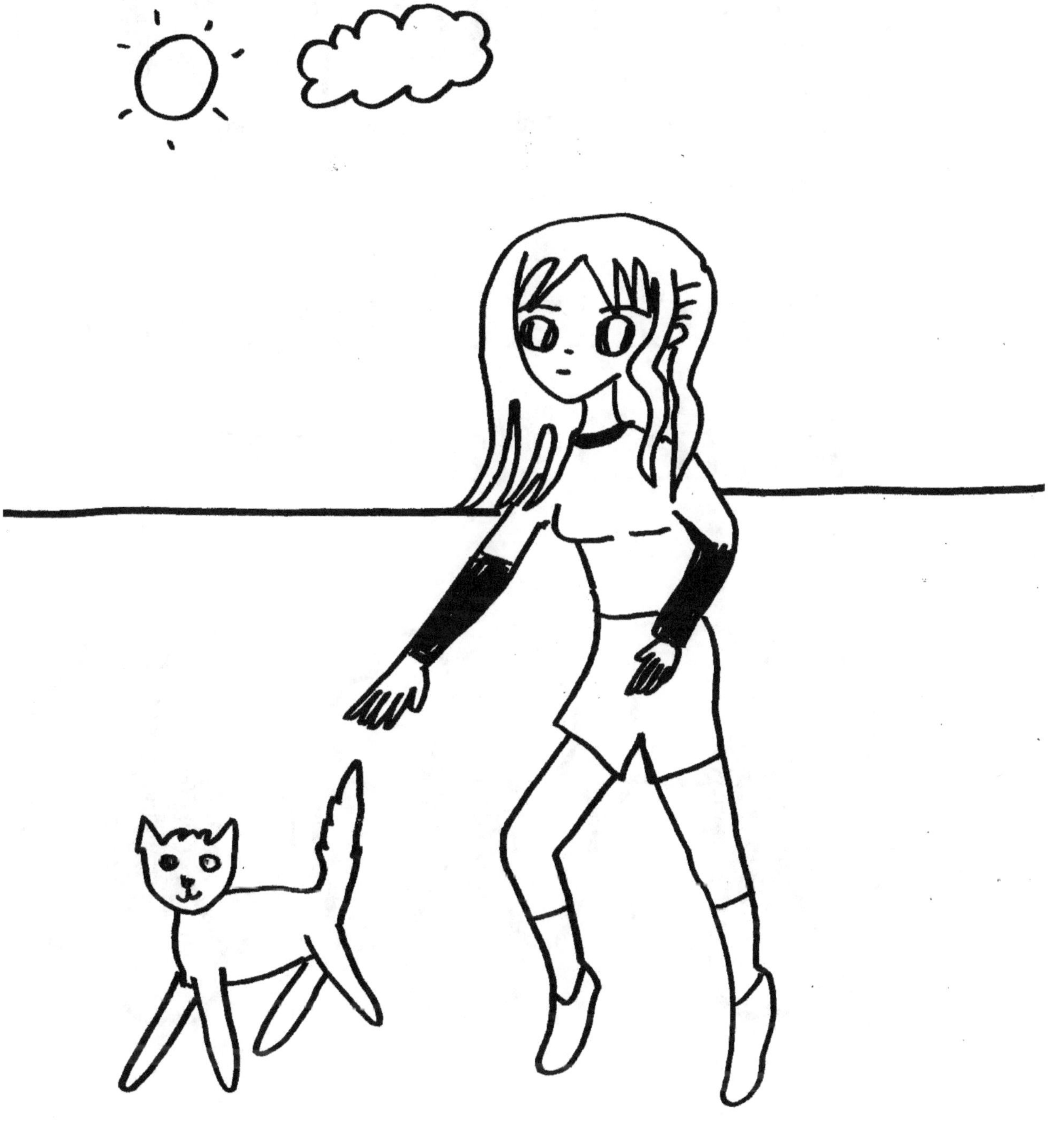

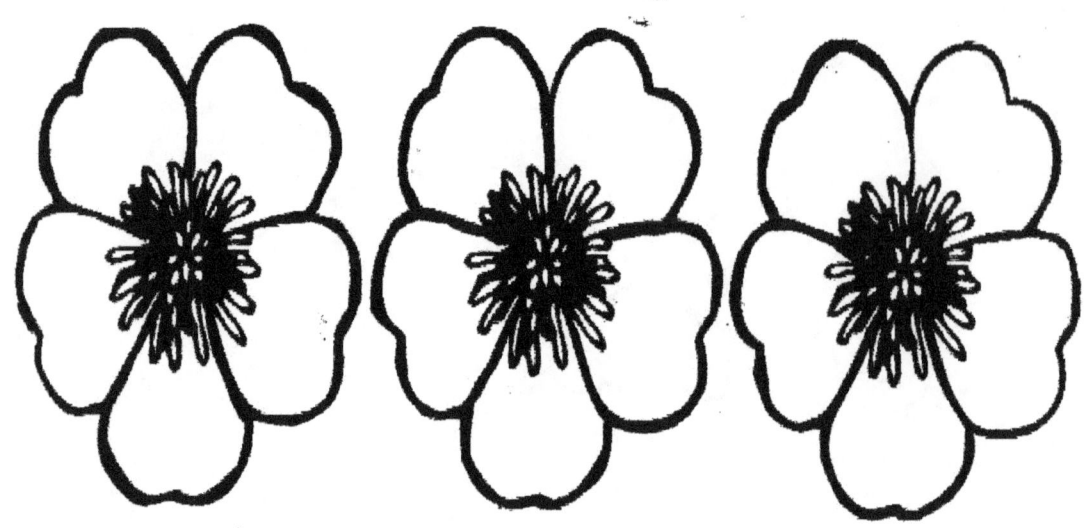

And kicking the kittens about.

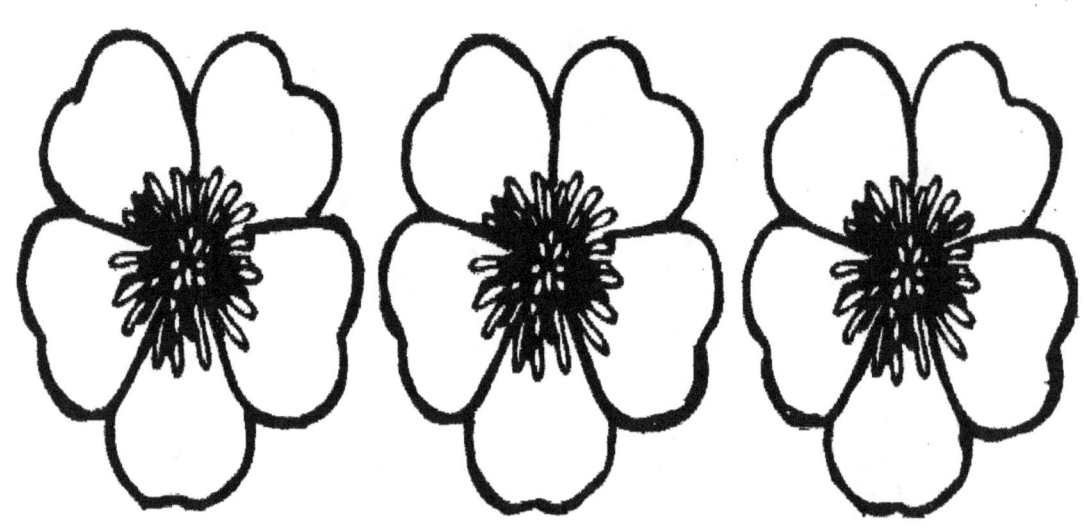

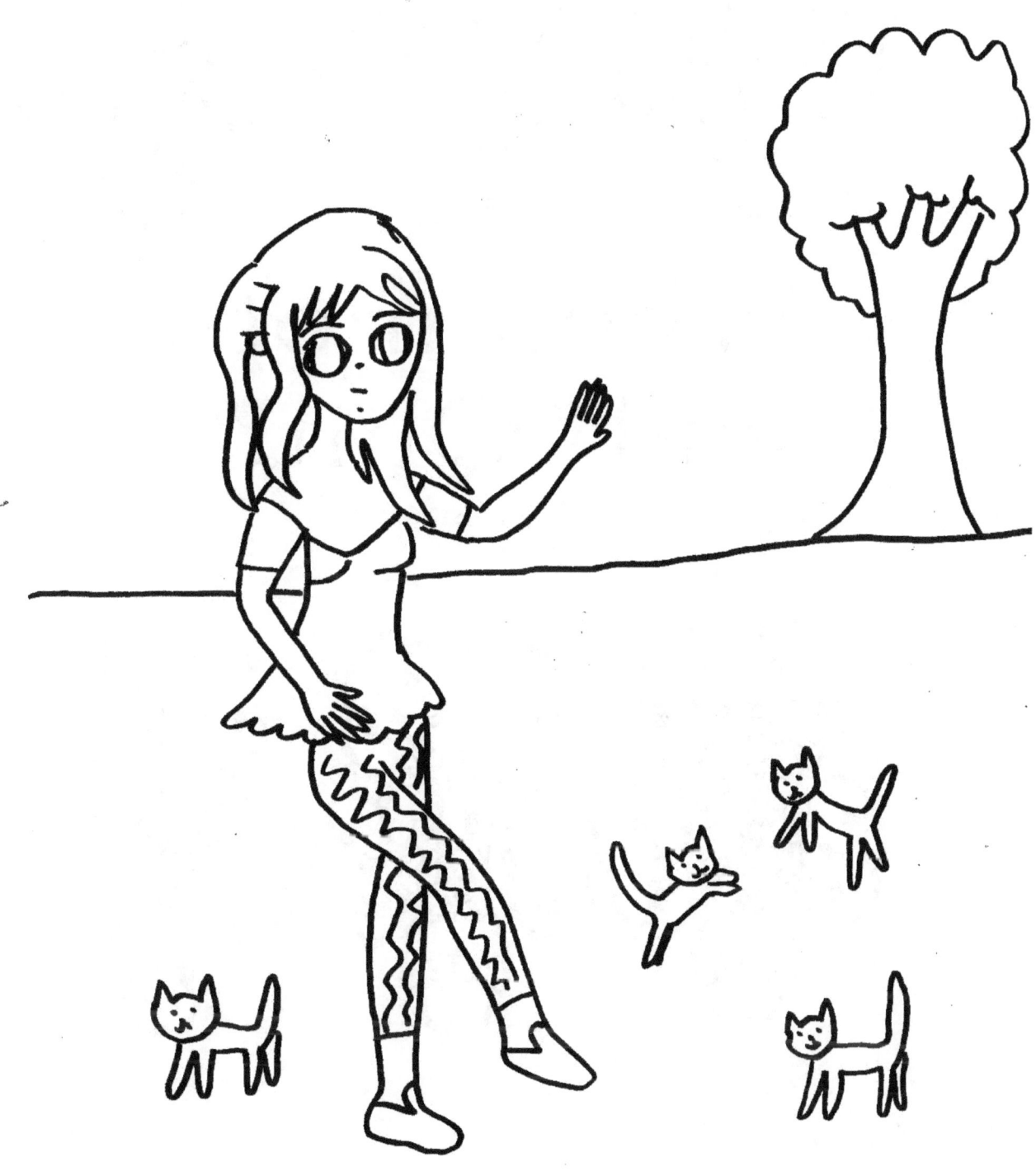

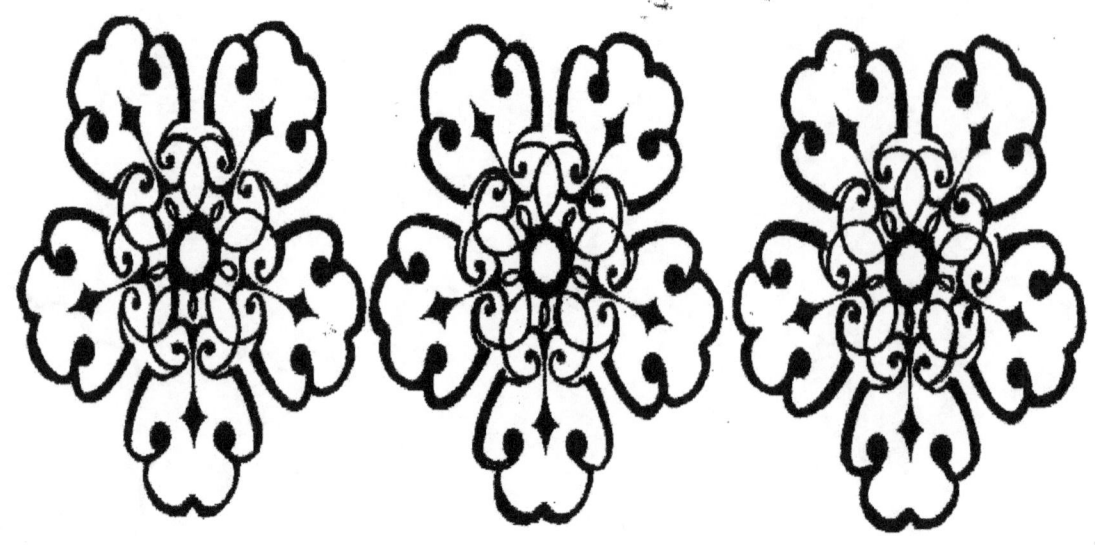

When mother said "Quit!"

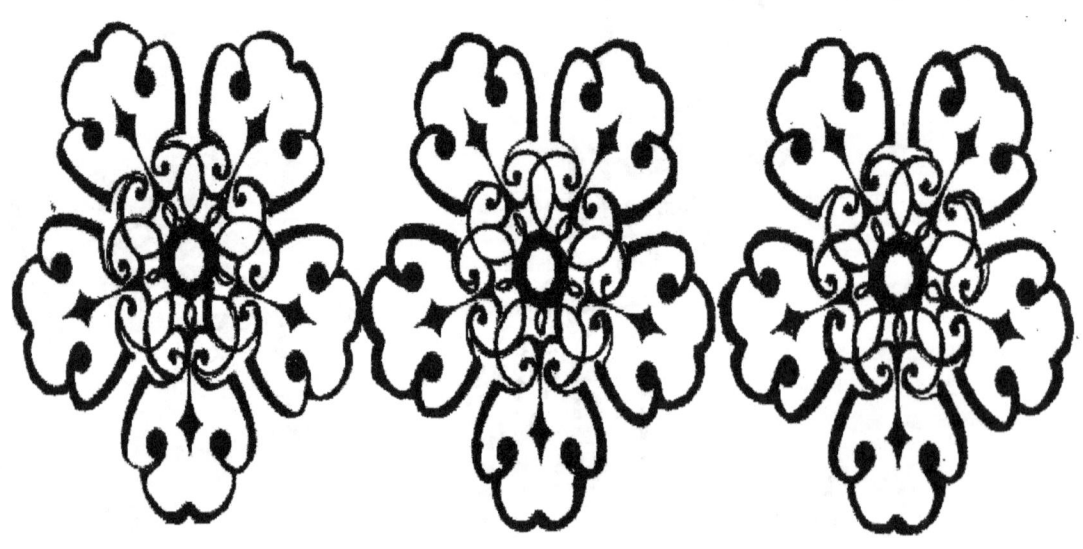

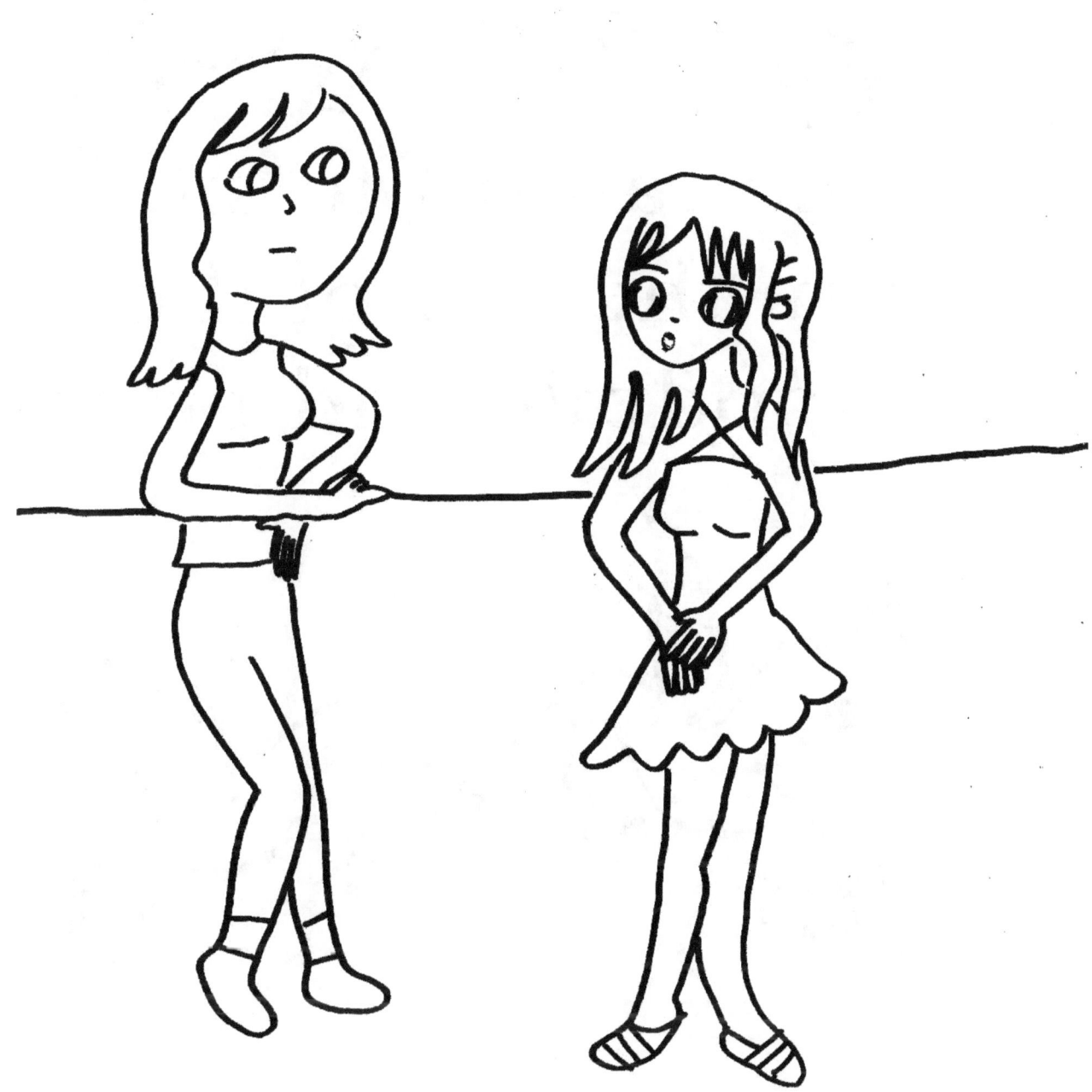

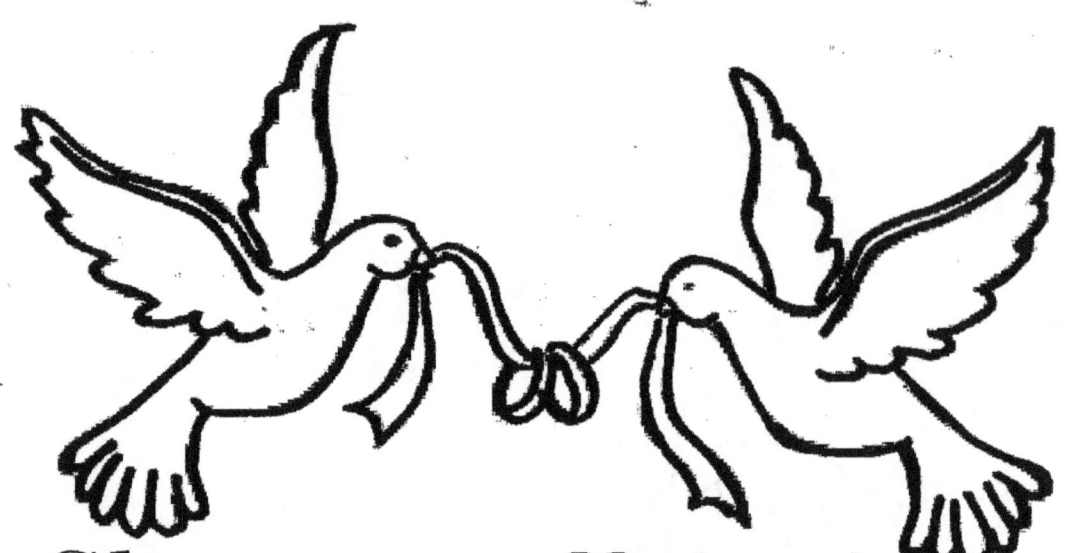

She ran off to sit
On the top of the
woodpile and pout;

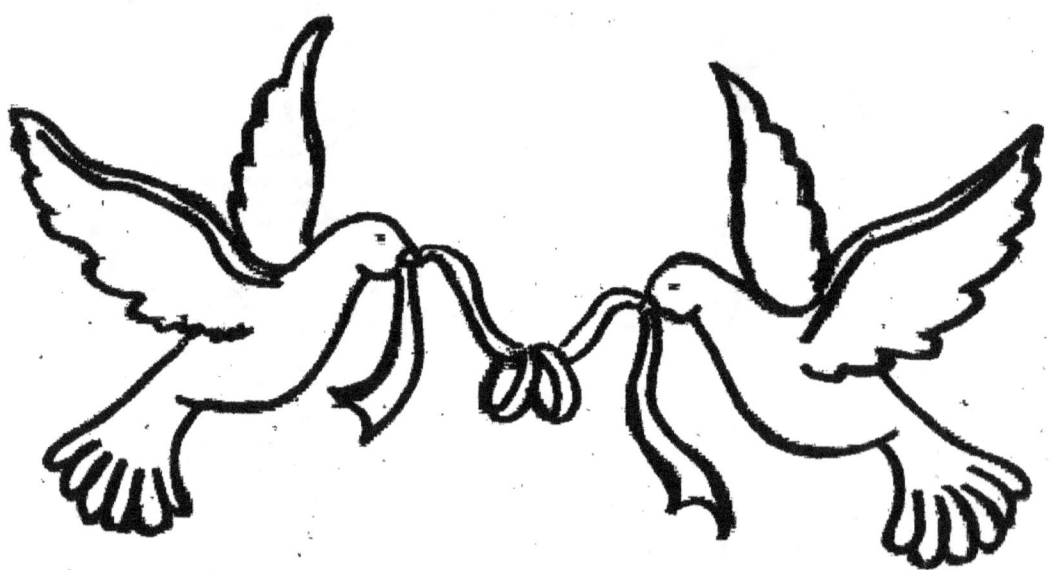

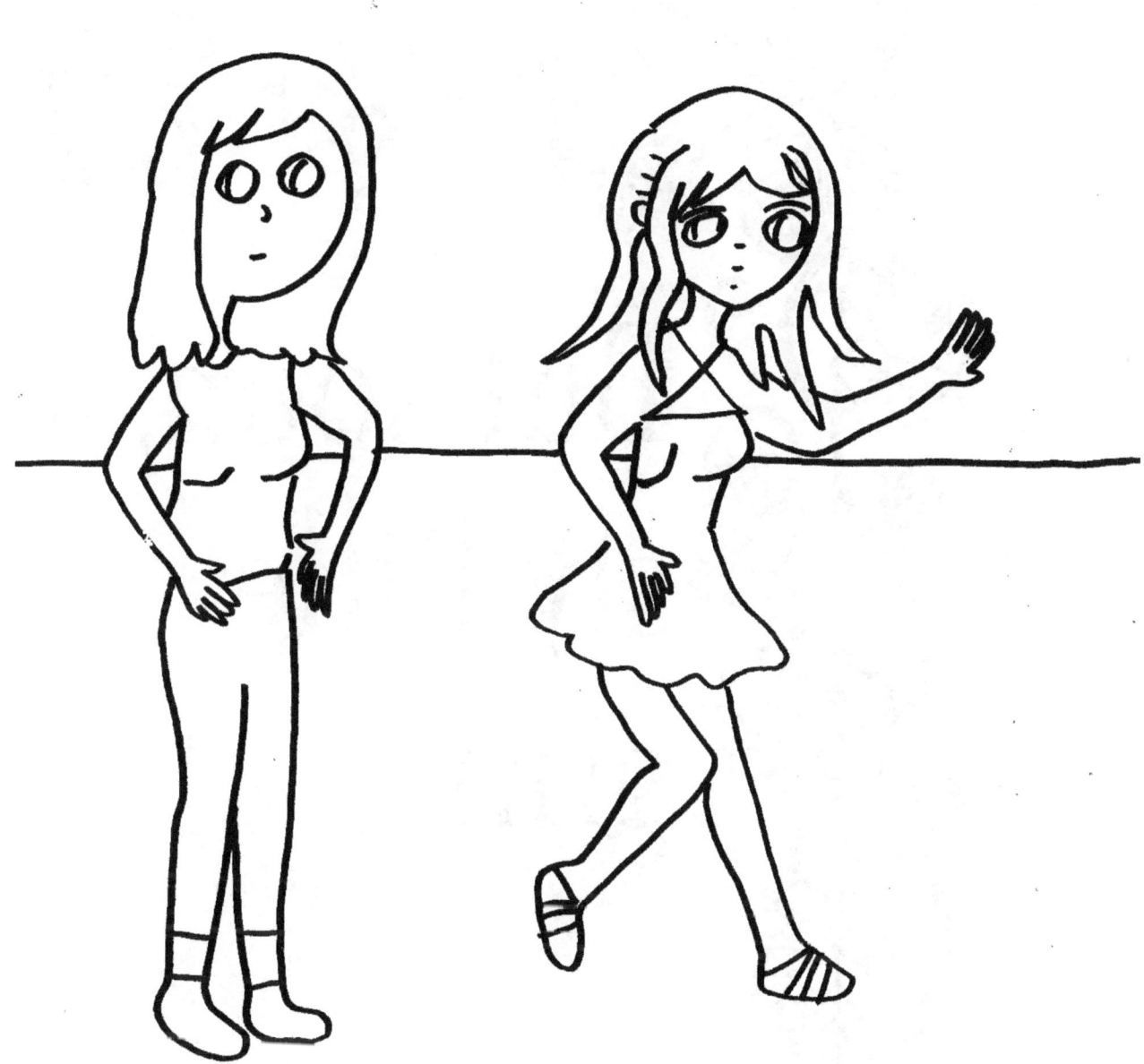

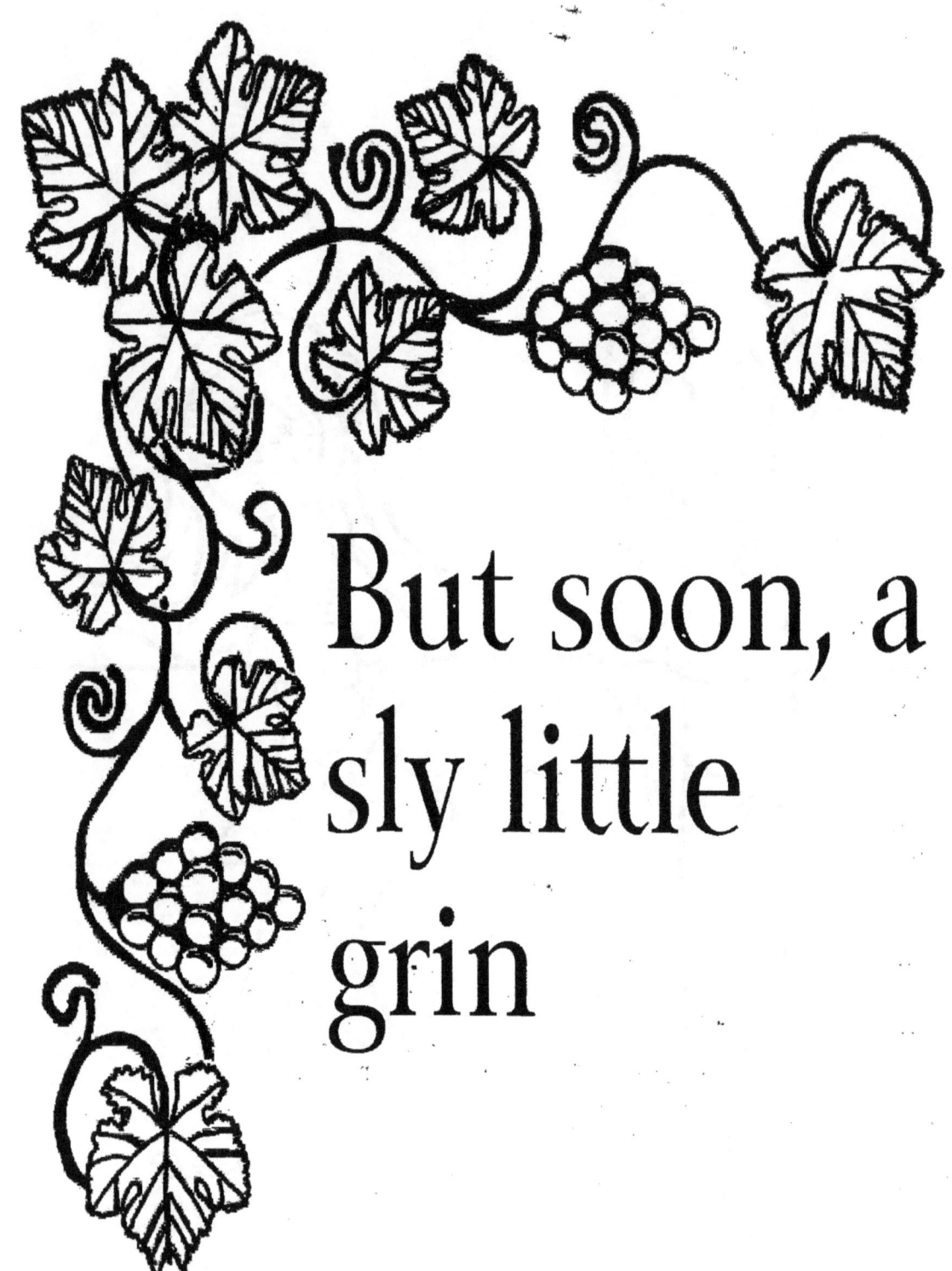

But soon, a
sly little
grin

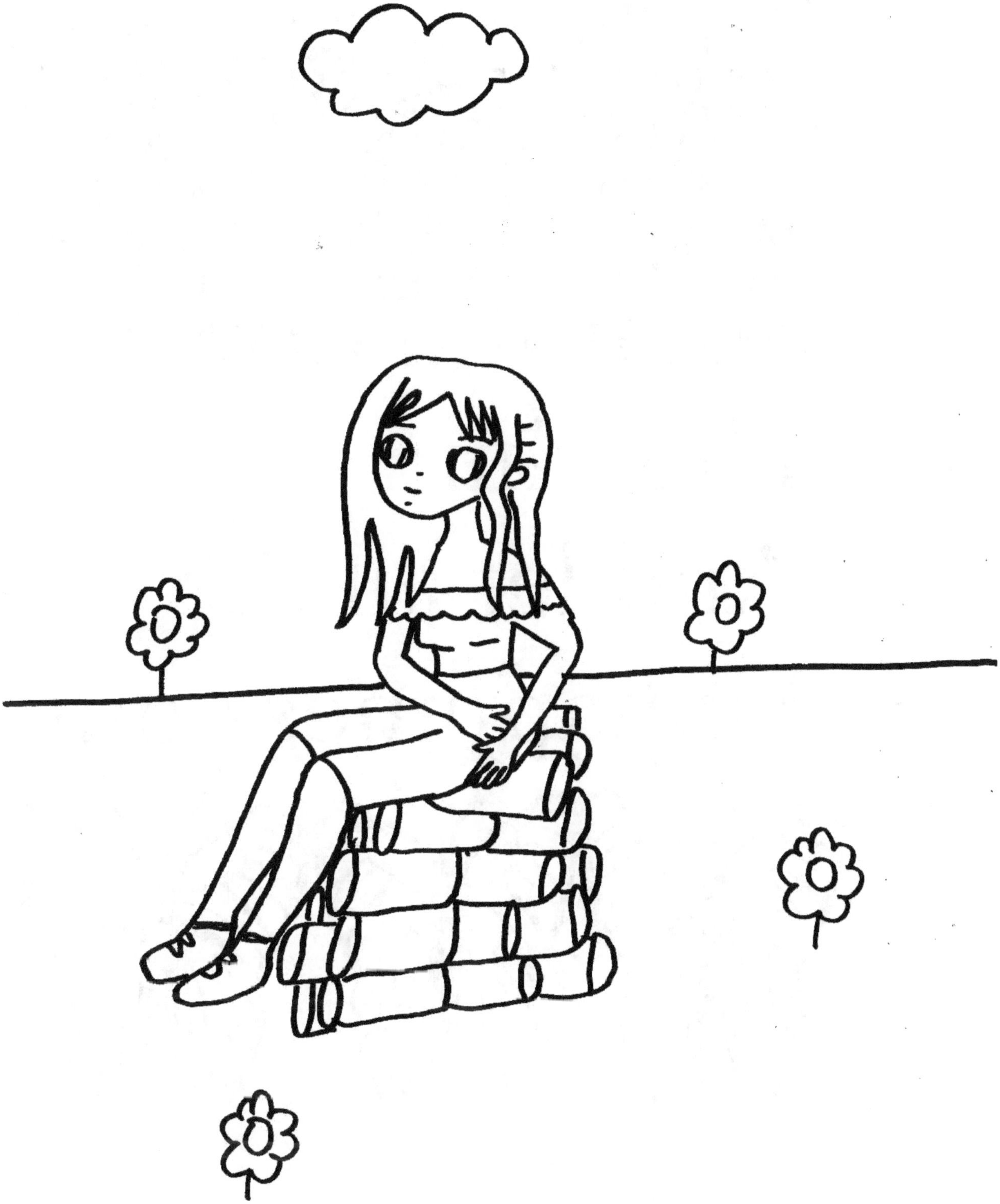

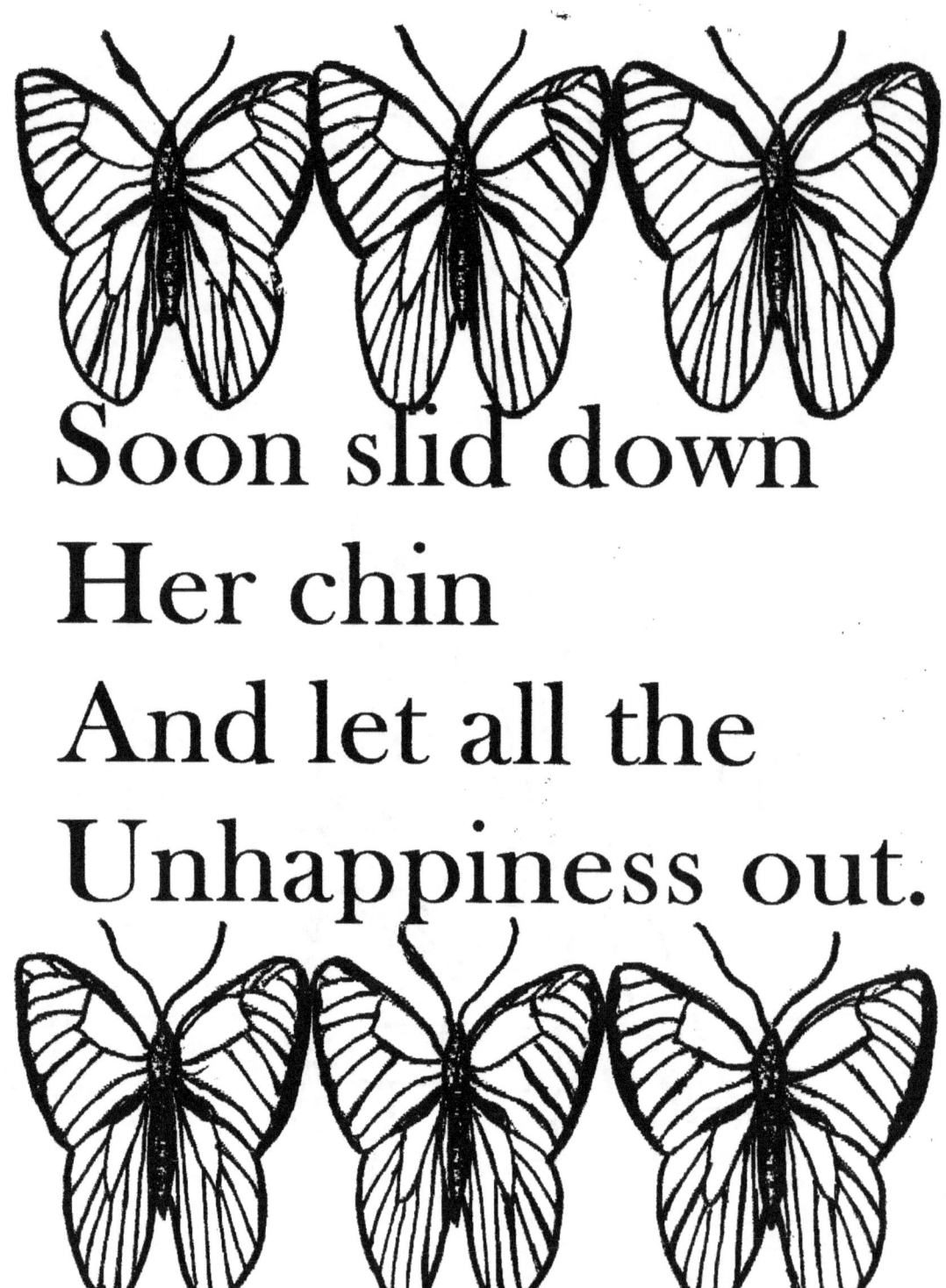

Soon slid down
Her chin
And let all the
Unhappiness out.

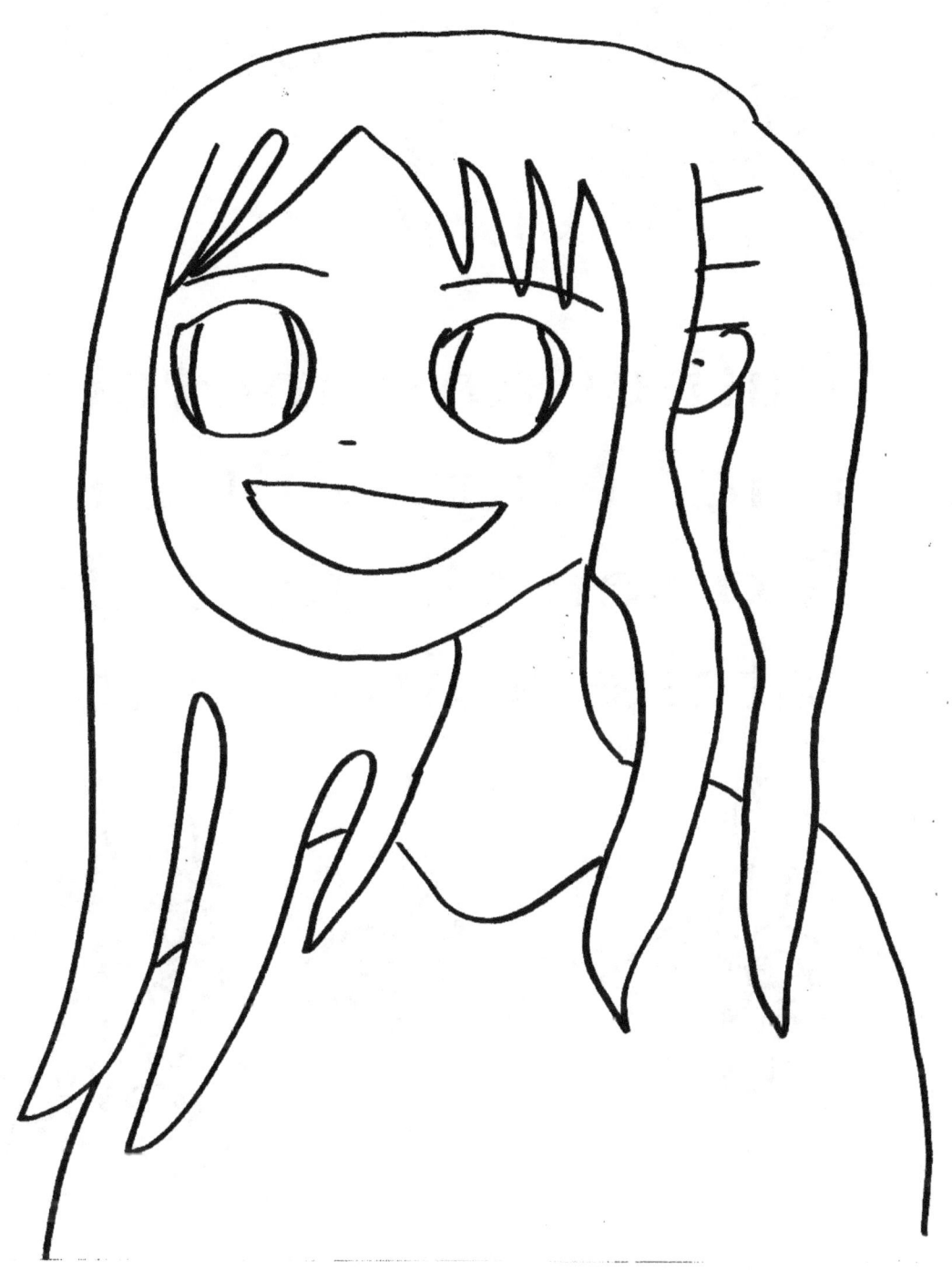

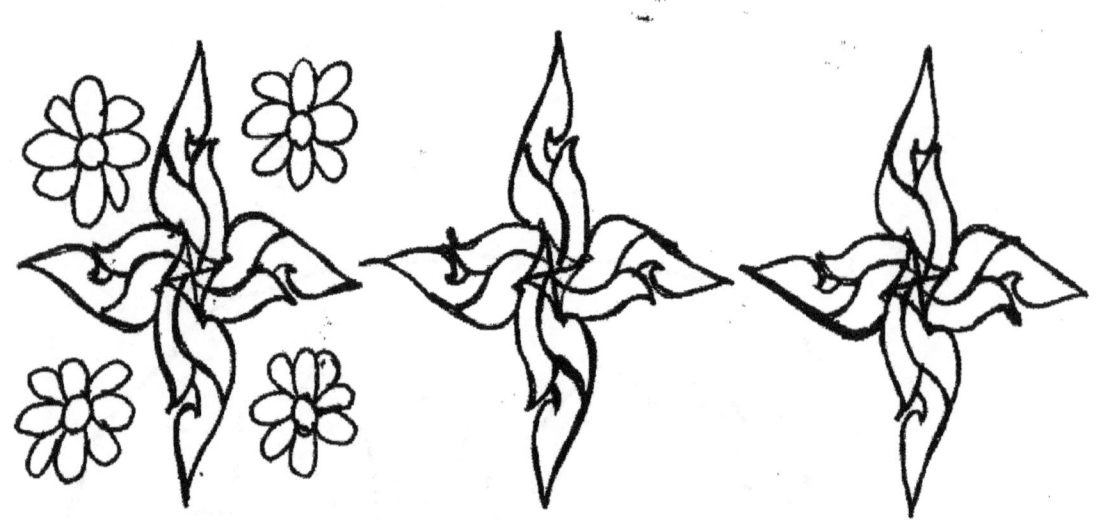

Father and mother
and Mary will go
To see all the sights
at the animal show.

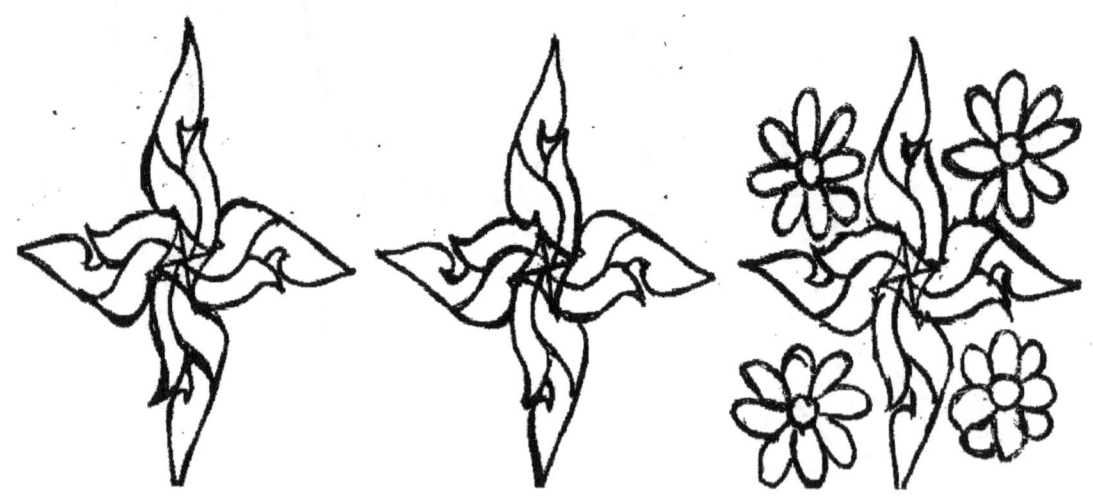

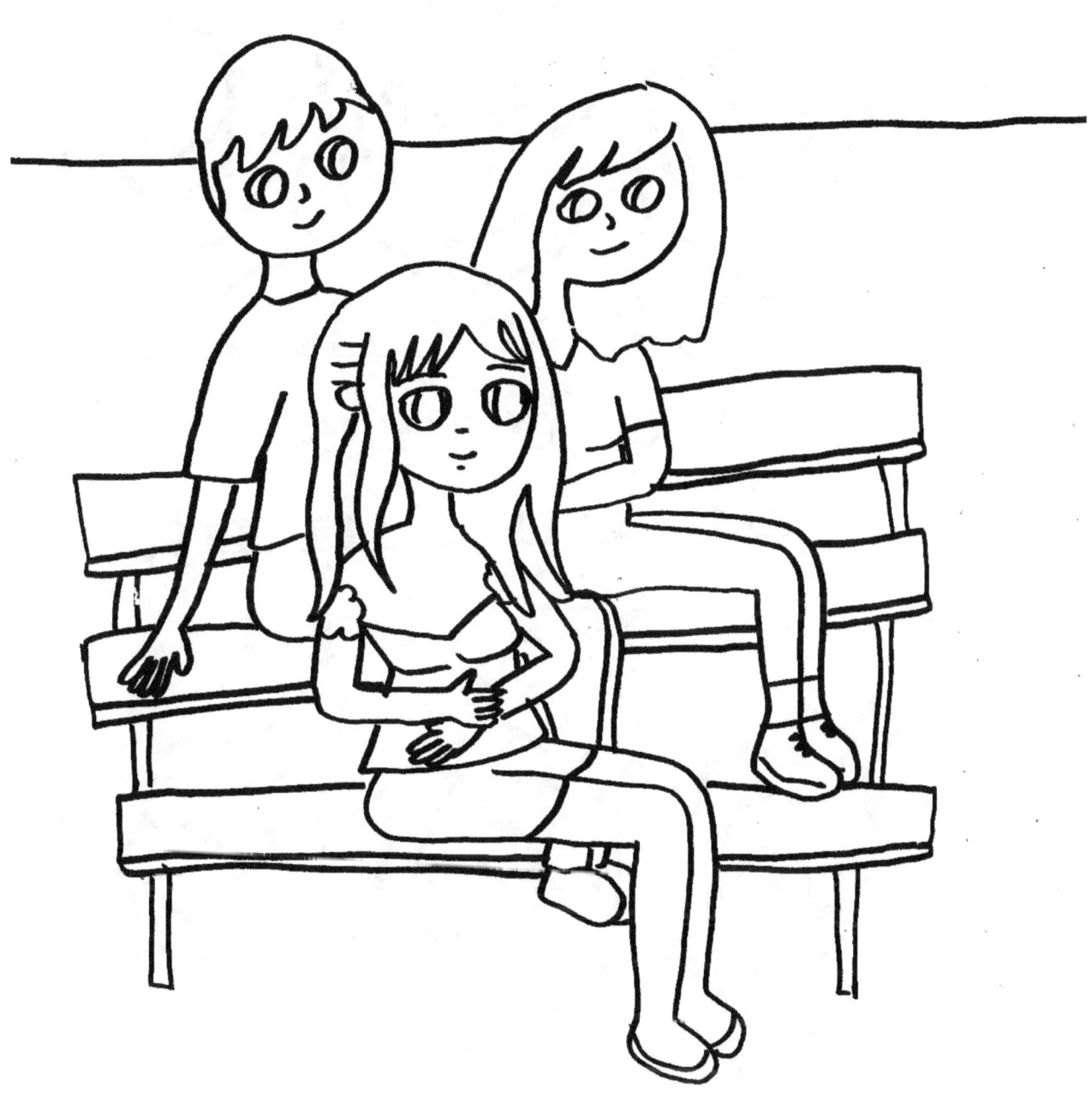

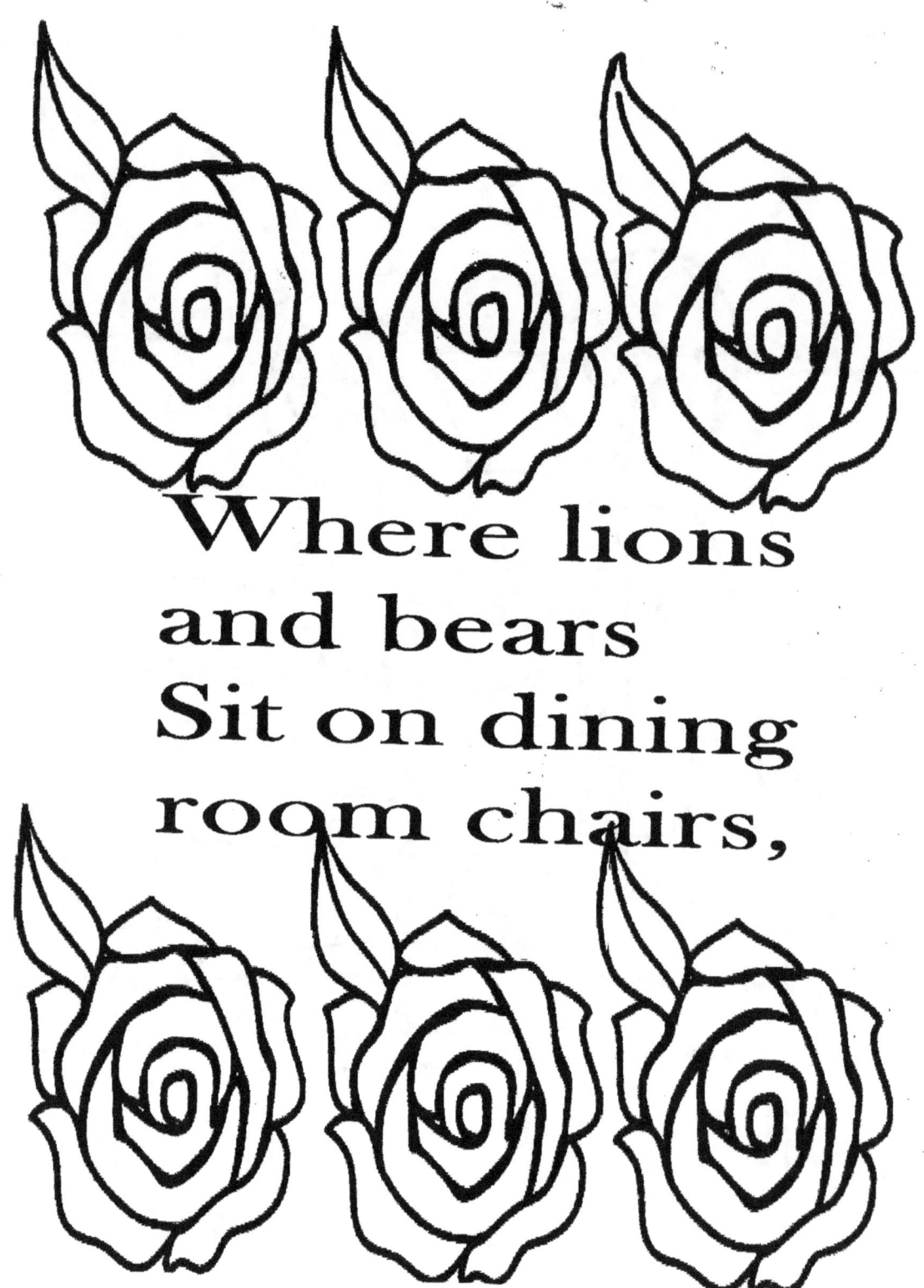

Where lions
and bears
Sit on dining
room chairs,

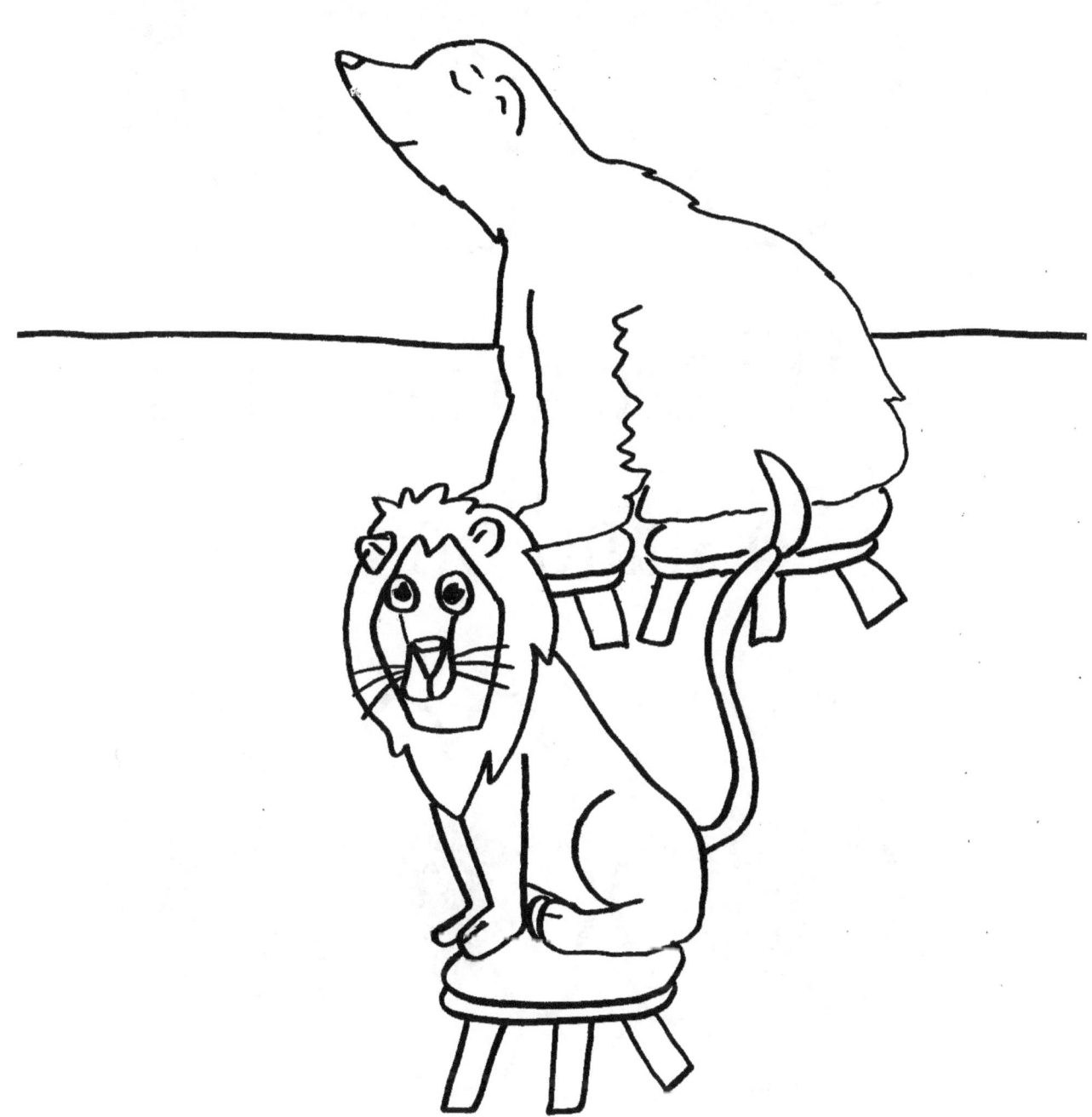

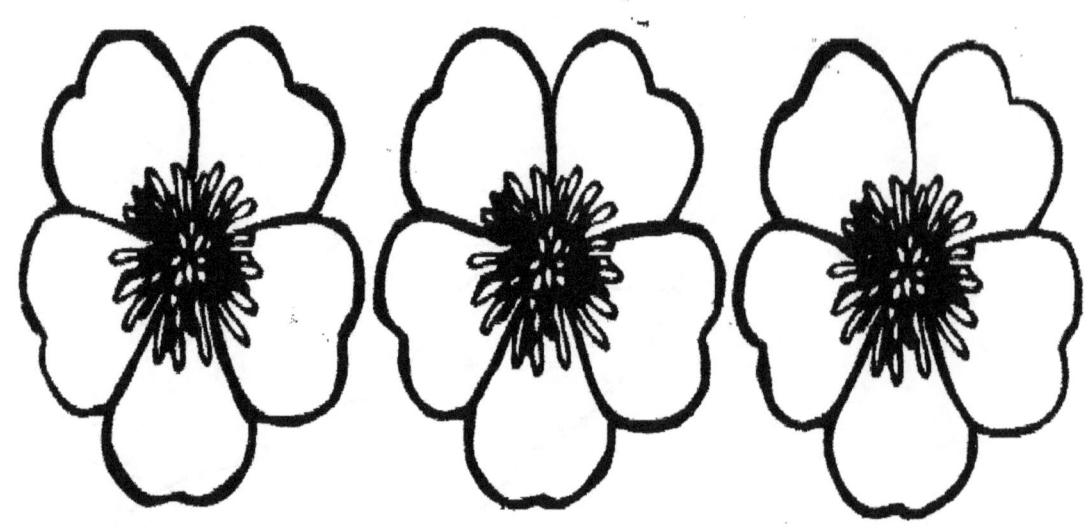

Where a camel is able

To stand on a table,

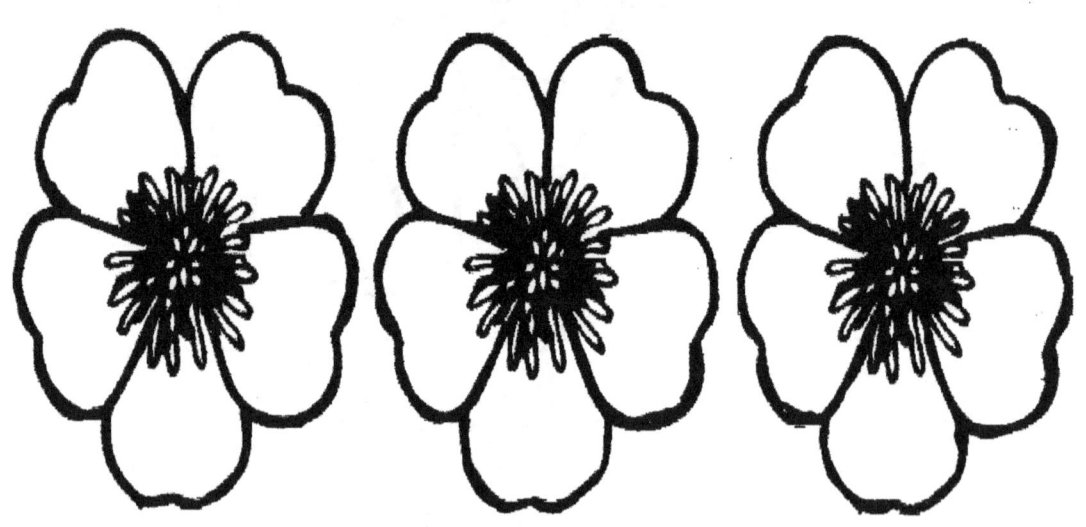

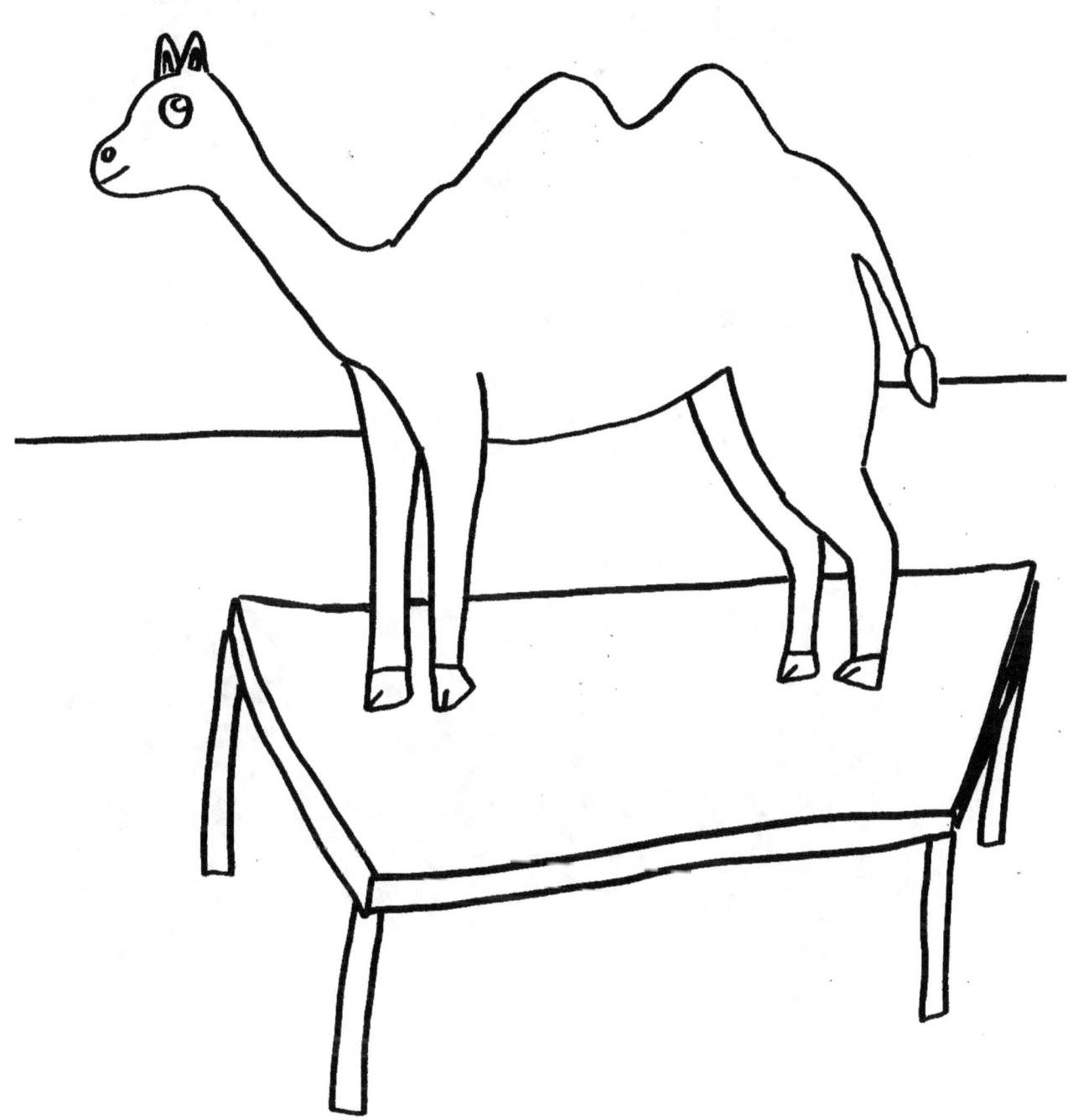

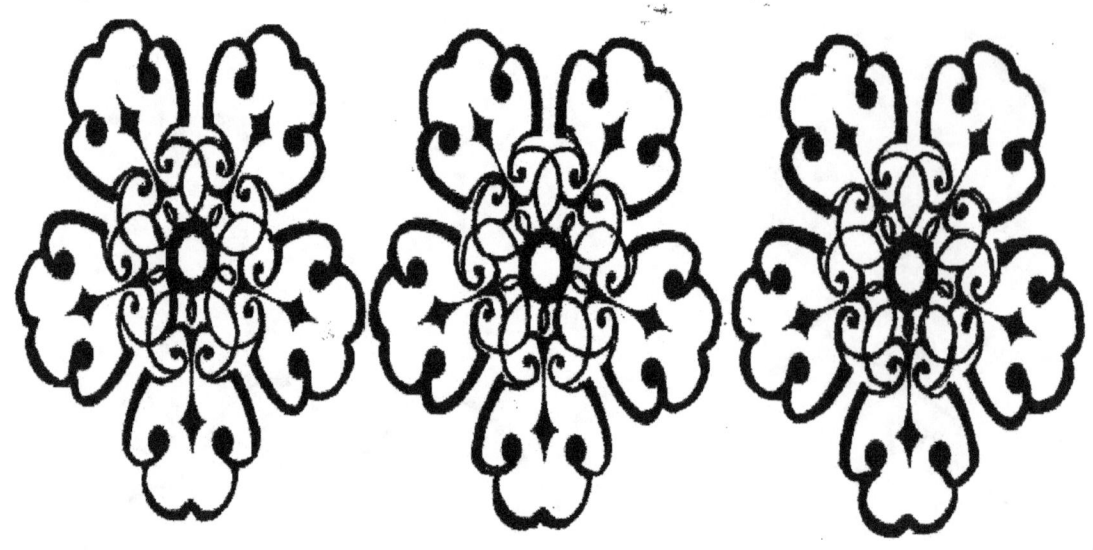

Where monkeys and seals
All travel on wheels,

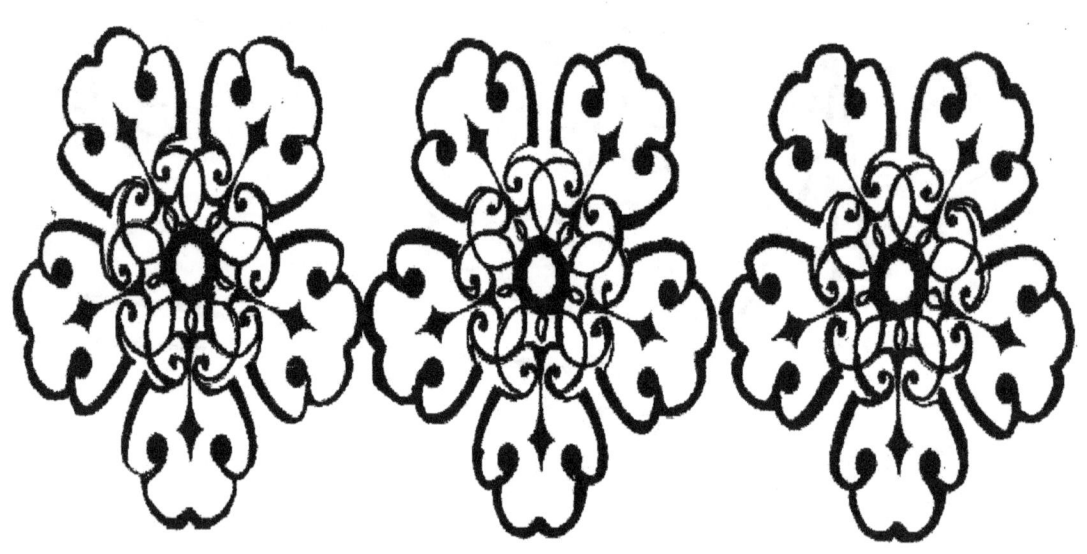

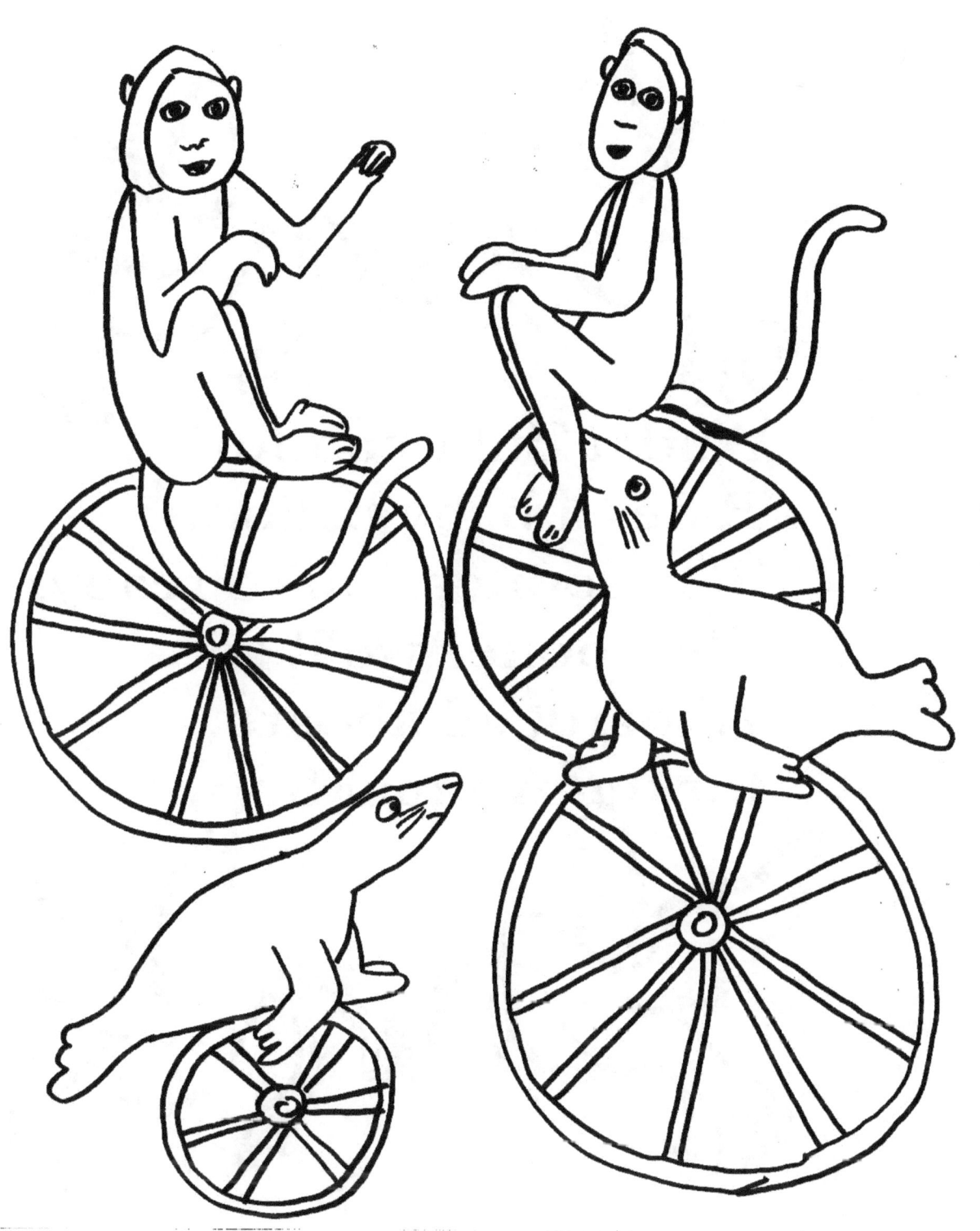

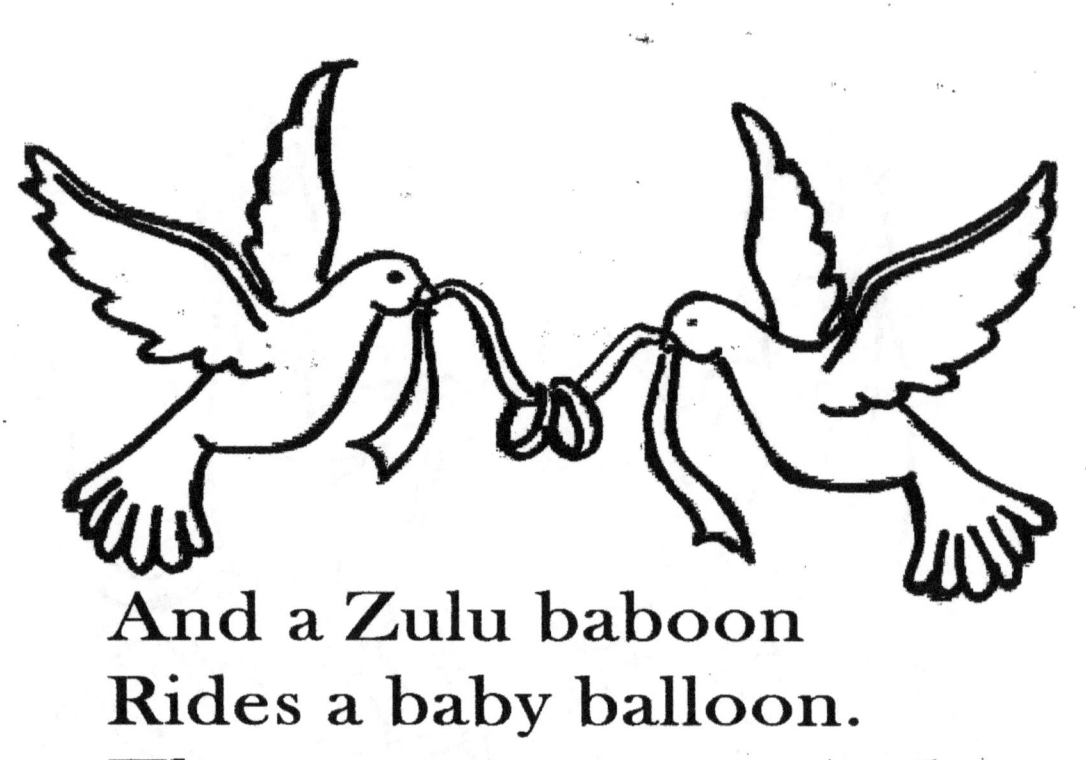

And a Zulu baboon
Rides a baby balloon.
The sooner you're ready,
 the sooner we'll go.
Aboard, all aboard,
 for the Animal Show!

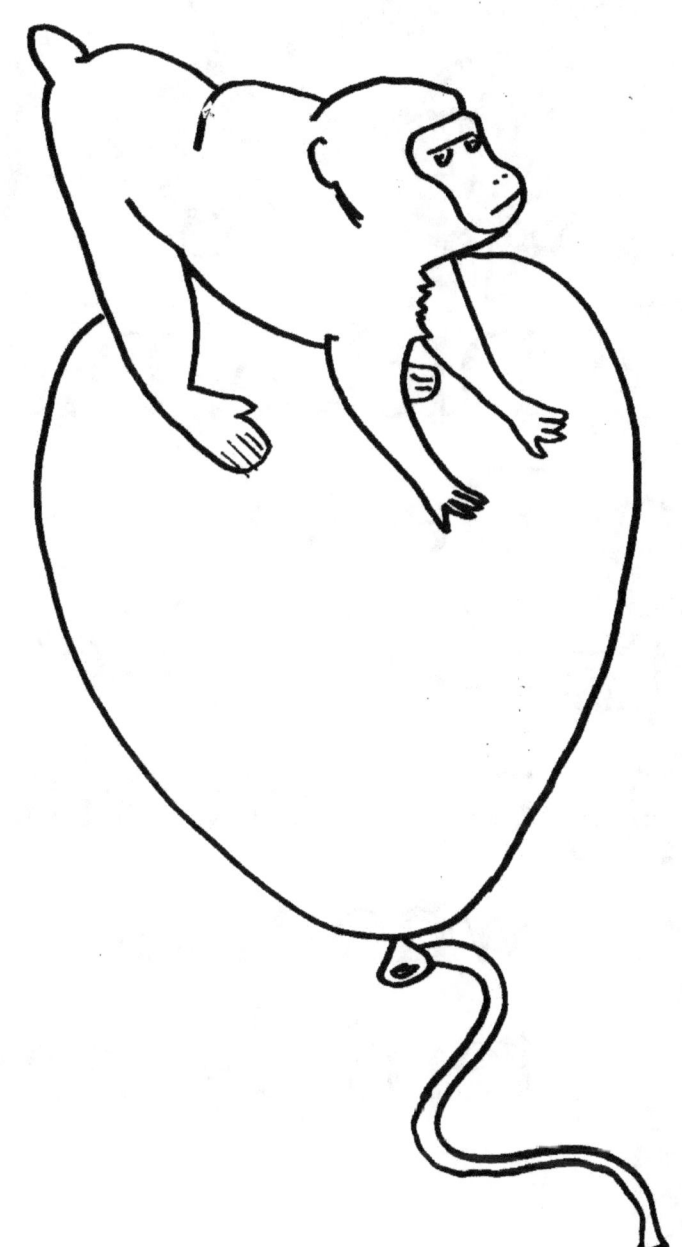

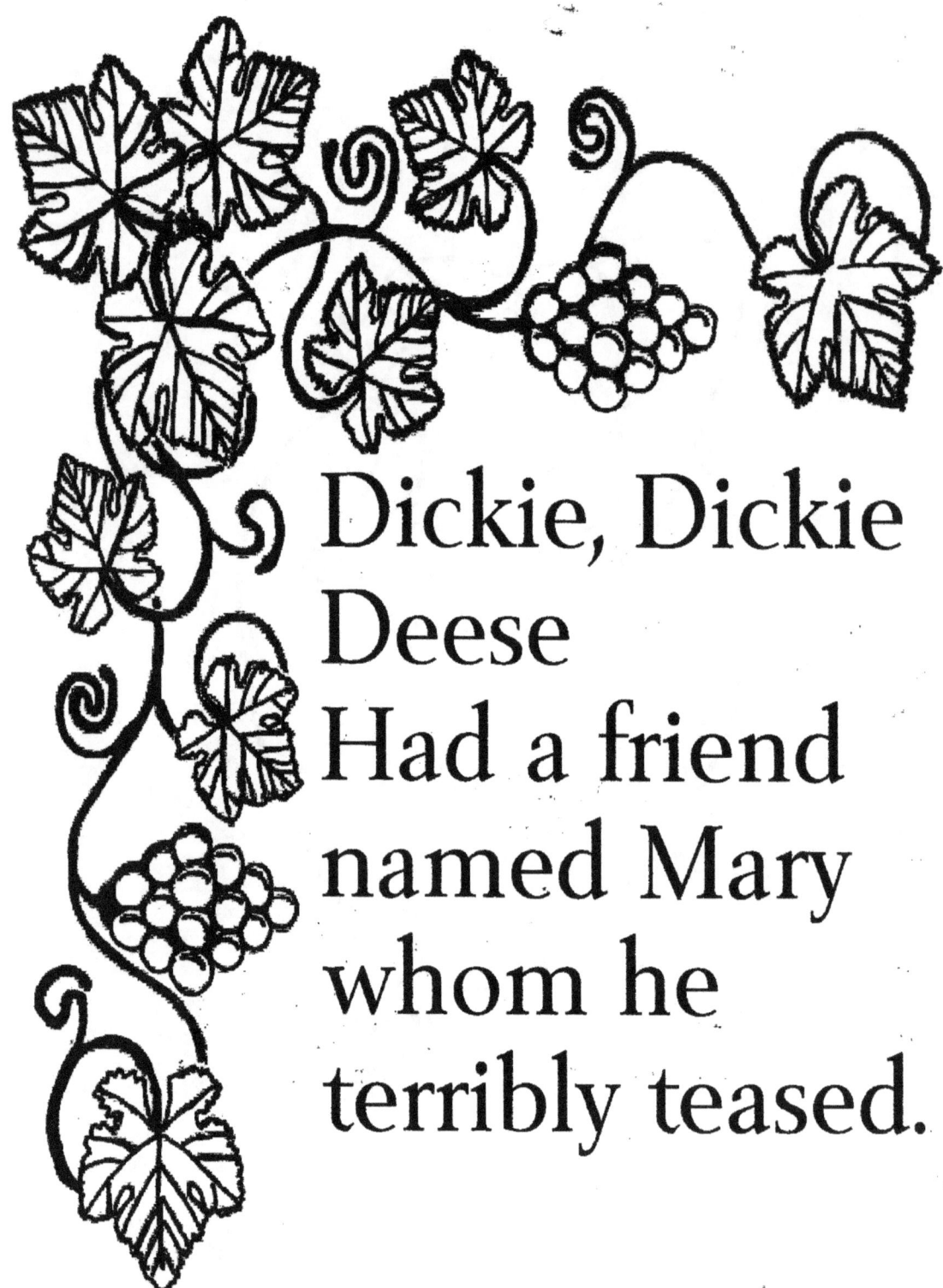

Dickie, Dickie
Deese
Had a friend
named Mary
whom he
terribly teased.

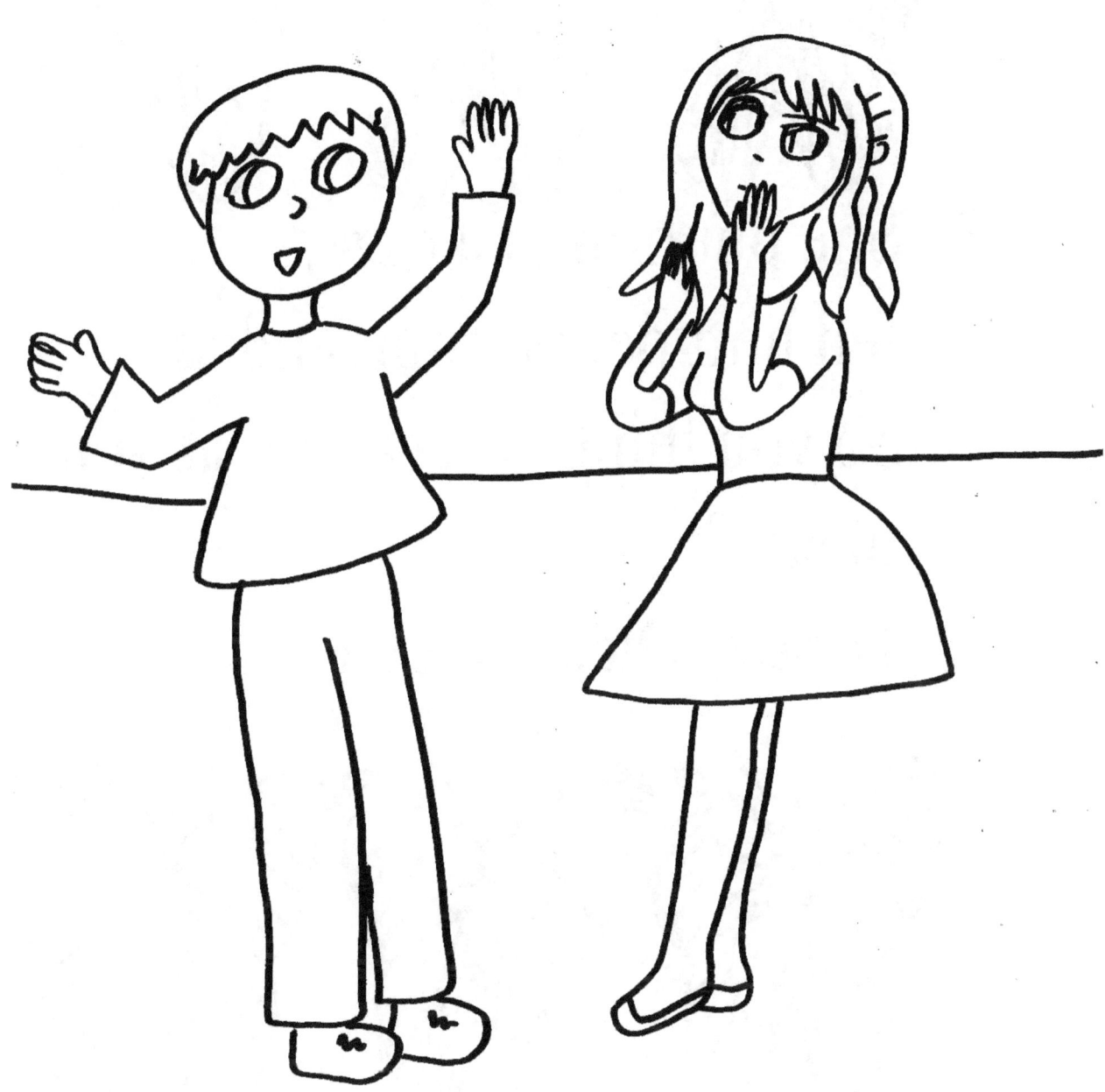

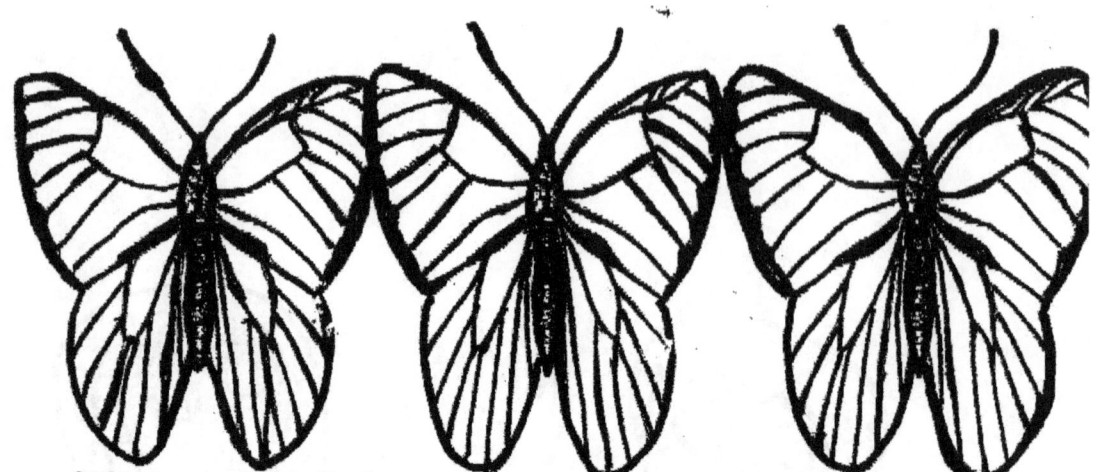

She put him in a cage,
fed him peppermint and sage.
So you think you can do as you
please?
Dickie, Dickie Deese.

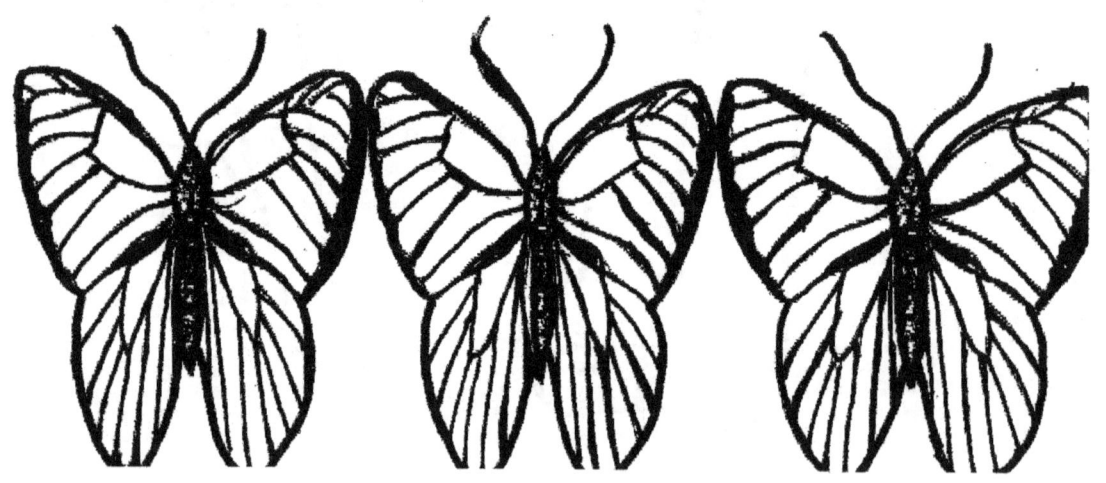

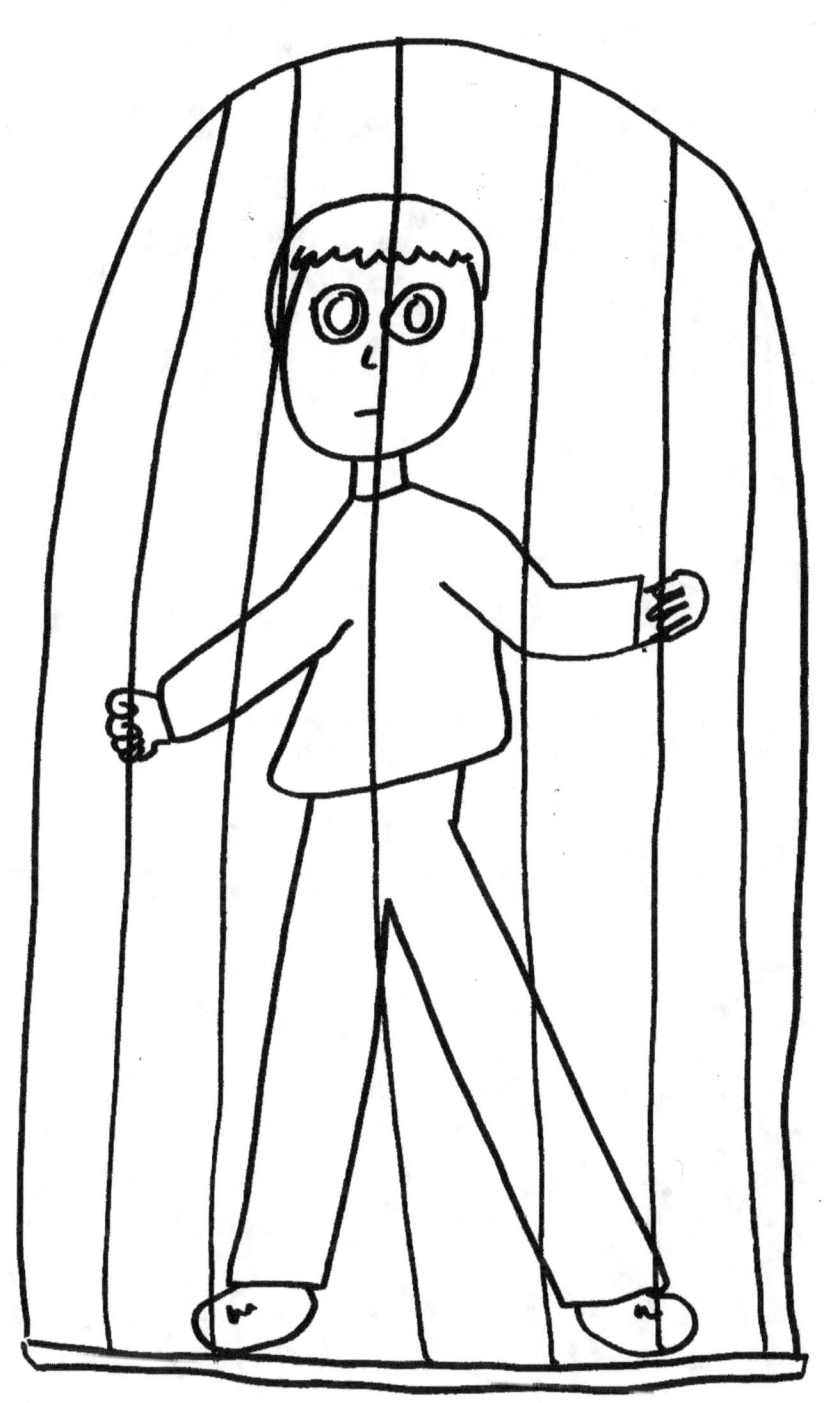

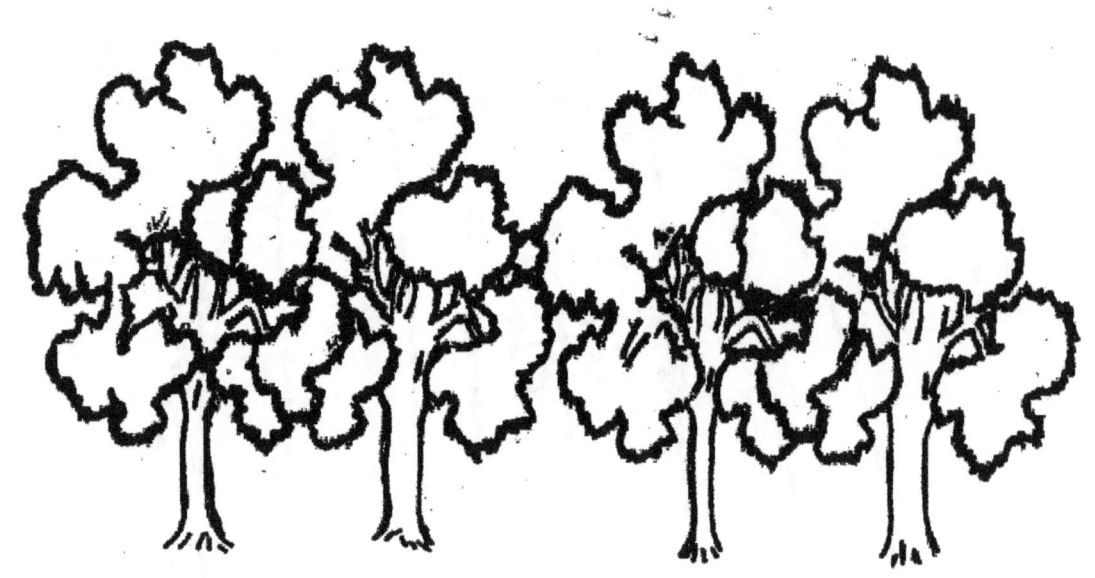

On the road to
Tattletown
What do I see?

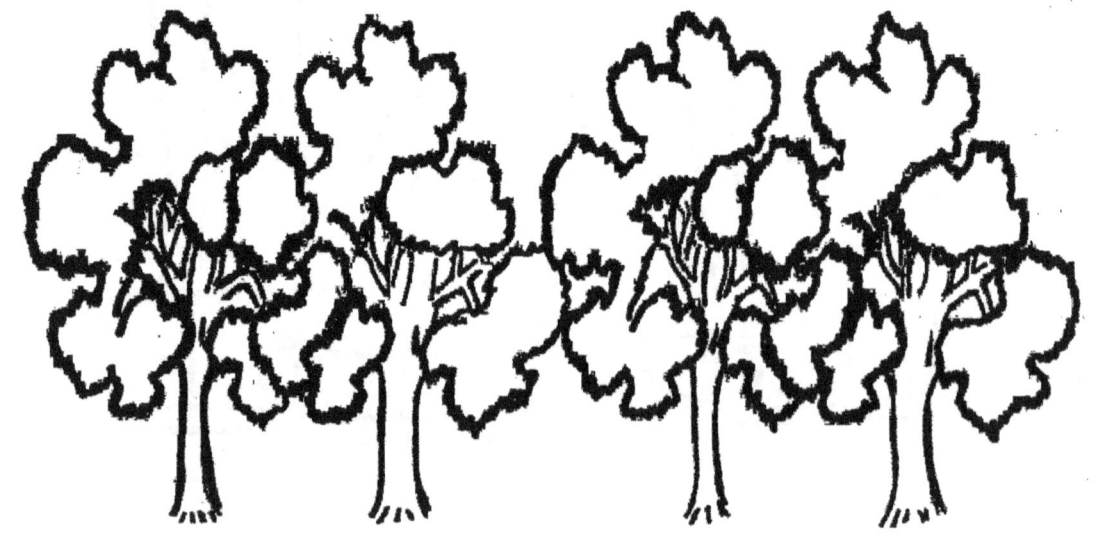

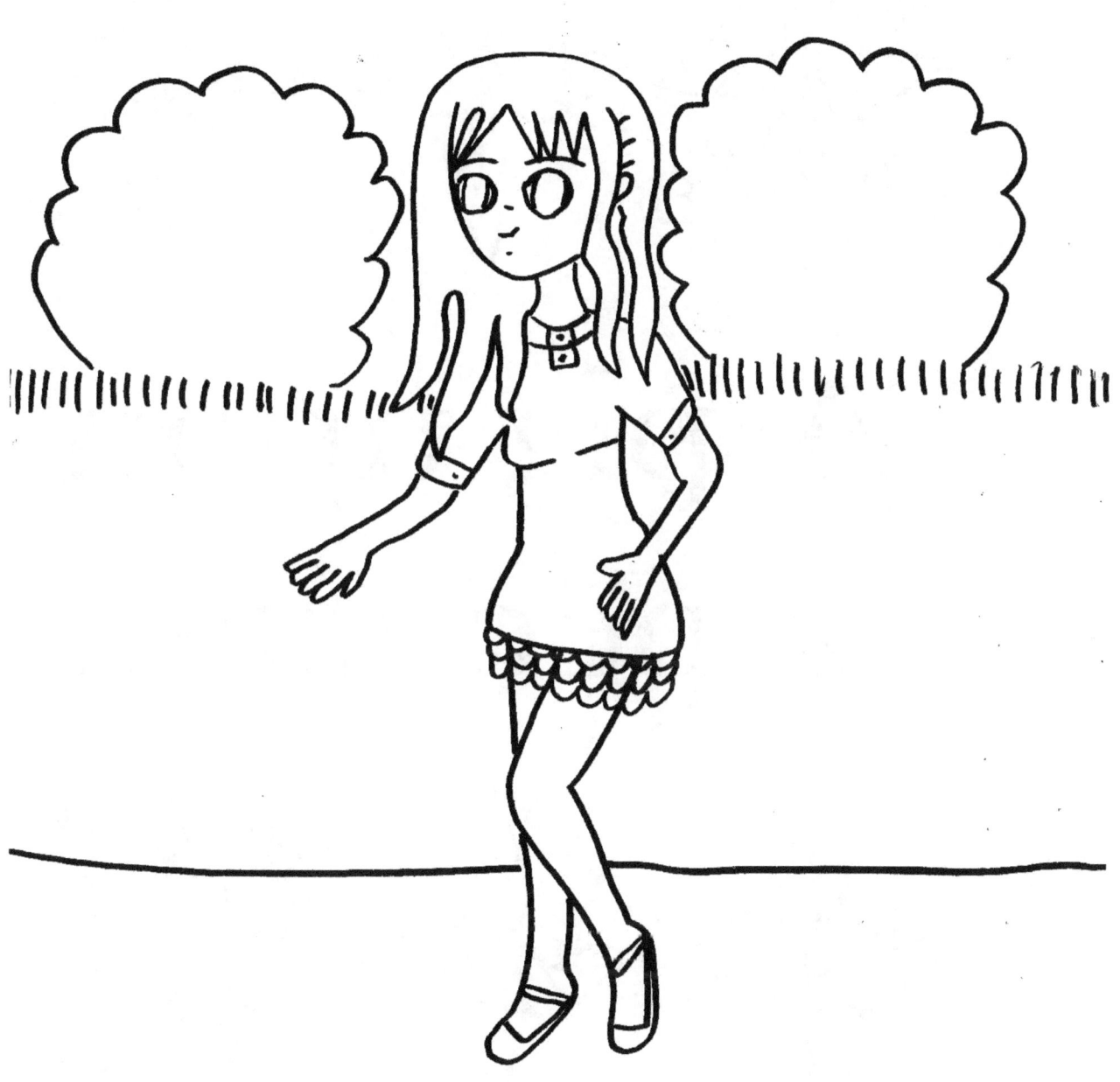

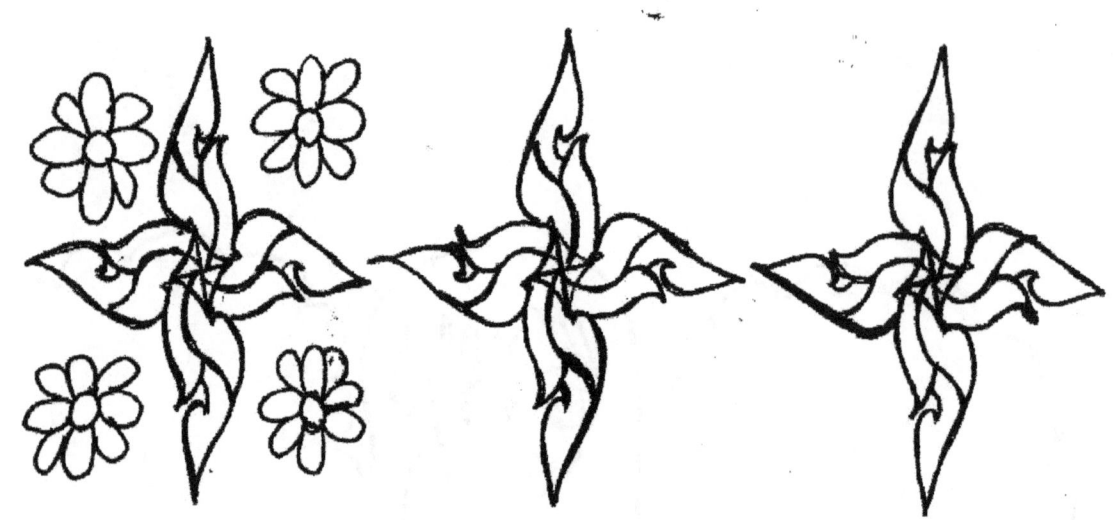

A pig upon
a pedestal,

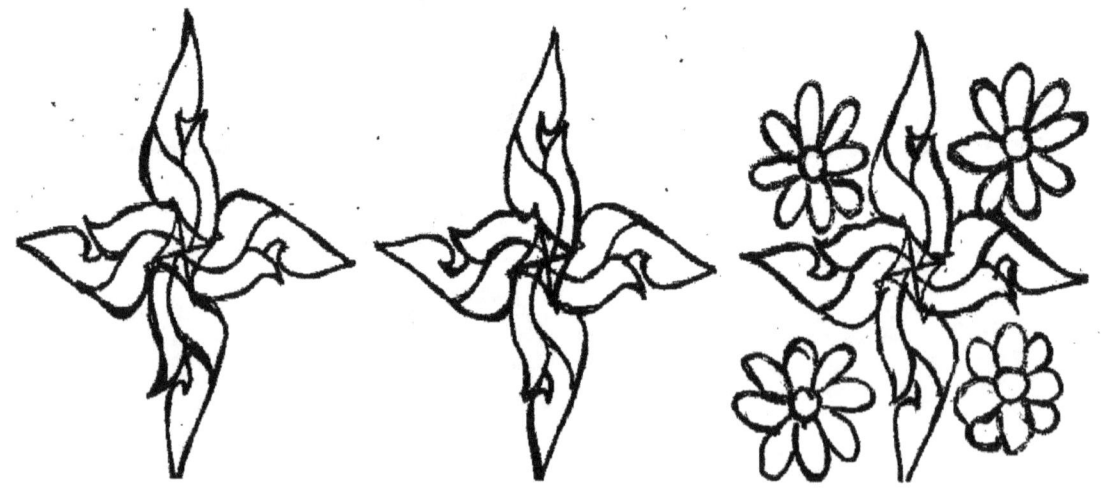

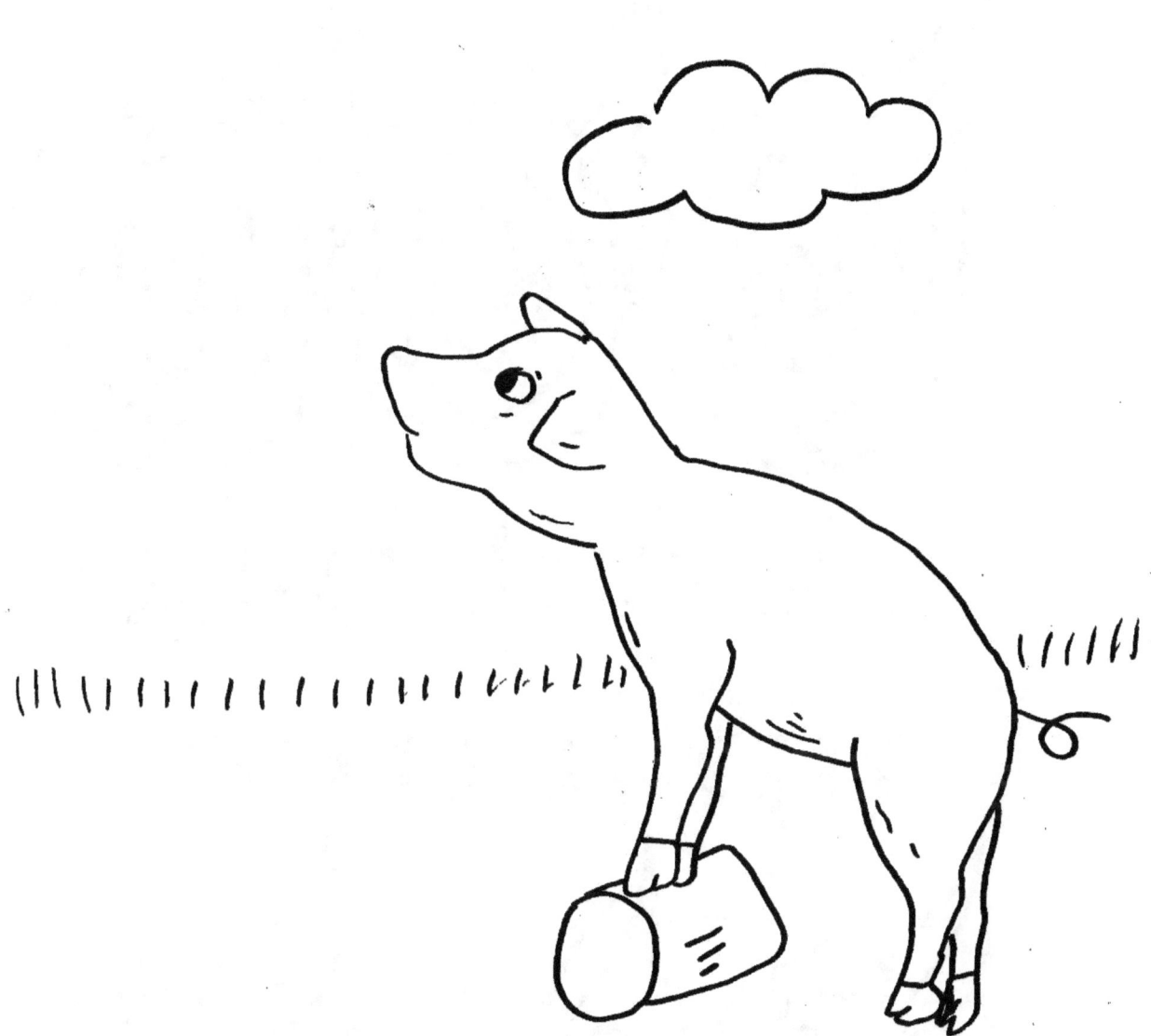

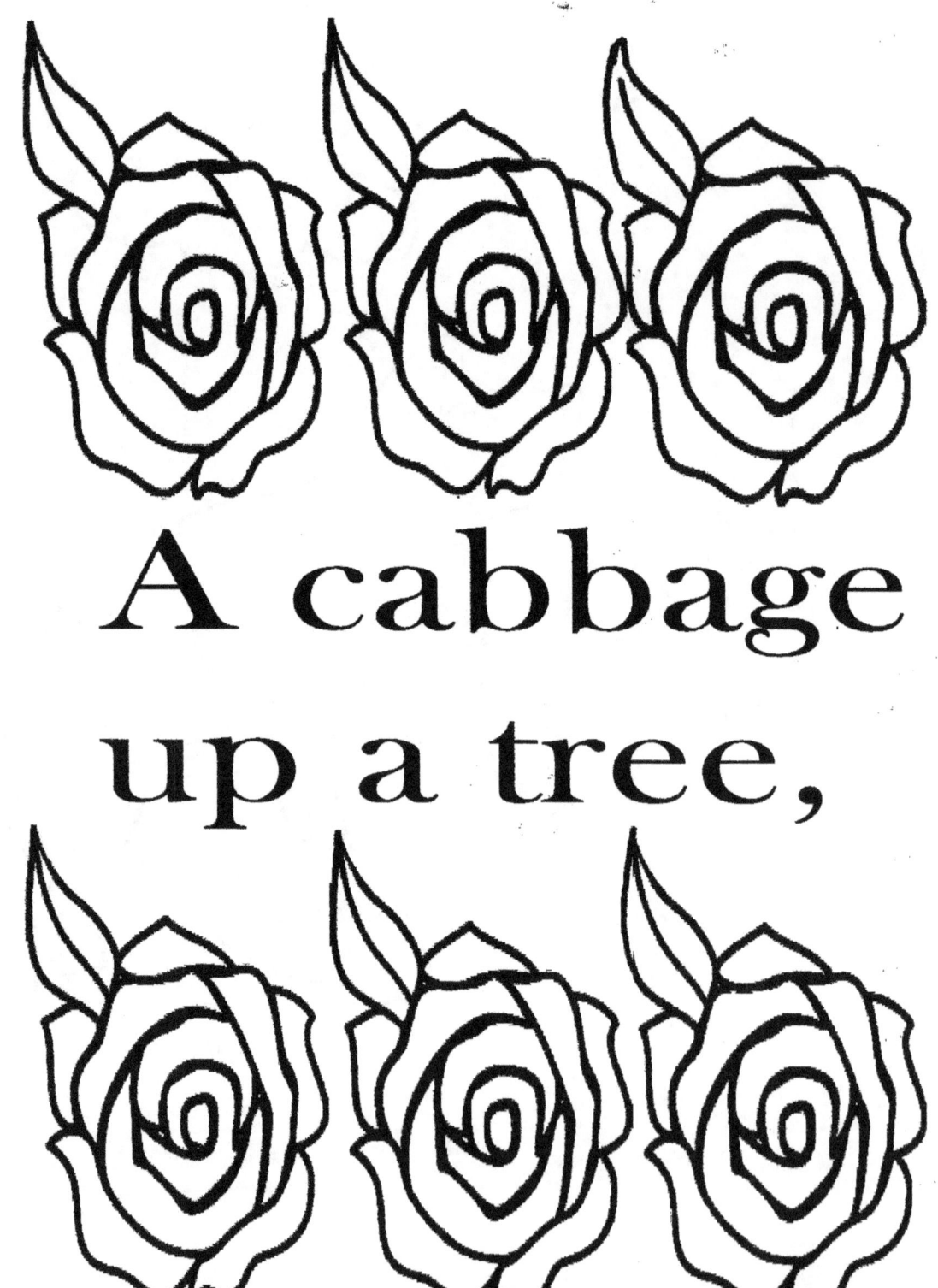

A cabbage

up a tree,

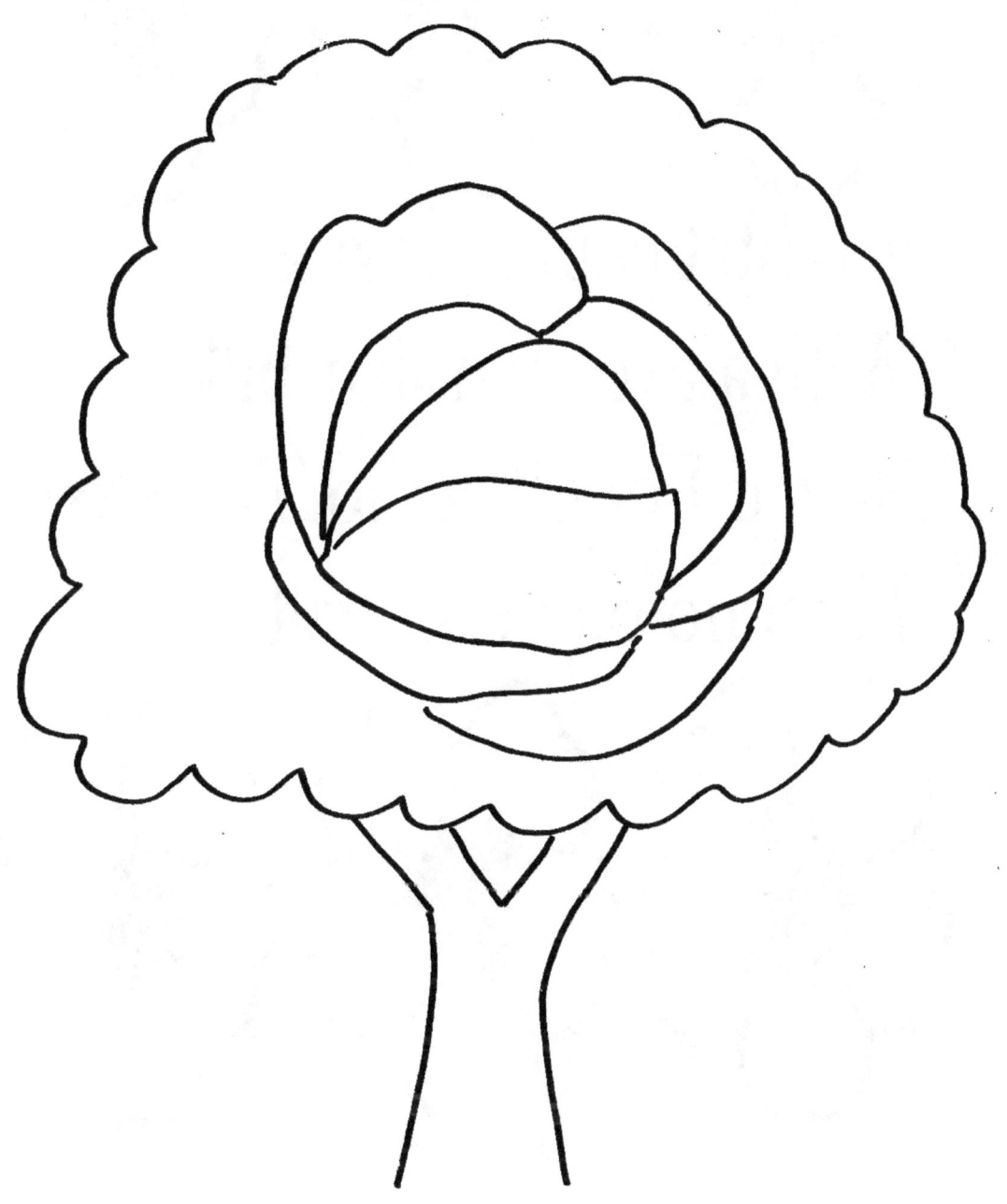

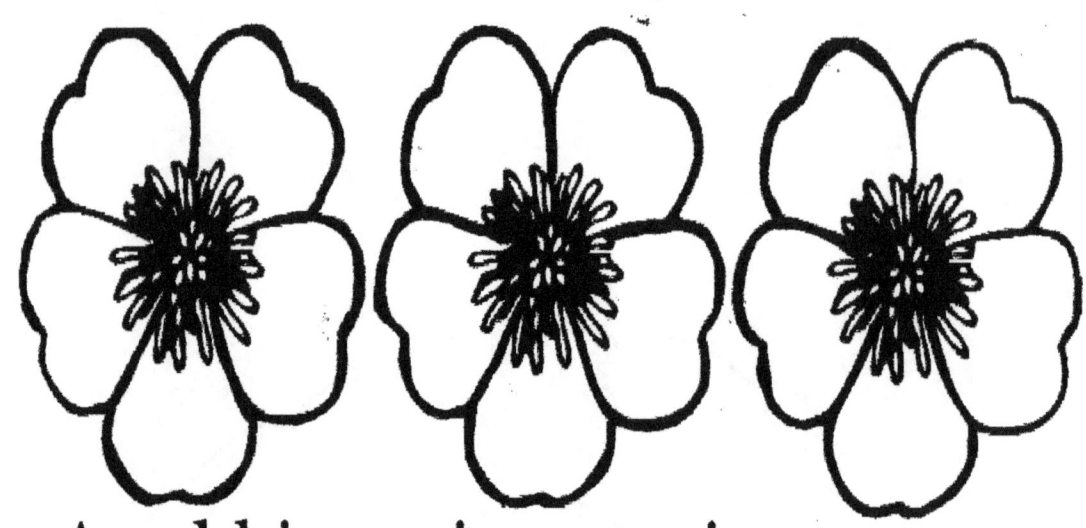

A rabbit cutting veggies
With a twenty dollar bill–
Now if I don't get to Tattletown
Then no one ever will.

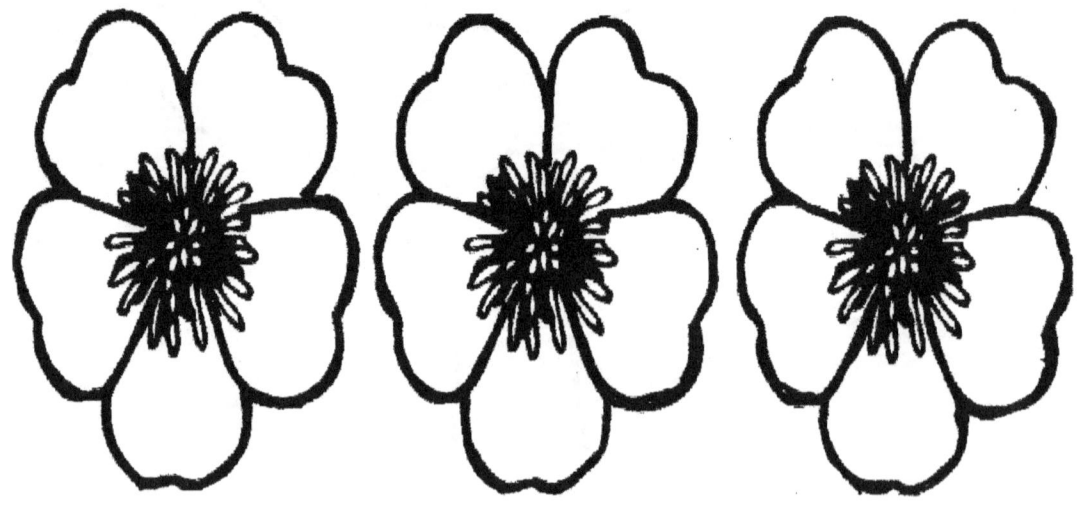

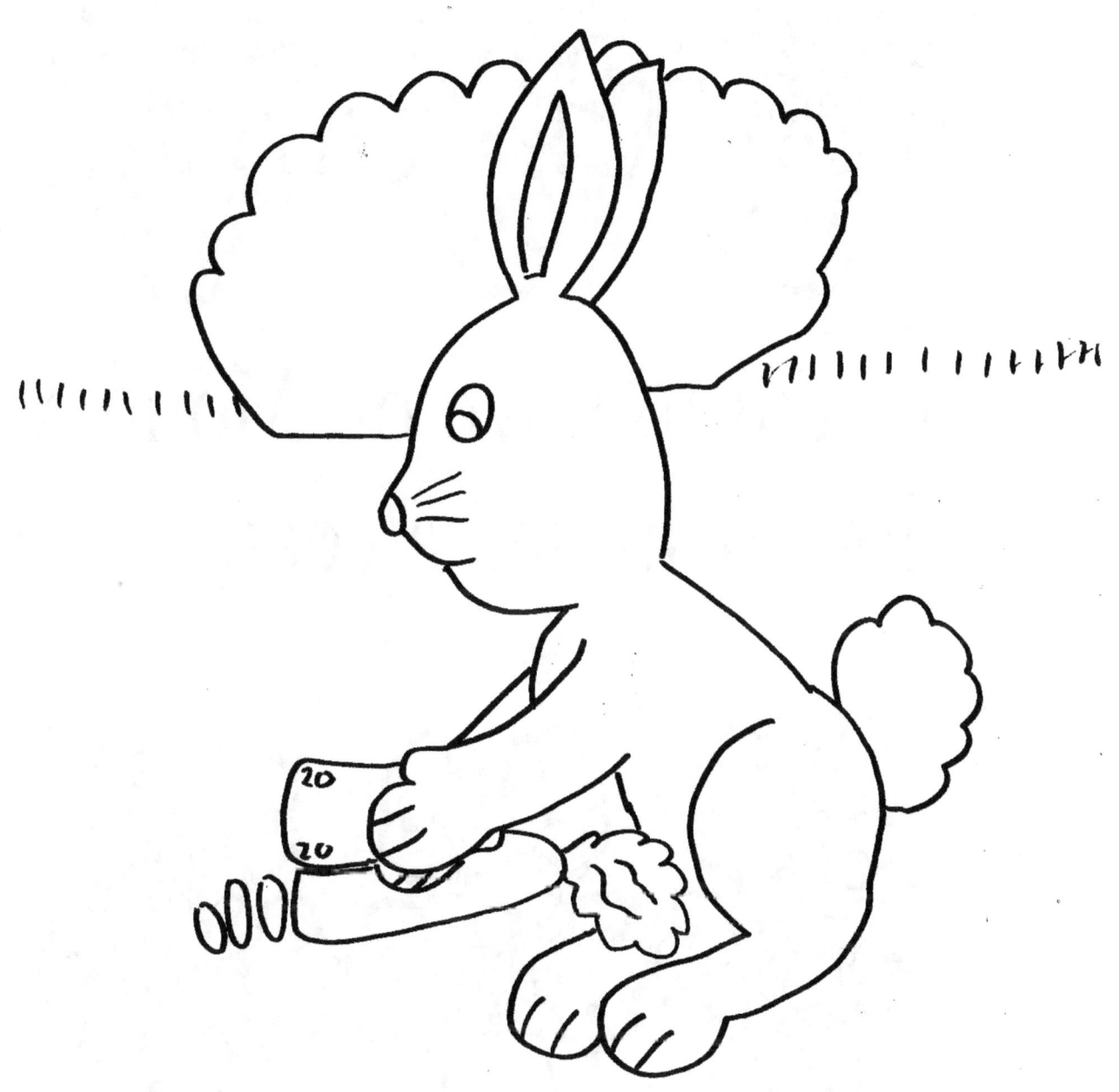

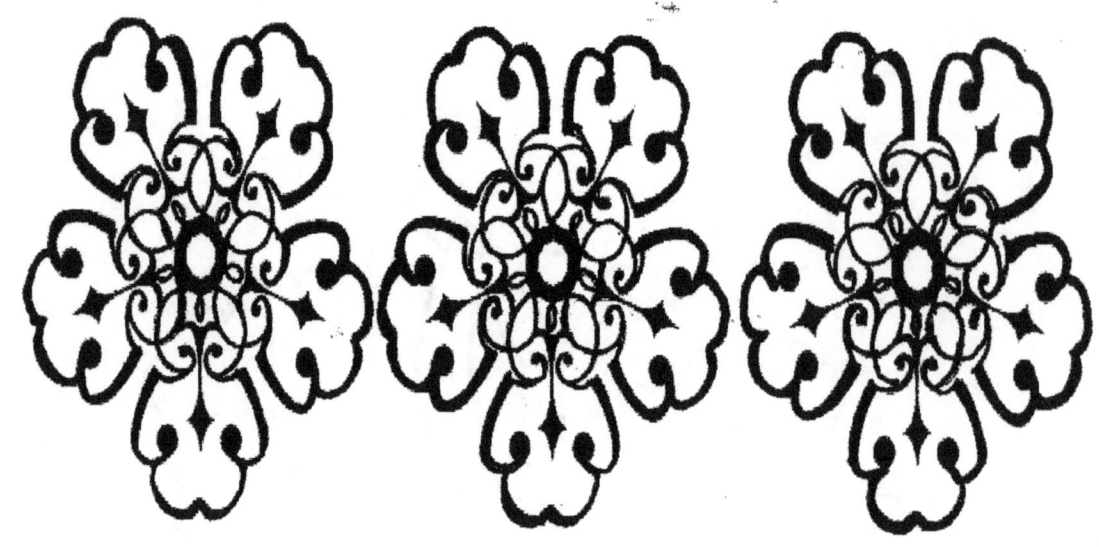

I went to town on Monday
To buy myself a coat,

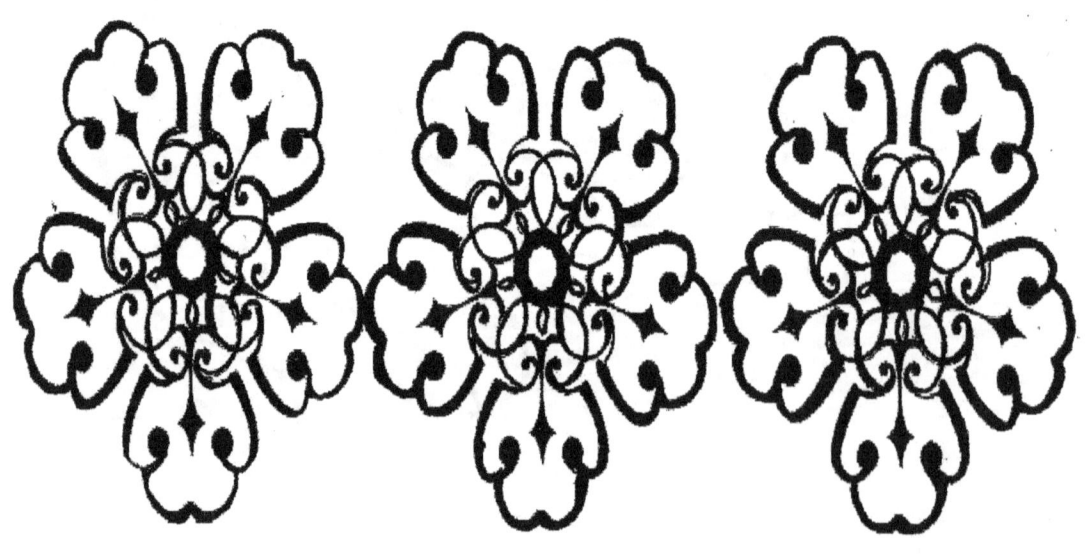

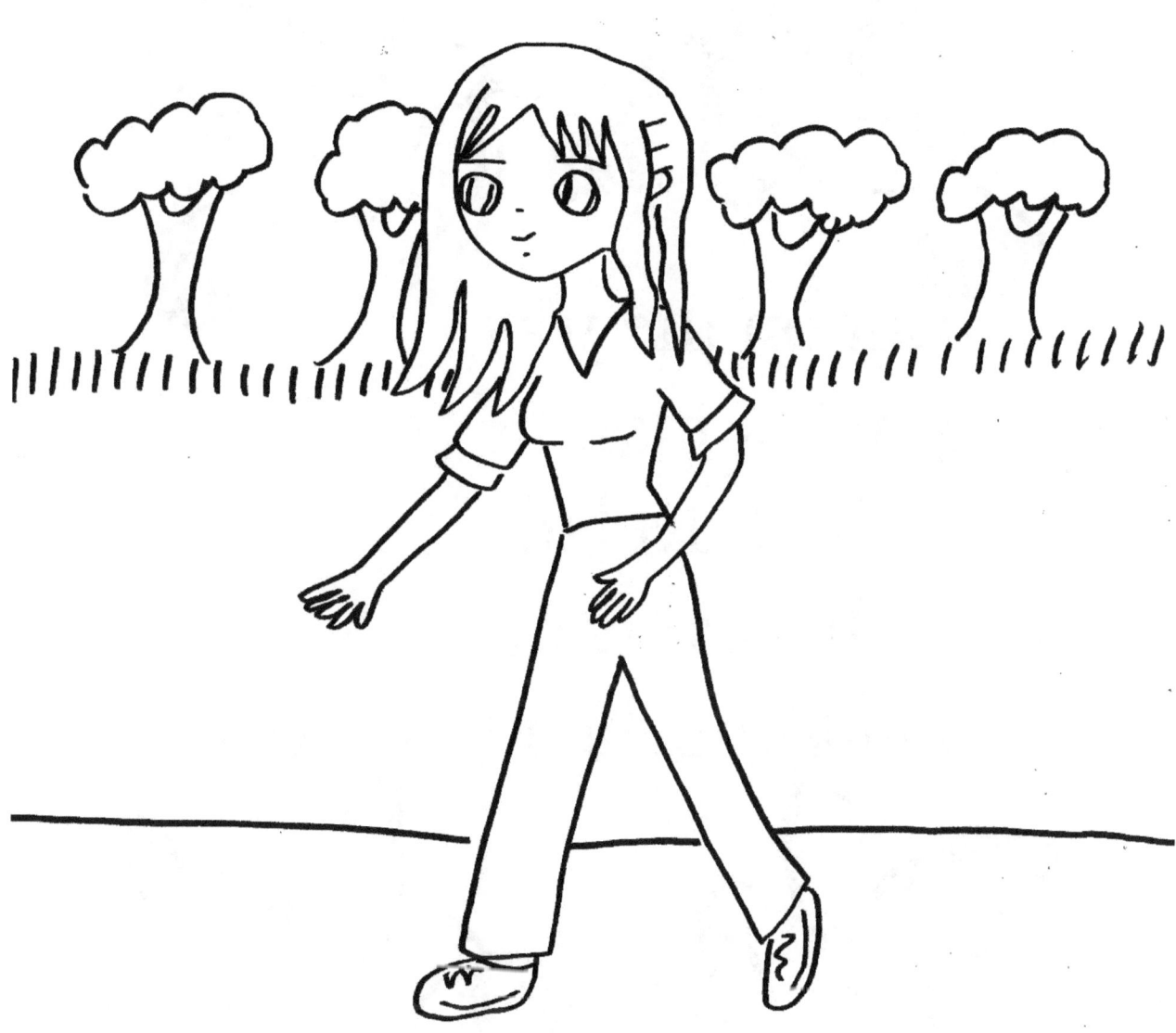

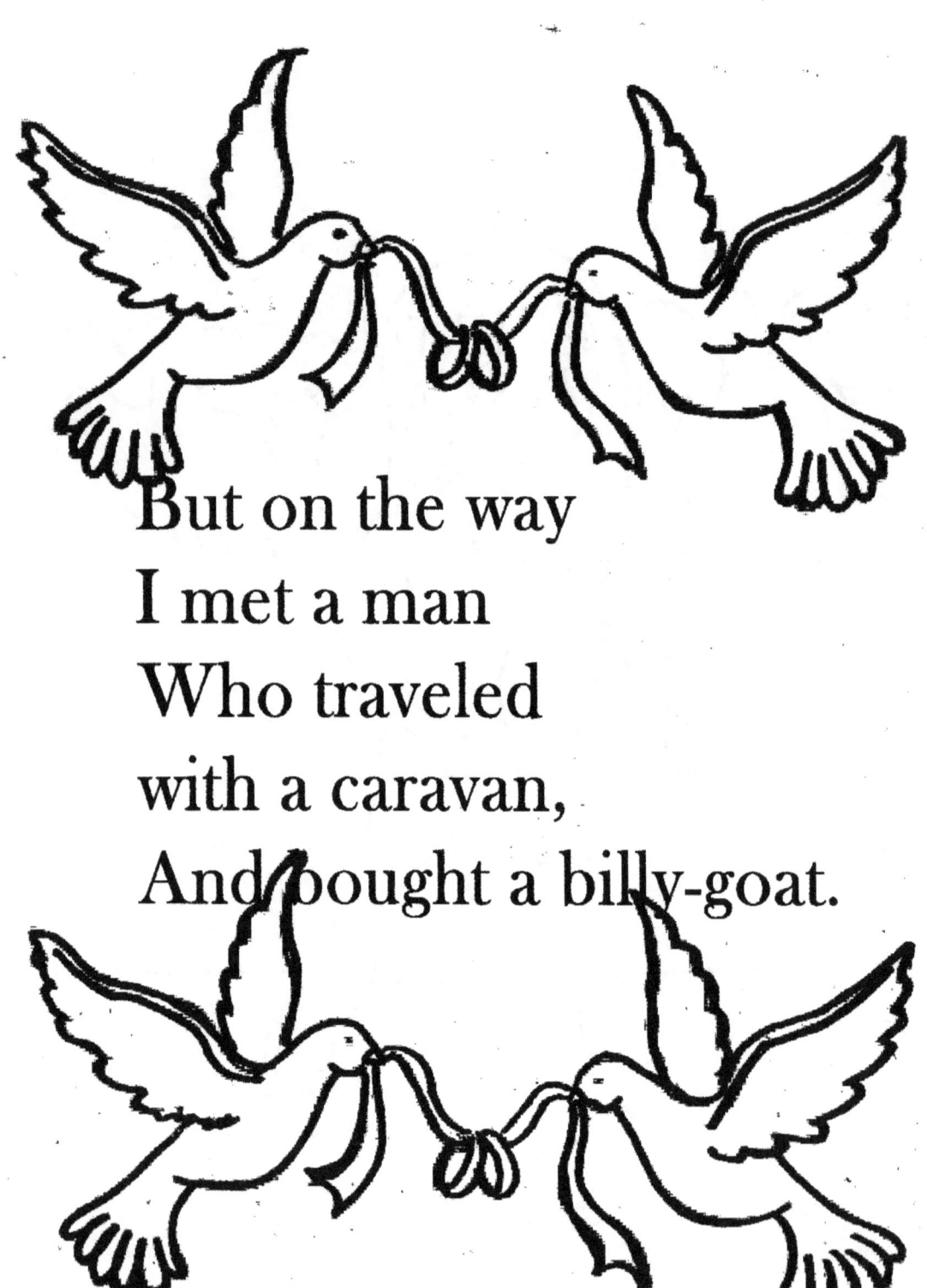

But on the way
I met a man
Who traveled
with a caravan,
And bought a billy-goat.

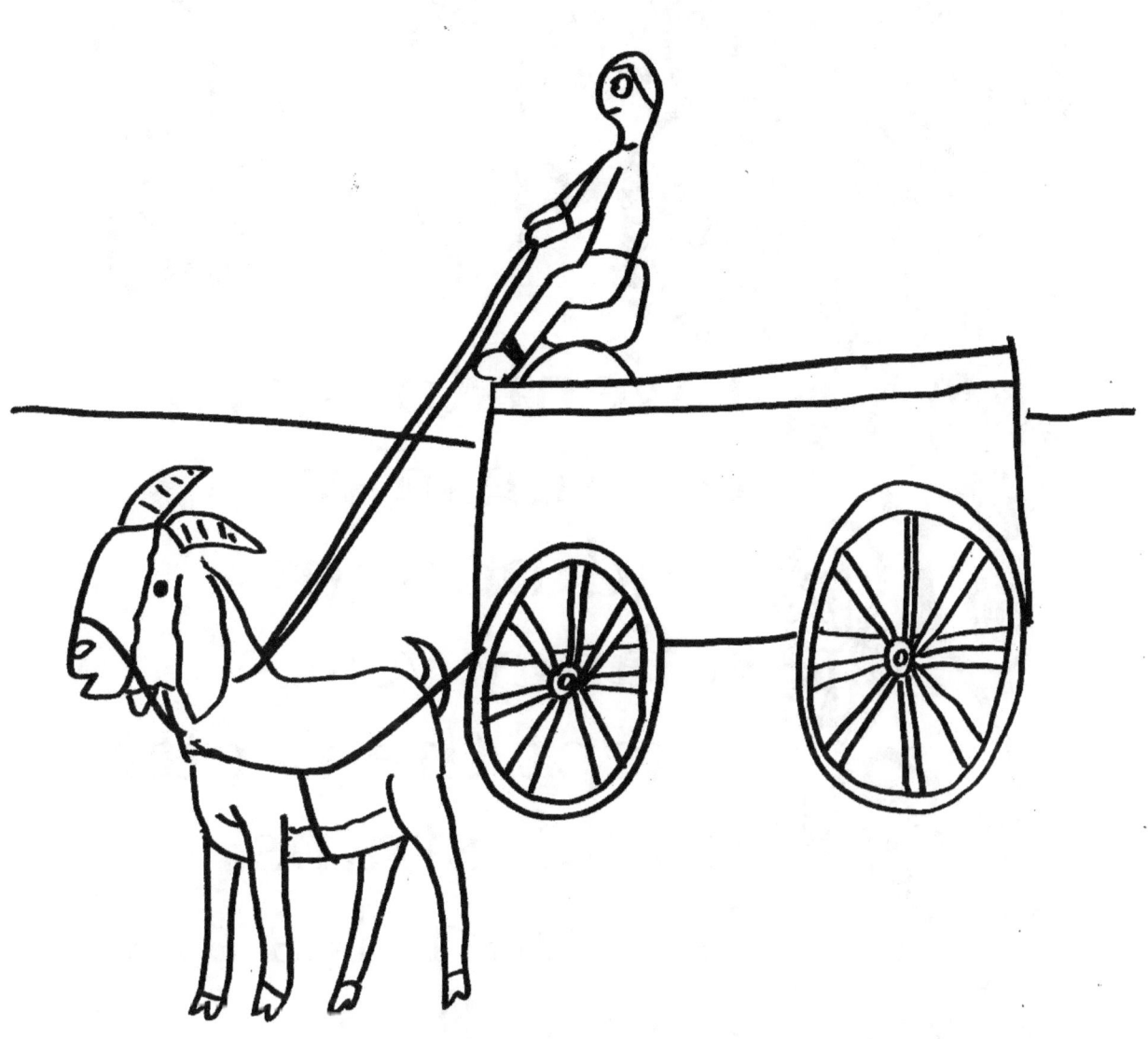

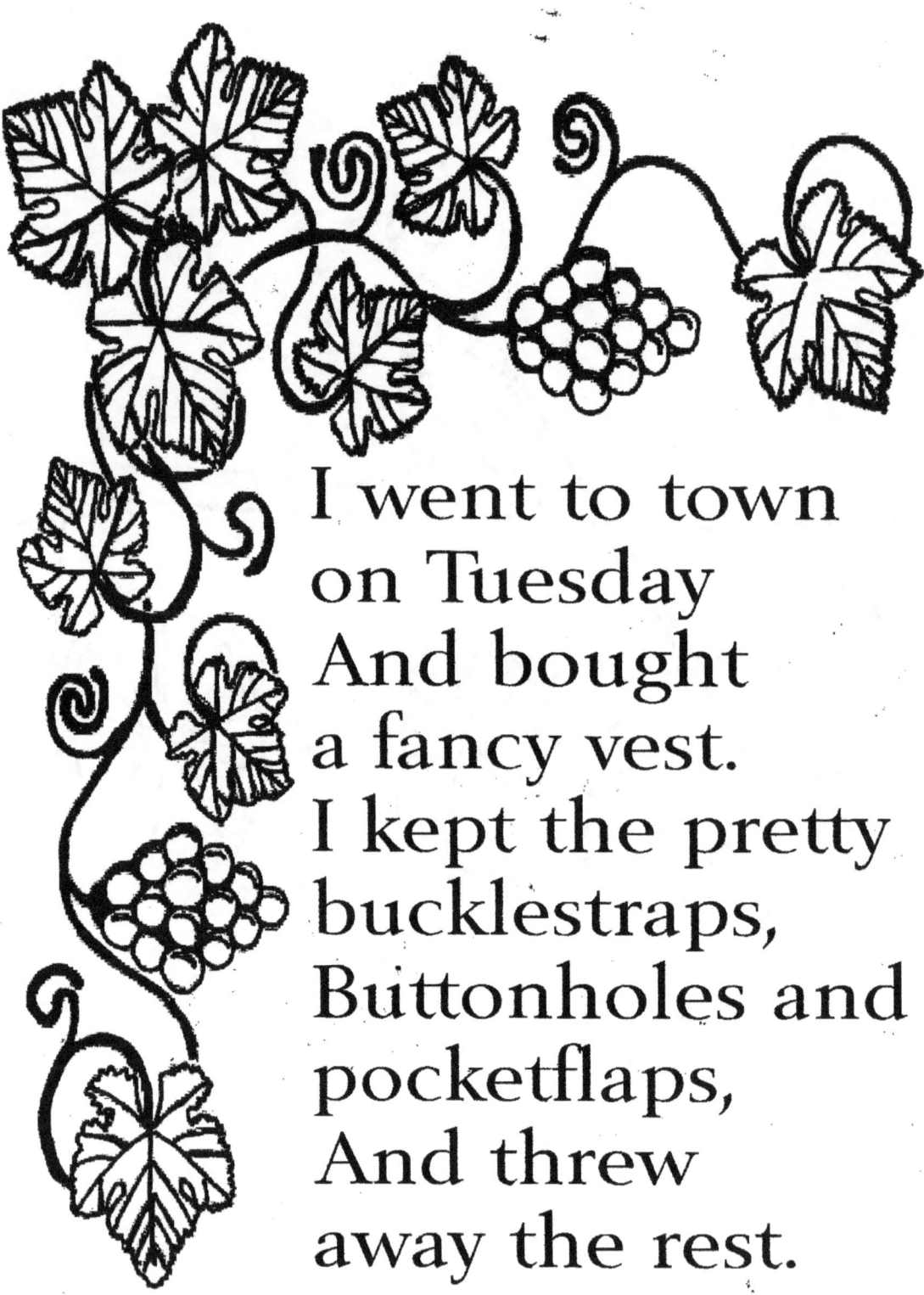

I went to town
on Tuesday
And bought
a fancy vest.
I kept the pretty
bucklestraps,
Buttonholes and
pocketflaps,
And threw
away the rest.

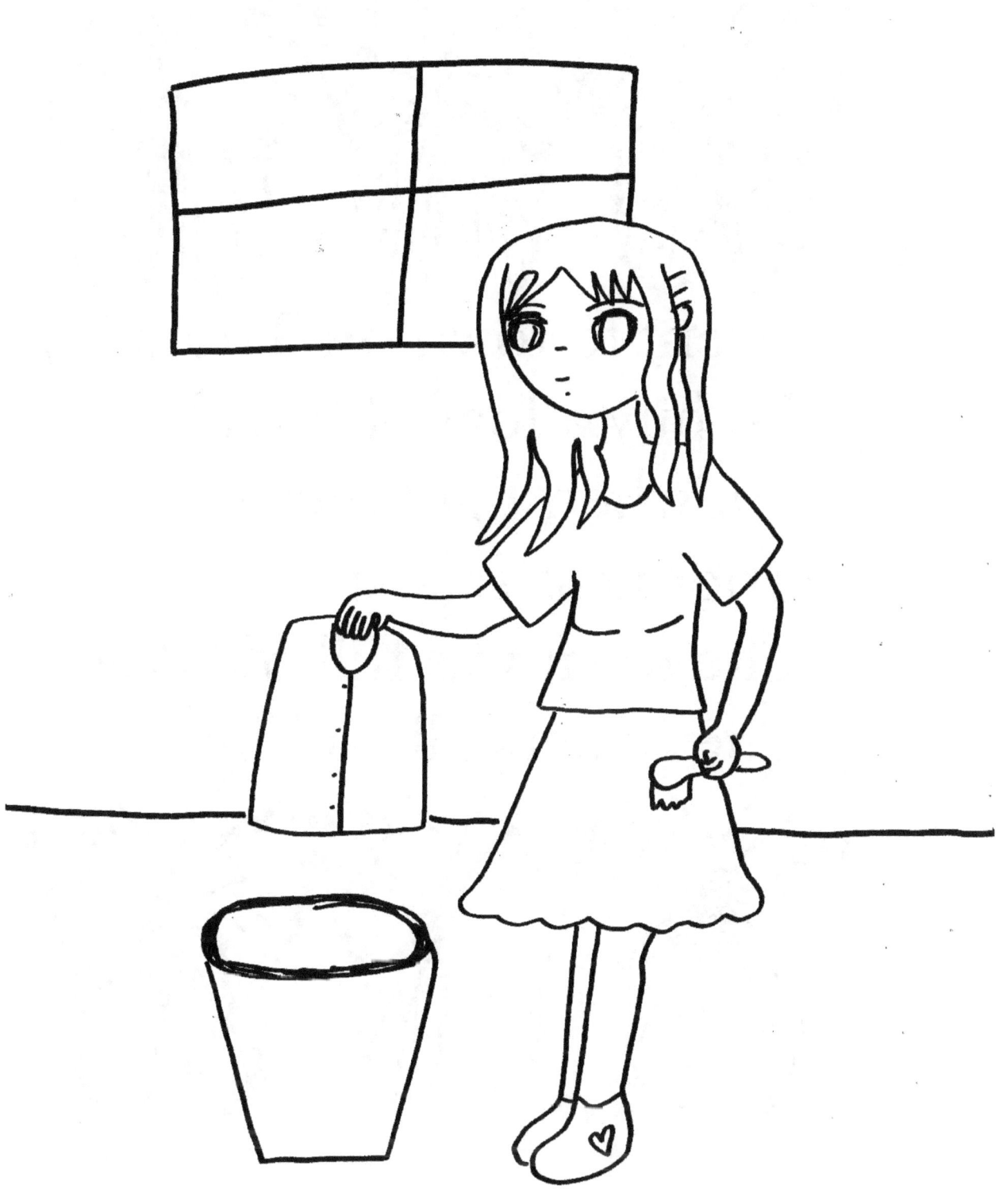

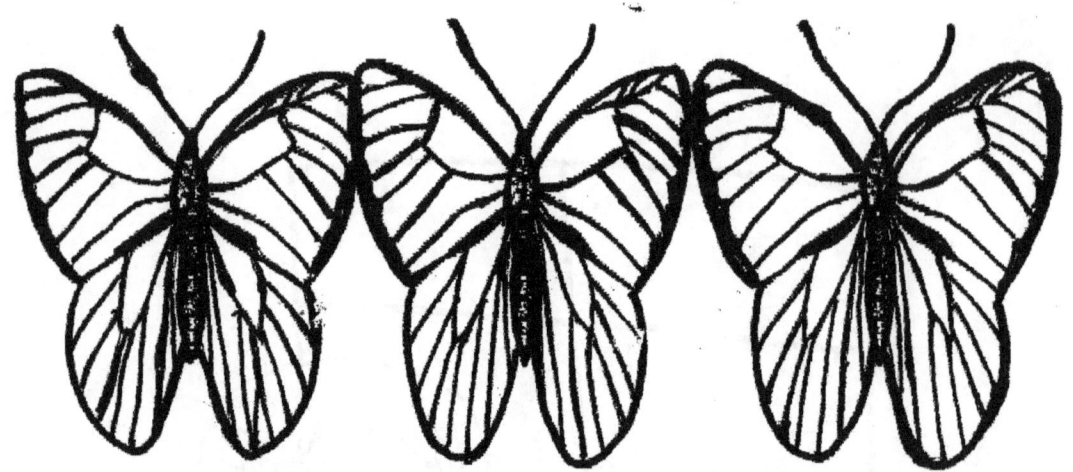

I went to town on Thursday
To buy a loaf of bread,
But when I got there,
Goodness sakes!
The town was full of lakes—
The bakers all had fled.

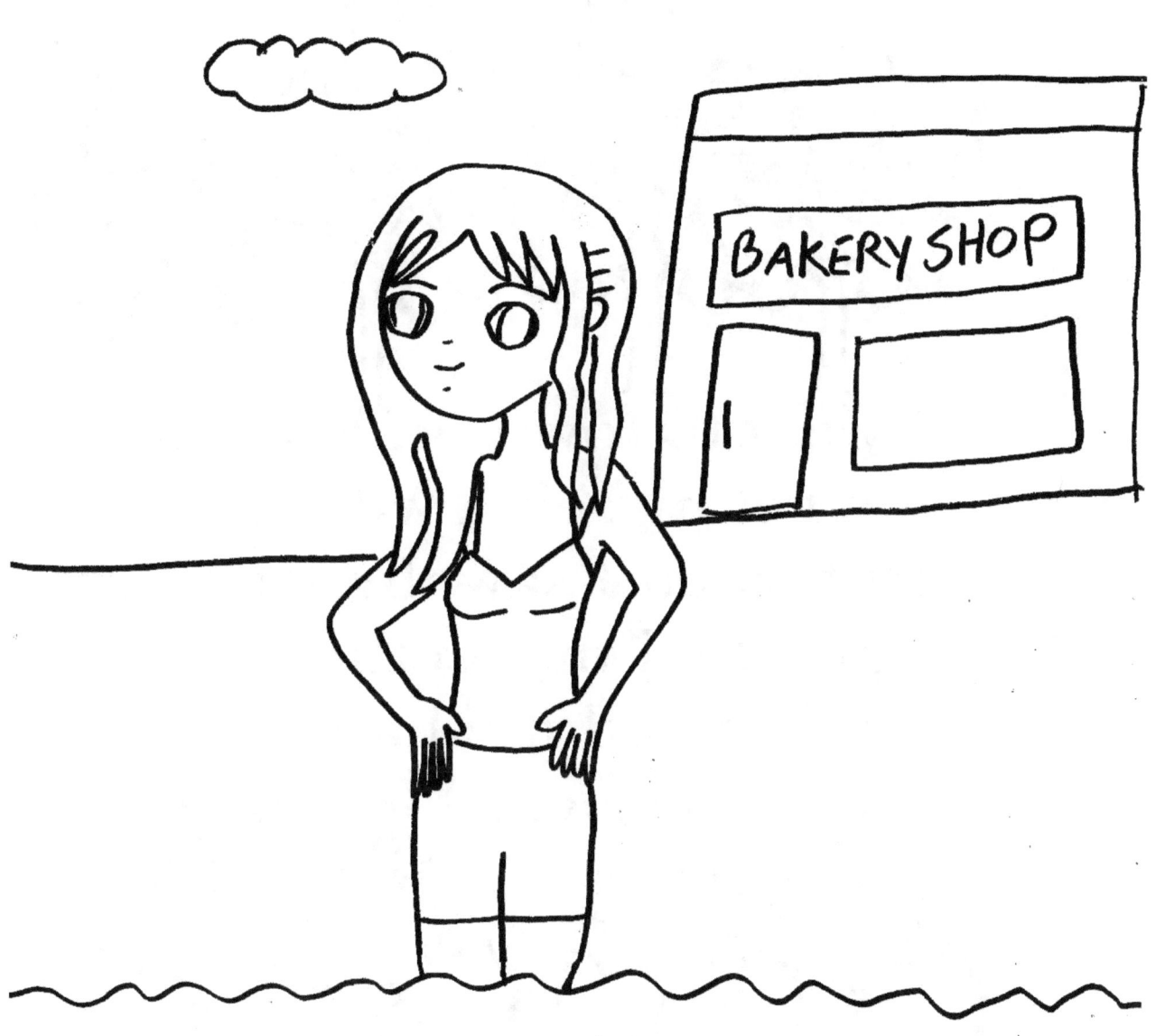

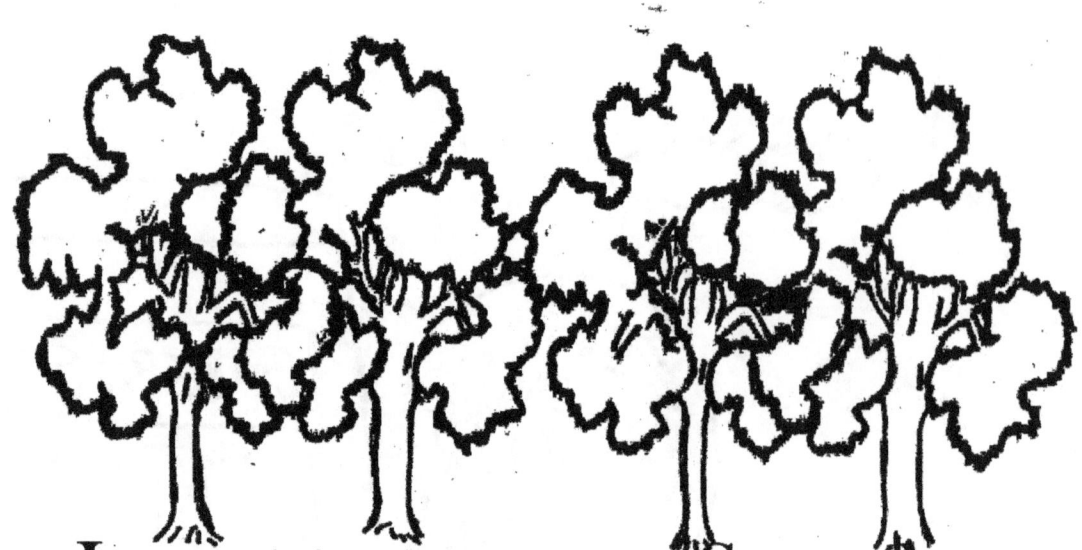

I went to town on Saturday
To get myself a wife,
But when I saw the lady fair
I gnashed my teeth
And pulled my hair
And scampered for my life.

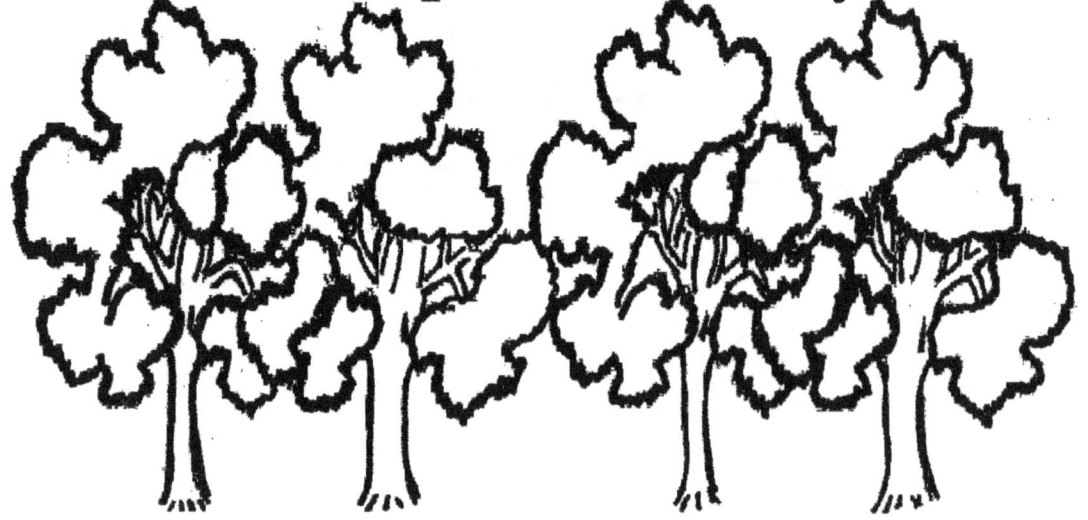

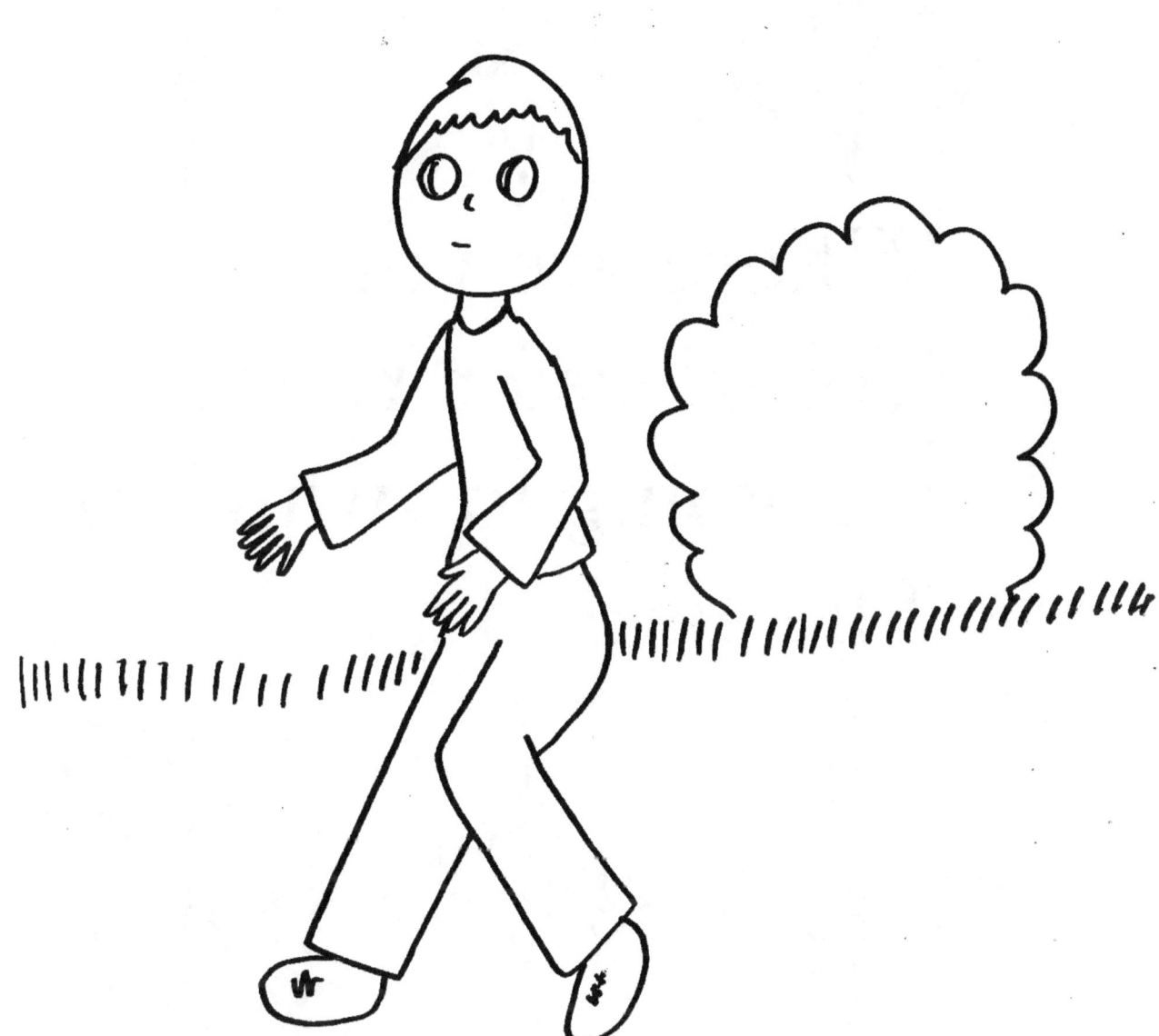

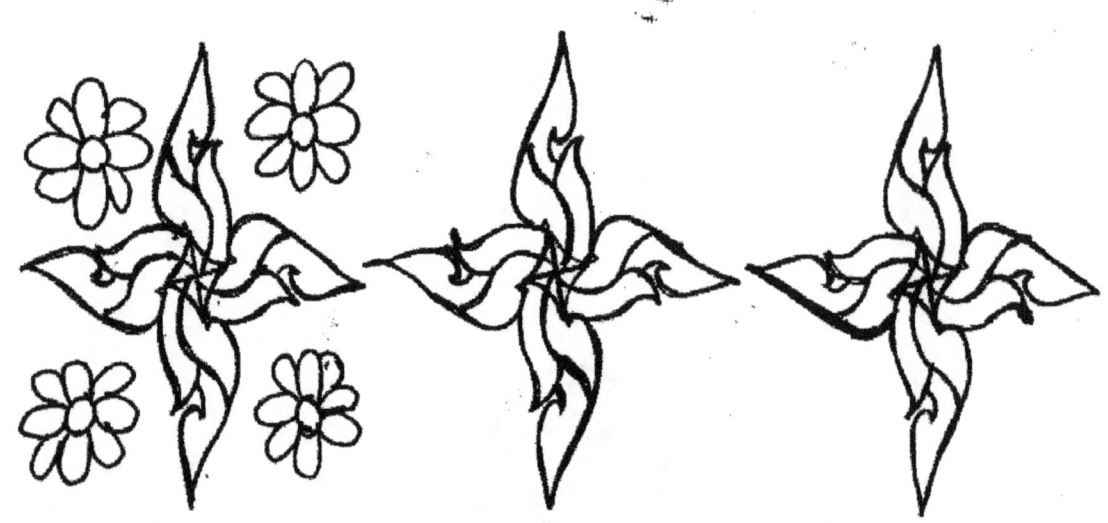

Where are you
Going, sister Kate?
I'm going to swing on
The garden gate,

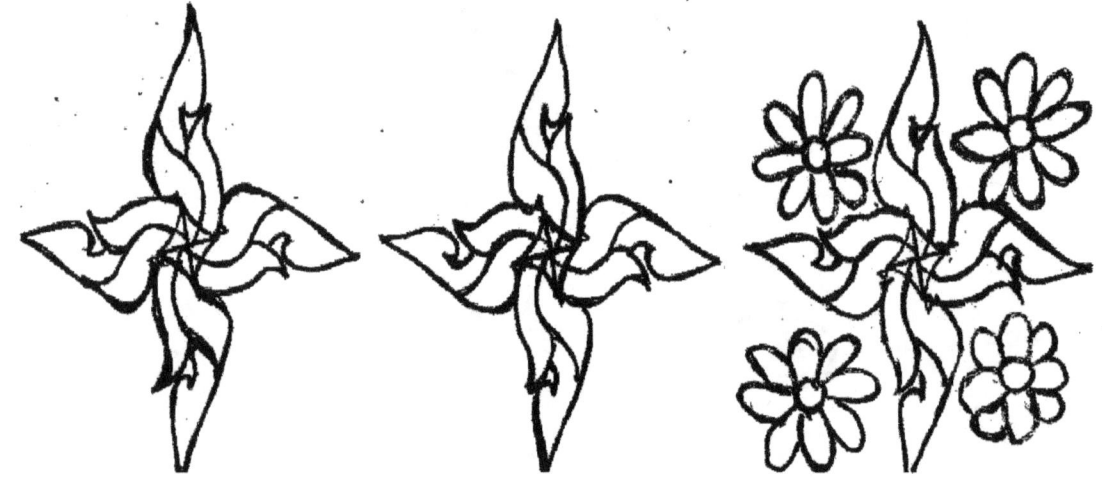

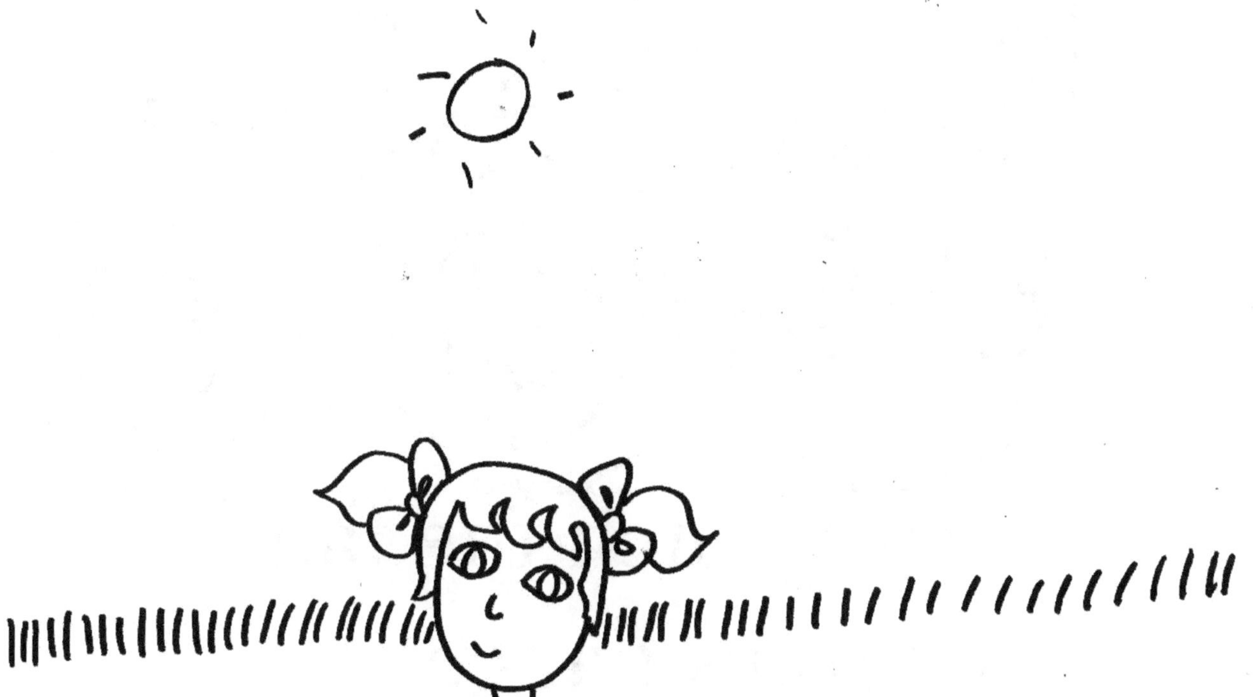

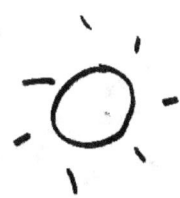

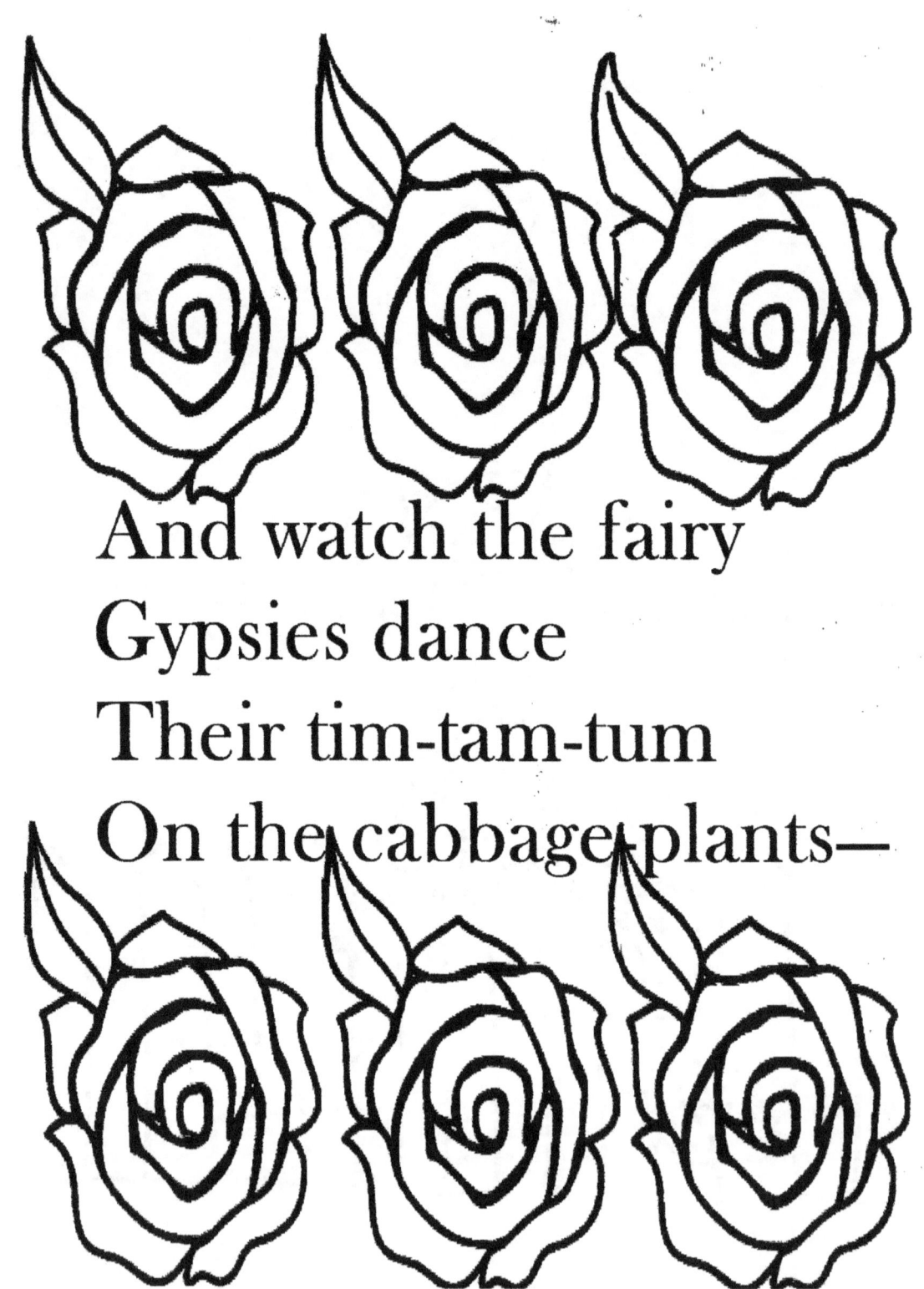

And watch the fairy
Gypsies dance
Their tim-tam-tum
On the cabbage plants—

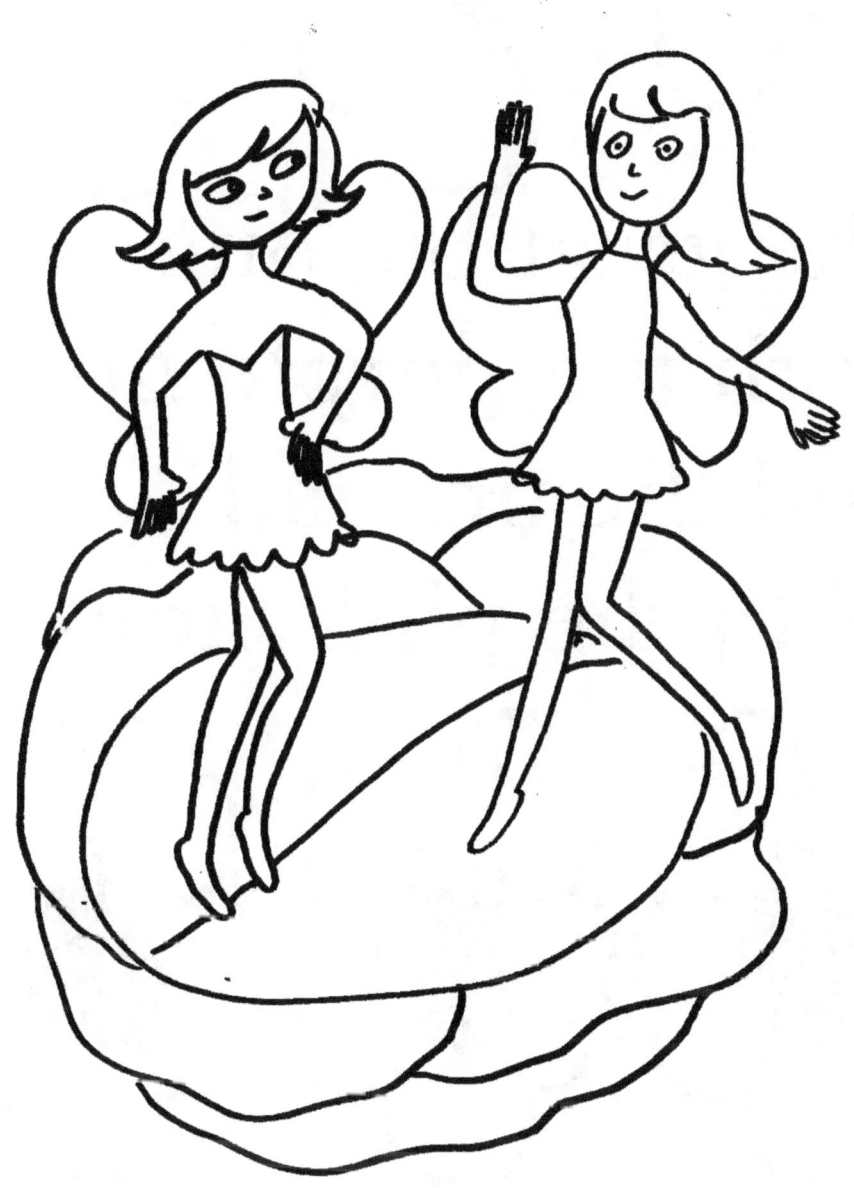

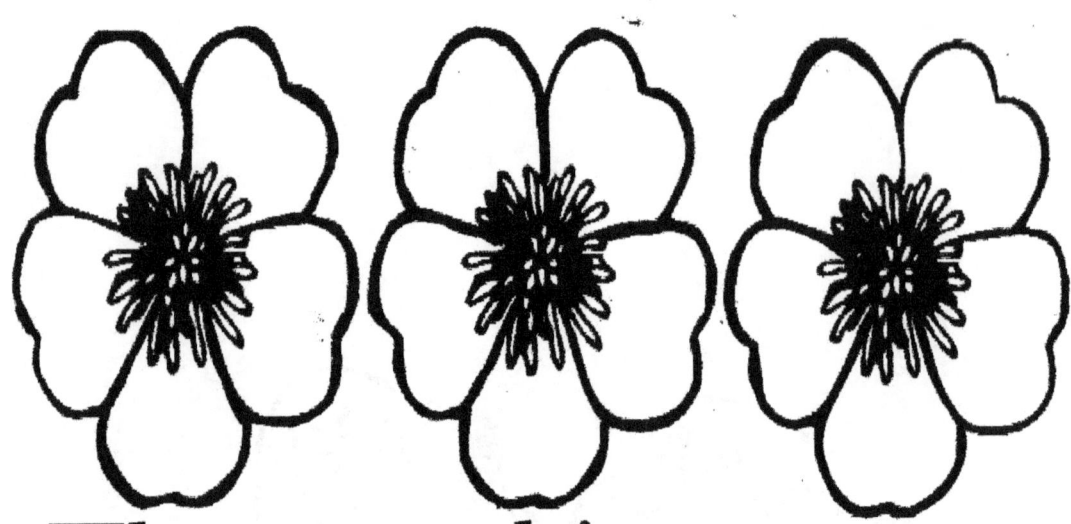

The great big one
With the purple nose,
And the tiny tad
With the pinky toes.

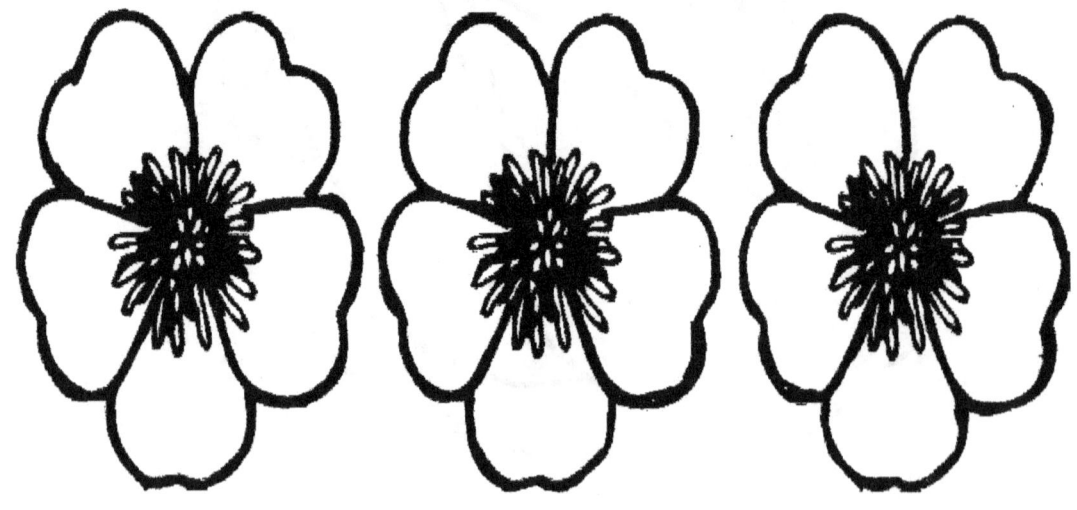

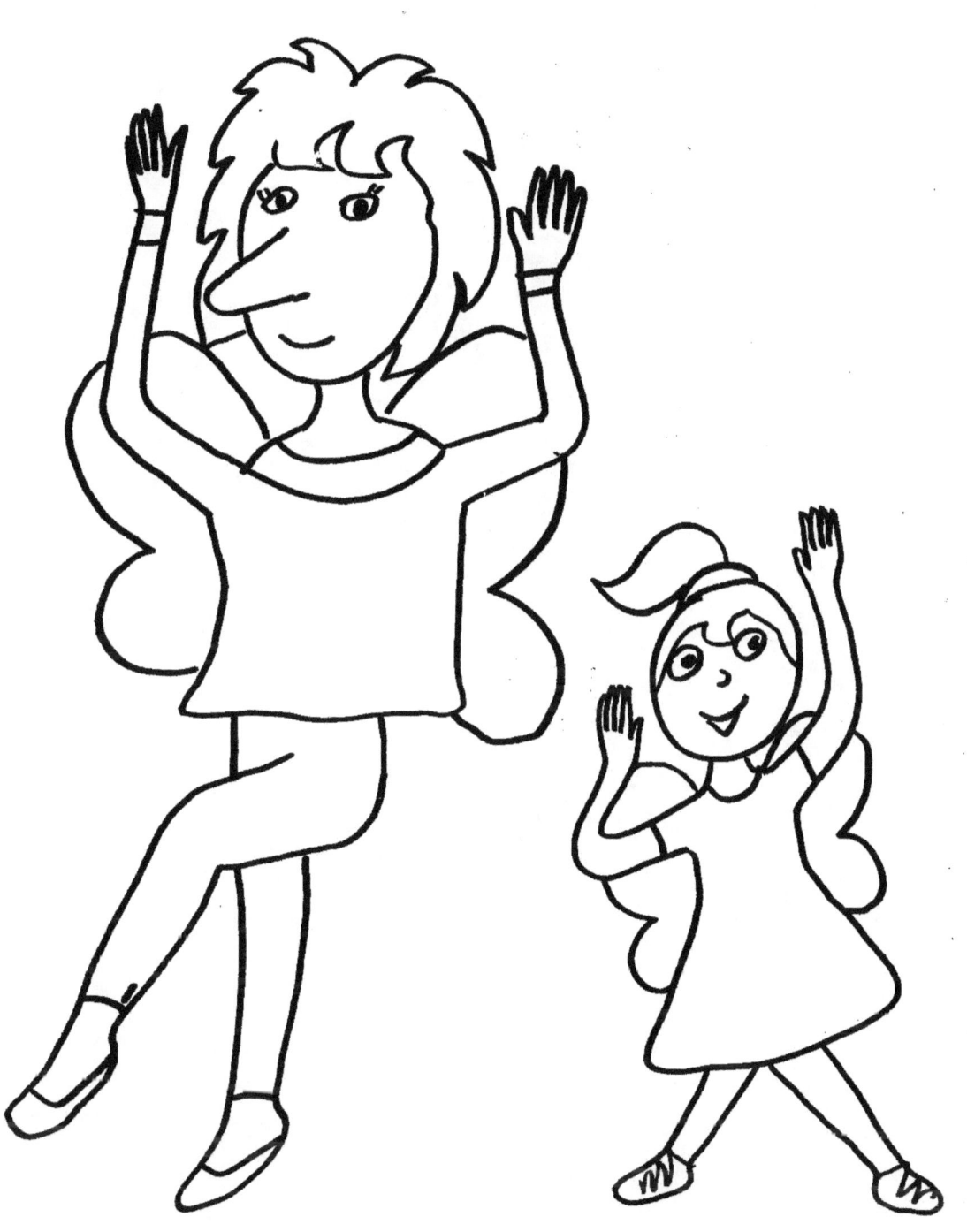